DEGREES of
DIFFICULTY

SPORT AND SOCIETY

Series Editors
Aram Goudsouzian
Jaime Schultz

Founding Editors
Benjamin G. Rader
Randy Roberts

A list of books in the series appears at the end of this book.

DEGREES of DIFFICULTY

HOW WOMEN'S GYMNASTICS ROSE TO PROMINENCE AND FELL FROM GRACE

GEORGIA CERVIN

UNIVERSITY OF ILLINOIS PRESS
Urbana, Chicago, and Springfield

Parts of this book were previously published as the following:
    "Making Meaning of the 1970s East-West Gymnastics Tours,"
Sporting Traditions 31, no. 2 (November 2015): 85–100, available at
https://digital.la84.org/digital/collection/p17103coll10/id/15590/
rec/1. Copyright Australian Society for Sport History.
    "Gymnasts Are Not Merely Circus Phenomena: Influences on the
Development of Women's Artistic Gymnastics during the 1970s,"
International Journal of the History of Sport 32, no. 16 (January 2016):
1929–46, available at https://www.tandfonline.com/doi/abs/10
.1080/09523367.2015.1124859. Copyright Taylor & Francis.
    "Ringing the Changes: How the Relationship between the
International Gymnastics Federation and the International Olympic
Committee Has Shaped Gymnastics Policy," *Sport History Review*
51, no. 1 (April 2020): 46–63, available at http://dx.doi.org/10.1123/
shr.2019–0041. Copyright Human Kinetics.

Library of Congress Cataloging-in-Publication Data
Names: Cervin, Georgia, author.
Title: Degrees of difficulty : how women's gymnastics rose to
    prominence and fell from grace / Georgia Cervin.
Description: Urbana, Chicago : University of Illinois Press, [2021] |
    Series: Sport and society | Includes bibliographical references
    and index.
Identifiers: LCCN 2020051329 (print) | LCCN 2020051330
    (ebook) | ISBN 9780252043772 (Cloth : acid-free paper) |
    ISBN 9780252085765 (Paperback : acid-free paper) | ISBN
    9780252052675 (eBook)
Subjects: LCSH: Gymnastics for women—History. | Gymnastics—
    Social aspects. | Gymnastics—Corrupt practices. | Gymnastics—
    Moral and ethical aspects.
Classification: LCC GV464 .C46 2021 (print) | LCC GV464 (ebook) |
    DDC 796.44082—dc23
LC record available at https://lccn.loc.gov/2020051329
LC ebook record available at https://lccn.loc.gov/2020051330

CONTENTS

PREFACE

Being a Gymnast, Being a Historian

This book has developed from the two major undertakings of my life: train-ing to be an elite gymnast and training to be a historian. As a historian, I wanted to understand how world systems were created and structured, how nations were constructed and how they related to one another, and how people created meaning from their pursuits. As a gymnast, I wondered why anyone would invent a balance beam so narrow and what motivated the bold first attempts at now-common risky maneuvers. This book started at the intersection of these curiosities, but it has gone far beyond these questions.

Learning about the histories of other sports and the social structures that underpin them cast gymnastics in a new light. When I engaged with sports scholars who were not historians, I realized there is a great need for historical discussion to inform their analyses of contemporary issues in sport. But it was equally apparent that historical inquiry needs to ask the right questions to really be of use in making sport better. In recent years, scrutiny of gymnastics has grown in the wake of the Me Too movement and allegations of all kinds of abuse in the sport. The absence of any full-length historical analysis of gymnastics formed a gaping hole in this discussion. Where did these issues come from? What has been socially acceptable in this sport? Why?

Originally, I concluded that the development of gymnastics was the result of a balance of power. Looking at relations between judges and gymnasts, federations and countries during the Cold War, I saw collaboration despite conflict—the careful balancing of diverse national and organizational interests. But as the horrors of US team doctor Larry Nassar's crimes became public, I realized that the gymnasts themselves were absent from this analysis, beyond their achievements. In fact, some of those I interviewed had questioned why I might even talk to gymnasts, as they were only children. It dawned on me that this silencing was a major factor in the abusive culture of gymnastics. And I realized that I had the materials ready to consider the historical context that allowed this culture to happen. I reassessed my original research with new questions about femininity, feminism, and power. This reexamination, detailed in this book, led me to conclude that women's gymnastics is, in fact, fundamentally shaped by an imbalance of power, between those who do it, and those who teach and govern it.

This book begins a historical analysis of women's artistic gymnastics. Although it builds on the work of historians who have looked at non-sportive gymnastics, it is one of the first books to examine the history of women's gymnastics as an international sport. It aims to do this in the context of international sport and global politics, as well as the social norms that have been constructed within the sport. Hence, the book fluctuates between looking inwardly at the sport and outwardly at gymnastics' place in the world. It reviews the origins of gymnastics and its position in the Olympic movement, how it was governed and the reasons behind the rules, where the sport fits into nationalism and international relations, who teaches gymnastics and how they do so, and what it all represents about class, gender, and race. The breadth of this work is intended to inform discussion of contemporary women's gymnastics and to launch further research and debate on the sport's history.

Degrees of Difficulty is but one version of gymnastics' past, and one reading of what it might mean. As historian Dave Day explains, "irrespective of the sources utilized, historical research is not an uncontested arena and when historians examine and discuss issues . . . each researcher brings their own perspective to bear on the topic which, in turn, engenders further debate."[1] Christophe Prochasson argues that there is an inevitable "entanglement of those who analyze with what is being analyzed."[2] On this basis, I too, have written about the need for historians to be forthright about their positionality when doing history.[3] If you know who is talking—and something about who they are, their perspectives, and the experiences that underpin them—you can better appreciate and critique the analysis that follows. So, in this preface, I want to explain my journey through this research, which began well before I visited my first archive or did my first interview.

My status as a former international gymnast gave me access to people and places that might not otherwise have been available for this research. I approached the Fédération internationale de gymnastique (FIG)—the international governing body for the sport—to help with sources for this research. Knowing I was a gymnast, the staff there told me they had watched a video of me before I visited the office. They provided me with the books they had about gymnastics, access to minute books, a list of contacts for interviews, and a media pass for me to conduct research at the 2014 world championships in Nanning. Through the FIG as well as my own networks, I connected with ten coaches, judges, officials, and former international gymnasts to undertake oral histories.[4] In person, on the phone, and by e-mail, I asked them questions about their time in the sport and, in some cases, their experience governing it.

Being a former gymnast has also meant that I speak the language of gymnastics. I am familiar with the terminology, the rules, and the culture of the sport. From this perspective, it has been easier for me to understand sources, easier to empathize with the people I spoke to, and easier for me to share in the lore of the sport. Many in the gymnastics world are skeptical of outsiders, territorial and protective of their sport, their life's work. But as a former gymnast, I was trusted.

I have been a gymnast all my life. I do not really remember starting; I do not remember ever not doing the sport. My parents tell me I started with baby gym. I did gymnastics at school and at my local club. I was in my first competition when I was five years old. I was OK. I came from a club that dominated competitions at the time. When I was seven, I came last at most competitions. By the time I was nine, I won most of them. I joined the national team when I was eleven, competing in my first international competition that year. I was training twenty-seven hours a week. A year later, it was up to twenty-nine hours. By the time I was thirteen, and for the rest of my career, I was training over thirty-two hours a week. I remained on the national team for six years, traveling around the world for competitions. In sum, I have always been a gymnast, but my competitive career was only thirteen years long.

My coaches were Russian. When they first arrived, they could only say "yes, no," and "one, two, three." Over time, they learned more words, and my teammates and I learned piecemeal Russian. We would begin and conclude each workout with pleasantries in Russian, and quickly learned gymnastics-specific instructions for the hours in between: "straighten your arms, work harder, why are you sitting down?" I felt so lucky to work with them. They were by far the most experienced in the country, having coached gold medal–winning Olympians. They had been through university level courses in gymnastics, and they had incredible technical knowledge. But they also endured a lot of animosity from their new compatriots in the West. Their experience on both sides of the Iron Curtain sparked my interest in how the Cold War might have influenced gymnastics.

For my first three senior international competitions, I was injured shortly before I was due to perform. When the final injury ended my career, I was devastated. Gymnastics was my first love. I mourned the sport for years, grieving over it as if I had lost a dear friend. I missed the training and the competition. Most of my friends had already quit, but I missed the days when we trained together, bonding through the shared struggle of daily workouts. I missed the status that being a gymnast gave me. It justified my small stature. It excused me from other commitments; I had training instead, working toward an important goal. But mostly, I missed how it felt. Soaring through the air, free from the forces of gravity that restrained everyone else. Completing complex movements in the air, and landing perfectly, not an inch off balance. The nervousness of learning a new skill, but the rush of adrenaline on successfully sticking the landing. The way my body could do anything I instructed it to do because it was so well-conditioned and prepared. I felt light and free and powerful and unstoppable. I could fly and I excelled at it.

This experience colors the analysis in the book because it is a sport that I am fond of. When I analyze gymnastics, I do it from this frame of reference. I would wish everyone the opportunity to enjoy gymnastics, as well. I want to promote the sport so that others can experience these thrills. But at the same time, I know firsthand the dangers of the sport. This is the foundation of my critique. The sport is problematic in many ways, and I know it can be better. It must be better. But change can happen only if the problems are revealed. This has already begun, through the accounts published by some gymnasts in their autobiographies. But being singular experiences, gymnastics administrators have been able to dismiss concerns, alleging that the experiences revealed in those works were exceptional, they were not normal for gymnastics. Nonetheless, the work has continued through the tireless investigations of journalists at papers like the *Orange County (CA) Register* and the *Indianapolis Star*. The latter exposed the Larry Nassar scandal, where the US team doctor was accused of sexually abusing hundreds of gymnasts, from the club to the elite levels. In 2020, gymnasts took up the torch themselves, publishing their own accounts of abuse in gymnastics on social media. In doing so they proved that these issues are not limited to certain people or certain countries: there is something awry in gymnastics around the world. This is where historical analysis comes in. Such a scale of abuse did not emerge from nowhere but was rather a result of the values and culture that have been normalized within the sport for decades.

So, it is my hope that this book offers insights into why women's gymnastics is the way it is. I have tried to show where the sport began, and the road it traveled to become what it is today. Along the way, I visit key people and key moments in the sport's history. As a historian, I analyze the sport in terms of global contexts and social structures. I hope it inspires you to think critically about the relationship between sport and society, and that it might cause you to look at women's gymnastics in a new light. More so, I hope it begins a new and ongoing conversation about the history and the future of women's artistic gymnastics.

ACKNOWLEDGMENTS

This research began at the University of Western Australia, where Mark Edele and Tony Barker consistently supported and encouraged this work. I am forever thankful for their teaching and mentoring, which really are the foundations of this book. Tony, in particular, has continued to support me as I transformed my research into a book, always willing to read my drafts and give his insightful advice, and I offer my sincerest gratitude to him.

My thanks also go to the wider discipline group of history at the University of Western Australia, which was an excellent environment to undertake the research for this book. I benefited from several scholarships from the University of Western Australia, without which this research would have been impossible. I completed much of this research under the auspices of an Australian Postgraduate Award and University of Western Australia Top-Up scholarship. Funds from the Graduate Research School enabled me to undertake the first research trip for this project, and funds from the Broeze Award enabled a second trip to collect oral histories. The Postgraduate Students Association topped up this award, so to them I also extend my appreciation.

I owe a great debt to the team at the Olympic Studies Centre in Lausanne, and their award of a grant to complete this research. In an old villa above the lake, these are more than the most beautiful archives in the world, they are a haven for the sport historian, and the friendliness of the staff there enhances the experience. Thanks to Nuria Puig for arranging my visit and to the staff for their unfailing positivity and helpfulness, particularly Stephanie Moreno and the entire archivist team. Additionally, the team behind the Olympic Multimedia Library have been incredibly patient and helpful, generously providing the images that illustrate this book. In this regard, I also extend my gratitude to the United States Olympic Committee and the Fédération internationale de gymnastique (FIG), which graciously granted permission to include these images in this book.

I also wish to acknowledge the staff at the FIG, particularly Nicolas Buompane and Philippe Silacci. These two took an interest in this work, provided a list of names and contact details for oral histories, and organized a media pass to conduct interviews at the 2014 world championships in China. Nicolas also continued responding to my ad hoc questions since then. Thanks also to all those in the international gymnastics community who were willing to engage in interviews with me, particularly Hardy Fink, who answered my questions throughout the project.

It has been a joy to discuss this sport with scholars from a range of different disciplines around the world as part of the international sociocultural women's artistic gymnastics research group. I am particularly grateful to Natalie Barker-Ruchti and Roslyn Kerr for their ongoing support and the variety of perspectives they provide.

I am similarly grateful to my friends who are part of the Réseaux d'études des relations internationales sportives. I am privileged to be part of this group of early career scholars specializing in sport history, not least because it has provided a pathway into critical scholarship beyond that which exists in the English language. This exposure to international discourse has introduced me to new ideas underpinning my analysis of gymnastics, while members of this group also provided insightful critiques, challenges, and feedback on this research. Special thanks must go to my friend Claire Nicolas, who read and commented on draft chapters of this book; and to Gregory Quin, who welcomed me into this network and was always keen to compare notes about the different gymnastic disciplines.

My colleagues in New Zealand also took an interest in my work. I am thankful to David Haines in particular, who read and commented on early drafts of this book.

I also wish to extend my gratitude to the team at University of Illinois Press for taking on this project in its early form and overseeing its transformation into the book before you. This is not least in part due to the robust feedback provided by the reviewers, whose comments and ideas really did transform the book. This would not have been possible without editor Daniel Nasset taking on the project and continuing to offer his ideas and support as it continued. I must also acknowledge the keen eye of Deborah Oliver, whose skillful editing ensured the accuracy of this book. And thanks too to Tad Ringo for shepherding this manuscript through the publication process.

I especially want to thank Lindsay Parks Pieper, whose comments really reshaped the book and who went above and beyond to help me, along with Jaime Schultz, who also reached out to encourage me. I must also mention the thoughtful suggestions I got from my friend, Johanna Mellis, who directed me to important research in which to situate my findings, as well as providing general comments that enhanced the final version of the book.

I also wish to thank the editors of *Sporting Traditions*, the *International Journal of the History of Sport*, and *Sport History Review*, who allowed me to derive parts of this book from articles I have published in these journals.

Finally, I would like to thank my friends and family for their unwavering support, belief in me, and patience. Janet Klee, your encouragement has been crucial. Neil Cervin, all those times you answered my simple questions with long lectures, thank you for beginning my interest in history. Greta Cervin, thank you for being a constant supporter since my gymnastics days and now throughout my writing. Poppy, thank you for keeping me company for every word I wrote. And finally, thank-you to Christopher Heydon, who helped conceive of this work and has been my biggest supporter along the way.

DEGREES of DIFFICULTY

INTRODUCTION

In 1973, a seventeen-year-old from Grodno, Belarus, found herself standing beside Richard Nixon in the Oval Office. Dressed in a white frilled blouse, with two thin white ribbons holding her hair back in loose pigtails, Olga Korbut barely reached the shoulders of the man towering beside her. In front of flashing cameras, President Nixon joked to Korbut that her remarkable skill of landing on her feet was something he would to do well to learn as a politician. After a pause for translation, Korbut laughed, her smile revealing perfect white teeth.

Korbut represented the transition from women's gymnastics to girl's gymnastics. She also popularized the sport in the United States, beginning its meteoric rise as the sport of choice for young girls. The shift from sport for women to one for girls laid the foundation for some of the most heinous abuse seen in any sport—emotional, physical, and sometimes sexual abuse that was sustained around the world despite decades of national investigations. But the shift from women to girls, from feminism to oppression, must be understood in its multiple contexts, foremost of the which was the Cold War.

In the midst of the Cold War, a team of Soviet gymnasts standing in the White House was unprecedented. While sporting contests had long been a surrogate for all-out war, gymnastics' global popularity provided opportunities to engage in a new form of diplomacy between East and West. The attractive, feminine, and later, young, gymnasts that populated the sport presented no threat to world leaders. Moreover, these gymnasts had the support of the public, as their adoring fans cemented gymnastics' place in popular culture and by proxy, its political value. Far from being what *Life* magazine once called "an athletic ritual pursued by crackpots, muscle-bound culturists, and misguided persons named Ivan," gymnastics had become one of the Olympic Games' most popular sports.[1]

The story of women's artistic gymnastics constitutes a unique chapter in the history of elite women's sports. Since the 1960s, it has been one of the most-watched Olympic sports on television, attracting a global audience. Where a goal in soccer or a victory on the track presented moments of triumphant emotion, television offered continuous close-ups of the intensity and drama of gymnastic competition. The different formats for men and women produced equally compelling performances by both, but the diminutive size and astonishing athleticism of the women made their achievements especially surprising. Viewers could admire the skill of somersaults on a narrow beam, marvel at the risks in ever more daring vaults or in breathtaking swings and plunges between the uneven bars. It was easy for viewers to understand the success of a "stuck" dismount off any of the apparatuses—the gymnasts planting down confidently on the ground without a hint of a stumble—before turning triumphantly to "salute" the judges. Spectators could also sympathize when achievement fell short of expectations, as crying young gymnasts were comforted by coaches acting as surrogate parents. By the end of the century, women's artistic gymnastics had moved far from its early emphasis on graceful, flowing movement more akin to ballet and other forms of dance. But it had developed in a manner removed from the priorities of feminism. Mainly small, mostly very young, athletes were more likely to seem victims than standard bearers of campaigns for gender equality.

Despite its popularity during the Olympics, throughout most of the twentieth century large crowds did not attend domestic gymnastic competitions, nor was there a similarly lucrative international league. Therefore, gymnastics had no chance of attracting the television coverage that was providing modest professional earnings to female basketballers and other athletes in the West. By contrast, women's artistic gymnastics had been shaped by the hard, contemporary reality of Eastern domination that saw gymnasts from the Soviet bloc win almost every world championship and Olympic gold medal until the end of the Cold War. Gymnastics competitions were part of the global contest between Cold War adversaries and of the radically different sports systems behind them. Victory meant ideological and national supremacy.

While Americans yearned for, and eventually found, gymnastics heroines of their own, it was inevitable that when the first superstars emerged, they were from the Eastern bloc. The popularity of Olga Korbut challenged hostile prevailing stereotypes of the Eastern-bloc medal-winning machine. Korbut's charm was at odds with Western impressions of relentless and humorless Soviet training methods. The unmatched achievements and subsequent history of the Romanian Nadia Comăneci were, for many, an unexpected insight into cracks in the presumed solidarity of the Eastern bloc.

The Eastern bloc's state-funded system of training athletes, and the prominence of women within it, brought accusations that it flouted the Olympics' amateur rules. But as the Olympic movement professionalized, US athletes soon accepted advertising and television contracts off the back of their gymnastic success. Combined with new training systems adopted from the Eastern bloc, the Americans began challenging the East's domination. By the end of the Cold War, the United States had progressed from virtual irrelevance to the world's best.

Degrees of Difficulty charts these shifts in geographic dominance, as well as the transformations taking place within gymnastics; in style, in equipment, and in participants. It draws extensively on primary sources from the Olympic archives and the records of the international gymnastics federation in Switzerland, as well as oral histories from around the world. The central thesis is that both conflict and collaboration during the Cold War shaped the development of women's artistic gymnastics. Gymnastics emerged as a global sport, shaped by—and perpetuating—European ideals of race, gender, and nationality. It was uniquely created as a space appropriate for women within the man's world of sports. Global conflict catalyzed innovation and competition, transforming gymnastics from balletic to acrobatic. Cold War rivalry created secrecy and animosity and fueled an unyielding imperative to win, even if doing so required cheating or abuse. As girls replaced mature women in the sport, coaches, governing bodies and nations began to sacrifice any duty of protection over the gymnasts, instead prioritizing gold medals and national glory.

Despite these conflicts, international cooperation, between coaches, judges, gymnasts, and even politicians, sustained the sport throughout the twentieth century. Officials from around the world came together to decide what social values the sport should demonstrate, what femininity meant, how it should be embodied and performed, and how gymnasts would be rewarded for it. Changing social and economic values transformed not only what the sport looked like, but who was doing it. The Fédération internationale de gymnastique (FIG) worked together with the International Olympic Committee (IOC), its coaches, judges, and gymnasts to disseminate these ideals. These two bodies acted as international nongovernment organizations, not only directing the sport but facilitating international cooperation and mediating sports diplomacy.[2] This book thus offers insights into how and why women's gymnastics developed the way it did, including insights into how dangerous sporting cultures are created, as well as challenging what we know about the Cold War and international relations throughout this period.

*   *   *

This history of gymnastics centers around the Cold War, the global cultural and ideological contest that defined much of the twentieth century.[3] In the absence of all-out military confrontation, cultural contest became a hallmark of the conflict, and sports its crowning jewel. Sports were used by governments to demonstrate virtue, progress, and superiority to win public approval and admiration, and above all, to prove international ascendancy at the quadrennial Olympic Games. These contests already carried nationalistic overtones, with competitors representing their country, their flag being raised if they won, while the national anthem played. Participation in the Olympic Games was an indication that a state was recognized by the international community.[4] Sports like gymnastics retained a link to the military, seen in terminology like "marching" between apparatuses and "saluting" to judges.

Both the United States and the Soviet Union used sports to tell stories about their nation; about what it meant to be a woman (or a man), what those societies valued (freedom, equality), and most importantly, national superiority.[5] Various scholarship has understood sports as a form of culture, reflecting political nous of the time. As historian Tony Shaw explains, during the Cold War "virtually everything, from sports to ballet to comic books and space travel, assumed political significance and hence potentially could be deployed as a weapon both to shape opinion at home and to subvert societies abroad."[6]

The Cold War elevated the stakes of Olympic competition, leading to a win-at-all-costs mentality that involved both physical violence and violation of amateur, anti-doping, and (allegedly) sex-segregation rules.[7] Scholar Toby Rider shows how the United States leveraged sports for its public diplomacy ambitions, effecting the defection of Hungarian athletes during the 1956 Olympic Games.[8] The US boycott of the 1980 Olympic Games in Moscow, then a similar boycott by the Soviet Union when Los Angeles was hosting the games four years later, reaffirmed the links between sports and political pressure.[9] Yet, sports, as a form of soft power, also offered opportunities for "moments of collaboration" between representatives from enemy states.[10] Indeed, this book responds to the call from historians to go beyond ideas of clash and conflict in the Cold War, instead showing how cooperation and collaboration existed despite the global war.[11] Moreover, it goes beyond a binary conception of the Cold War, finding multilateral cooperation and collaboration in the "ambiguous zones within which international organizations, states, sport leaders and athletes interacted in order to achieve their respective goals during the Cold War."[12]

Sports are contested not only on the field or in the arena, but also within the international bodies that govern them. Non-state actors involved in the governance of international sports—like the IOC, the FIG, and other international federations—played a crucial role in foreign relations and diplomacy through sports during this period.[13] Although the leaders of the IOC were genuinely committed to separate spheres for sports and politics, this book shows that the organization nevertheless had moments of active political investment. Not only did the IOC intervene with forms of soft diplomacy, the games also were an arena in which the rules of engagement were negotiated.[14]

Throughout much of the Cold War, amateurism was a defining feature of the sporting conflict between East and West. Athletes would be expelled from competition if they received payment or gifts for anything related to their sporting activities. Not only did this bar athletes from receiving sponsorship, it also prohibited them from activities like coaching, or even working in shops selling sporting goods. The amateur rule effectively meant athletes had to commit to another profession to earn money, which limited the time they had left to practice and compete. It also advantaged athletes from wealthy backgrounds who could afford to work less and devote more time to sports. Amateurism thus reflected class conflict as a way of excluding the working class from sports.[15] When the Soviet Union first participated in the Olympics in 1952, it represented the encroachment of the working class into international sports, taking class conflict to an international scale and giving the amateur rule new significance.[16] At its creation as an Olympic sport and for much of its history, gymnastics has carried the weight of the amateur rule.

While historian John Gleaves identifies continuing class conflict in the emergence of anti-doping rhetoric, another scholar, Paul Dimeo, argues that the discourse around doping had developed into crude international stereotypes: the Eastern bloc are all drug cheats, but Western dopers are individual black sheep. Doping, however, has rarely been a problem in gymnastics. Doping nonetheless had a role in women's gymnastics, as discussed in chapter 4. Between 1952 and 2000, the *FIG Bulletins* record fewer than five positive doping tests.[17]

Sports have not only been a site for class conflict, they have also been a place in which sex and gender were strictly defined, mediated, and segregated. During the Cold War, the question of women's role in sports was reinvigorated. There was widespread opposition to women's sports around the world, but when the Soviet Union counted on its large contingent of women athletes for its enormous medal hauls, many in the West began to take women's sports more seriously to meet the Soviet challenge. Training became more rigorous, demanding, and time-intensive, and the result of these efforts was a hardening and muscling of women's bodies. It was at this time, in the 1960s, that the IOC first introduced "femininity controls" to counteract the perceived masculinization of women athletes and ensure that no man could masquerade as a woman to win.[18]

These concerns about how women should participate illuminate the gendered assumptions on which modern sports have been built. When women were making advances in employment and suffrage in the early twentieth century, it prompted a "crisis of masculinity." But masculinity could be reinforced by exclusion. Sports were considered the "natural domain of men," where men could demonstrate "natural superiority" over women. Modern sports, then, excluded women and defined them in opposition to men. As the Olympic movement grew in the early twentieth century, sports were perceived to be a "fief of virility."[19] The appropriate, limited role for women in sports then was limited to activities that promoted femininity, physical attractiveness, and healthy bodies for reproduction.

Medical practitioners saw menstruation as a bodily weakness that rendered women less capable than men. At the same time though, women's role as mothers were so highly valued that their reproductive capabilities were carefully protected through medical advice against participation in sports, or participation only in light exercises.[20] Women were perceived as weak, in additional to being naturally passive and submissive. Moreover, the aggression, power, and competition that characterized modern sports were considered highly masculine. Women's participation in sports, then, had been irreconcilable with ideas about femininity, except for when that sport had been designed to appear effortless and to promote and perform femininity, like women's gymnastics.

In the early twentieth century, medical practitioners and pedagogues developed socially acceptable exercises and sports for women that would protect their femininity.[21] Sociologist Susan Cahn established that "educators created a respectable 'feminine' brand of athletics designed to maximize female participation while averting controversy." These efforts "effectively defined 'feminine' sport as a lesser version of male sport: less competitive, less demanding, and less skillful."[22] Institutions like the FIG and the IOC were crucial to normalizing hierarchies of social difference between men and women, preventing them from competing together and demanding that women use shorter distances, reduced times, and modified equipment.[23] Certainly, this can be seen in the origins of women's artistic gymnastics. It was designed specifically for women to participate in sports in a gender-appropriate way. It was conceived as a performance of femininity, and this purpose saw it swiftly accepted into the Olympic roster. While weightlifting and boxing had to wait until 2000 and 2012, respectively, to become Olympic sports for women, women's artistic gymnastics had already been an Olympic event for over half a century.

When women's artistic gymnastics first became an Olympic sport in 1952, the issues of Cold War sports and women's sports intersected immediately. From then until the end of the Cold War, the Soviet Union won nearly every gold medal in Olympic women's gymnastics. This was no small feat, with six events to contest, and eighteen medals to be won at each Olympics. Over the fifty years and ten times in which the Soviet Union competed in women's artistic gymnastics at the Olympic Games, it won a staggering ninety-two medals.[24] The paragon of its domination was a 100 percent gold medal rate in the prestigious team competition.

The Soviet Union had a well-devised medal-winning strategy, supported by serious investment into developing and training athletes.[25] Moreover, it didn't practice a gender differential, instead devoting as much attention to women's sports as to men's. Soviet traditions of physical culture combined with communist notions of gender roles to support their female gymnasts.[26]

Table I.1: Medalists in the prestigious team and all-around competitions at each Olympic Games between 1952 and 2000, by country.

	Team			All-Around		
	Gold	Silver	Bronze	Gold	Silver	Bronze
1952	USSR	HUN	TCH	USSR	USSR	HUN
1956	USSR	HUN	ROU	USSR	HUN	USSR
1960	USSR	TCH	ROU	USSR	USSR	USSR
1964	USSR	TCH	JAP	TCH	USSR	USSR
1968	USSR	TCH	GDR	TCH	USSR	USSR
1972	USSR	GDR	HUN	USSR	GDR	USSR
1976	USSR	ROU	GDR	ROU	USSR	USSR
1980	USSR	ROU	GDR	USSR	ROU/GDR	
1984	ROU	USA	CHN	USA	ROU	ROU
1988	USSR	ROU	GDR	USSR	ROU	USSR
1992	EUN	ROU	USA	EUN	USA	ROU

Key: CHN = China (from 1984 onward); EUN = Unified Team (1992 only, former Soviet Union team); GDR = German Democratic Republic; HUN = Hungary; JAP = Japan; ROU = Romania; TCH = Czechoslovakia; USSR = Soviet Union (not present at 1984 Olympics); USA = United States (not present at 1980 Olympics)

It took some time before the success of Soviet women forced many Western countries to see that the lack of female representation on their own teams undermined their Olympic efforts. While Soviet women's sporting success allowed their Western counterparts to gain more attention and acceptance, gymnasts like Věra Čáslavská, and Olga Korbut allayed concerns over sports' masculinizing effect and proved women could be triumphant in the world of sports.[27] Implicit in this development is a contradiction central to the sport and a common theme throughout this book. Women's artistic gymnastics helped women's sports by demonstrating that women could retain their femininity even if they became elite athletes. But it did this by demanding performances that conformed to traditional ideas about femininity, rather than challenging gender ideals.

Nadia Comăneci added the question of age to understandings of femininity when at fourteen she won nearly every medal at the 1976 Montreal Olympics. The Romanian gymnast achieved the first perfect 10 in Olympic competition and went on to repeat this feat a further six times. Comăneci's mastery was readily visible to the average viewer because it bore the hallmarks of what had always been considered excellent execution in gymnastics—straight legs, pointed toes, and stuck landings.

Of course, the judging is more complex than this, also requiring certain body positions at certain points in an element and requiring that specific

Table I.2: Medalists in the apparatus competitions at each Olympic Games between 1952 and 2000, by country.

	Vault			Uneven Bars			Balance Beam			Floor Exercise		
	Gold	Silver	Bronze	Gold	Silver	Bronze	Gold	Silver	Bronze	Gold	Silver	Bronze
1952	USSR	USSR	USSR	HUN	USSR	HUN	USSR	USSR	HUN	HUN	USSR	HUN
1956	USSR	USSR	SWE/HUN	HUN	USSR	USSR	HUN	TCH/USSR		USSR/HUN		ROU
1960	USSR	USSR	USSR	USSR	USSR	USSR	TCH	USSR	USSR	USSR	USSR	USSR
1964	TCH	USSR/EUA		USSR	HUN	USSR	TCH	USSR	USSR	USSR	USSR	HUN
1968	TCH	GDR	USSR	TCH	GDR	USSR	USSR	TCH	USSR	USSR/TCH		USSR
1972	GDR	GDR	USSR	GDR	USSR/GDR		USSR	USSR	GDR	USSR	USSR	USSR
1976	USSR	USSR	GDR	ROU	ROU	HUN	ROU	USSR	ROU	USSR	USSR	ROU
1980	USSR	GDR	ROU	GDR	ROU	GDR/ROU/USSR	ROU	USSR	USSR	USSR/ROU		USSR/GDR
1984	ROU	USA	ROU	CHN/USA		USA	ROU/ROU		USA	ROU	USA	USA
1988	USSR	ROU	ROU	ROU	GDR	USSR	ROU	USSR	ROU/USA	ROU	USSR	BUL
1992	HUN/ROU		EUN	CHN	EUN	USA	EUN	CHN/USA		ROU	HUN	ROU/EUN/USA

Key: BUL = Bulgaria; CHN = China (from 1984 onward); EUA = United Team of Germany; EUN = Unified Team (1992 only, former Soviet Union team); GDR = German Democratic Republic; HUN = Hungary; JAP = Japan; ROU = Romania; SWE = Sweden; TCH = Czechoslovakia; USSR = Soviet Union (not present at 1984 Olympics); USA = United States (not present at 1980 Olympics) types of elements are performed in each routine. But many requirements in gymnastics have been changeable because every four years its rule book is rewritten. At the beginning of each Olympic quadrennium, a new Code of Points is released, and judges, gymnasts, and fans need to relearn the new requirements. With the release of each new code, competitors strategize how to capitalize on the desired movements, looking for ways to earn the most points with the least effort or risk of mistake. Imagine if a sprinter had to run 80 meters one Olympics, and then 120 meters the next—everything about the training, strategy, and determination of the final outcomes would be different, although the fundamental demand to run fast would remain constant. In this way, the rule makers of gymnastics had the power to determine exactly the kind of movements they wanted to see, and as a byproduct of that, who was best suited to perform it. But gymnasts and coaches found new ways to interpret the rules, leaving the FIG often responding to, rather than leading, changes in the sport.

*   *   *

Degrees of Difficulty shows how women's artistic gymnastics went from a sport at the forefront of feminism to one notorious for its young athletes and abusive practices. Yet in the context of the Cold War, it shows how women's gymnastics developed as a result of conflict and collaboration between gymnasts, coaches, and governing bodies—the FIG and IOC. It reveals how these individuals and organizations navigated international politics and how the Cold War catalyzed advances in the sport. Cumulatively, it shows how changing economic, social, and political values all contributed to a decrease in the average age of gymnasts and a corresponding increase in power of coaches, officials, and organizations. It is the first extensive research to try to make sense of the history of women's artistic gymnastics, and in that way, it offers unique perspectives on how and why the sport developed the way it did. Moreover, it shows how gymnastics has transmitted and perpetuated social ideals, and the role governing bodies have played in shaping these bodily discourses. Indeed, with its use of FIG and IOC sources, this book offers important insights into the functioning of international sports more broadly. It also contributes to a growing body of research that understands the Cold War as more than a conflict, but rather, as a time of international collaboration too. Each chapter shows how different forms of conflict, cooperation, and collaboration were essential to the way gymnastics developed. The chapters span inward-looking examinations of the sport—historical origins, femininity, style—and outward-looking, bigger-picture analyses that situate gymnastics and its development within the cultural Cold War.

The book starts with an introduction to the creation of women's artistic gymnastics. The first chapter assembles a vast array of secondary sources on the history of gymnastics and physical education more broadly, to show how it developed into sportive gymnastics. It then looks at how the sport was modified and made acceptable for women, outlaying the gendered cultural foundations on which women's artistic gymnastics was built. The advent of women's gymnastics was an important milestone in proving that women could be active and competitive, while preserving and even promoting femininity. The chapter argues that despite vastly different national traditions and gender expectations, women's gymnastics was created and standardized as a result of international cooperation achieved in what had hitherto been considered a man's domain.

Chapter 2 explores the changing ideals of Olympic sports from amateur to professional, and how that shift impacted gymnastics. It argues that Olympic economic policy was a place of challenge in Cold War gymnastics, rather than cooperation, with opposing views on the question of amateurism extending from fans and media to the FIG and IOC. These differences ultimately increased the FIG's dependence on the IOC. It also shows how the amateur rule contributed to the rise of child athletes in gymnastics, and how economic incentives are inherently linked to gymnastics success.

Chapter 3 examines the importance of sports as soft power and the role that gymnasts played in cultural diplomacy. It shows how the Eastern-bloc gymnastics tours of the 1970s relayed the message of détente and highlighted the use of sports for political means. Moreover, it leveraged gymnastics' popularity, while also reaffirming the sport's values of femininity, diminutiveness, and compliance. The Olympic boycotts of the 1980s grew out of such sports diplomacy, but they resulted in unexpected shifts of power and influence within international federations. The chapter argues that the use of gymnastics in diplomacy provided moments of international cooperation and ultimately renewed the role of sports as a place for collaboration during the Cold War.

Chapter 4 looks at how the rules of gymnastics have been made and broken. On the one hand, it demonstrates that many FIG decisions that shaped the sport were actually made in response to IOC pressure. But on the other hand, it reveals how cheating—through excessive ties, score-fixing, age falsification, and doping—really put the credibility of the sport, and its inclusion in the Olympic Games, at risk. It argues that, while international judges and officials collaborated to break the rules, the FIG cooperated with the IOC to maintain gymnastics in the Olympic movement. In doing so it shows that, very early on in the sport's history, coaches and officials prioritized their own and their national interests ahead of gymnasts'.

Chapter 5 demonstrates how the rise of the child gymnast was intricately entwined with femininity and "race." Canvassing the physical presentation of gymnasts, their behaviors, and their gymnastics, the chapter shows how the performance of femininity has always been central to women's gymnastics. But that performance of gender has changed in tandem with broader social trends, the changing styles of gymnastics, and particularly acrobatization. The chapter argues that collaboration across borders can be subtle, as officials, technologies, gymnasts, and coaches worked together to define and redefine what femininity means in gymnastics. Ultimately it asks whether a sport that was designed and constrained as feminine can offer some kind of feminist experience for the gymnasts involved.

Chapter 6 looks at the role of coaches and administrators in potentially limiting the feminist potential of women's gymnastics, through discipline and control. As the Cold War came to an end, it sparked a diaspora of former Eastern-bloc coaches who built strong gymnastics programs in their new Western homes but have often been scapegoated as the source of abuse in women's gymnastics. This analysis shows that abusive coaching has a long history in sports around the world, and that a culture of fear has been normalized within gymnastics, not least in part due to age and gender dynamics between gymnasts and coaches and officials. However, this chapter also looks at the results that have been achieved using more positive, empowering relationships, arguing that it is true collaboration that get results in gymnastics. Chapter 6 concludes with recommendations that address the power imbalance at the heart of women's gymnastics' abusive culture.

Finally, the conclusion offers thoughts on the history and future of women's artistic gymnastics. It looks back over the twentieth century and observes that some of the nostalgia for a golden era of gymnastics was present even in the sport's first decades. This suggests that the ideals of the sport have often been rooted in times past. The conclusion uses this understanding of history to reflect on the current state of women's gymnastics and, ultimately, argues that the sport's feminist potential needs to be restored in order for gymnastics' credibility to be reclaimed.

1

THE ORIGINS OF WOMEN'S ARTISTIC GYMNASTICS

"Gymnastics is a term which has different meanings in different languages and refers widely to diverging concepts and practices ranging from gymnastics on apparatuses to expressive movement cultures," writes historian Gertrud Pfister.[1] So, a history of sportive gymnastics needs to begin with an exploration of the varied movement cultures that have evolved over the last two centuries into the sport that we know today. Presently, the broader sport of gymnastics hosts various disciplines, including women's artistic gymnastics, alongside men's artistic, rhythmic, acrobatic, aerobic, trampoline, tumbling, and parkour. In fact, it was not until the twentieth century that "gymnastics" came to refer to a sport. Before that—and occasionally into the twentieth century—the term was used as a catchall for physical activity, particularly when it had educative aims. Only in the late nineteenth century, as international federations organized for each sport and gathered around the Olympic movement, did the notion of a consistent, universal, standardized competition lead to the development of the sport known as gymnastics.

This chapter examines the origins and development of gymnastics as it became a sport that then diverged into various disciplines, including women's artistic gymnastics. It shows how women's gymnastics began as a feminist pursuit, leading the way for women's sports. Created by women, for women, and governed exclusively by women, gymnastics demonstrated that women could participate in physical activity and competition without comprising their femininity or health. To get to this point in the early twentieth century, gymnastics grew from various nationalist gymnastics traditions in Europe, including their ideals about race, masculinity, femininity, and citizenship. While European sports leaders negotiated and collaborated to develop a shared understanding of the ideals of women's gymnastics, ideas about how women should engage in sports more generally remained diverse. So, when women's artistic gymnastics finally debuted at the 1952 Olympic Games, women gymnasts in the Eastern bloc and the West represented radically different sports systems. Beginning with the nineteenth century, this chapter chronologically explores these developments, arguing that international collaboration—between sports leaders and IOC representatives—standardized, popularized, and expanded the sport in the twentieth century.

A Genealogy of Modern Gymnastics

The creation of modern gymnastics is innately tied to the Enlightenment. Philosopher Jean-Jacques Rousseau argued that physical experiences are closely connected to mental, personal, social, and moral issues.[2] With such thinking, physical education found a place in an emerging education movement. This was only bolstered by eighteenth-century scholars' fascination with antiquity as inspiration for ways of organizing society. Education was no longer a privilege for the few but rather a necessity for modern, enlightened societies. Education, including gymnastics, became an important part of European society.

Education was particularly important in the late eighteenth century, as much of Europe was engaged in nation building. Physical education then, was also linked to the need to support and strengthen men to become not only healthy citizens but strong soldiers. Gymnastics developed in this mixture of education, nationalism, and militarism. In various European nations, teachers developed methods of training the body, known as gymnastics. Each of these was inspired by the works of pioneering German educator, Johann Christoph Friedrich GutsMuths, but were shaped for their own national contexts.

Johann Christoph Friedrich GutsMuths

In the late eighteenth century, Johann GutsMuths began teaching gymnastics. Having studied pedagogy at university, the so-called Grandfather of Gymnastics was convinced of the connection between the body and mind in education. While working as a teacher, he developed the coursebook on gymnastics, *Gymnastik für die Jugend* (*Gymnastics for Youth*), with the hope that employing physical education in schools would contribute to moral strength. His lessons were popular, and by 1800 his coursebook had been published in Britain, and two years later, in the United States. GutsMuths drew on naturalism, as advocated by Rousseau, based on the gymnastics of ancient Greece: "Our gymnastics adheres closely to the culture of the intellect; walks harmoniously hand in hand with it and thereby ideally resembles the pedagogical skills that were practiced by the young men in the Academy of Athens."[3] The ideals of gymnastics were situated in reverence for ancient Greece, much like the modern Olympics were a century later when Baron Pierre de Coubertin established them. It is no surprise then, that "gymnastics" was the name given to this new exercise regime. The name came from the classic training of ancient Greek warriors and athletes, *gymnos* in Greek, meaning "naked"—a reference to the unclothed bodies that originally practiced the activity.[4] GutsMuths's gymnastics was established to counteract "effeminate education."[5] From the outset it aimed to promote masculinity.

GutsMuths designed gymnastics as "culture for the body," to be integrated into the school curriculum.[6] He focused on a wide array of movements, including climbing, dancing, jumping, running, swimming, and throwing. In this sense, the broad nature of his work can be seen as the foundation for physical education, and also some of the essential components of sportive gymnastics. Describing hoop and skipping exercises, dancing, vaulting, and balancing, GutsMuths touched on the apparatuses and skills that, two centuries later, became various disciplines of sportive gymnastics: men's and women's artistic gymnastics, and rhythmic gymnastics.

Pehr Henrik Ling

In Sweden, Pehr Henrik Ling was inspired by GutsMuths's teachings.[7] After completing medical training, Ling outlined his own system of gymnastics exercises, categorized into pedagogical, medical, military, and aesthetic. A former fencer, he was motivated by his own experience of the health benefits of physical activity. As a military instructor at Karlberg in Stockholm, he was upset that Sweden lost Finland to Russia in the Napoleonic Wars. One observer later wrote: "an ardent patriotism and love of country provided the hidden source of his struggle to further gymnastics." So, in 1813, he established the Royal Central Gymnastics Institute in Stockholm to train physical educators.[8]

Ling's gymnastics was primarily floor-based, without apparatuses. He did however, make use of the rope and the balance beam.[9] Some sources also credit Ling with developing the wall bars and box vaulting horse, which was used for somersaulting.[10] Pfister summarizes the essential principles of Ling's gymnastics: "The exercises should be simple, involve the whole body and encourage participation by everyone."[11] His style of gymnastics was known as light gymnastics, owing to the freer style in comparison to German gymnastics. Instead, Ling's gymnastics emphasized the integration of expression through movement, bodily development, and muscular beauty—in such ways it was akin to dance. As GutsMuths had championed, the point was to educate the body. The form was, nonetheless, authoritarian in nature, with a focus on training, drill, and precision of movement.

Ling's style of gymnastics was further developed by educators François Delsarte, Rudolf Bode, and Émile Jacques-Dalcroze, who were all concerned with training singers, musicians, and dancers. By the early twentieth century, dance to music with handheld apparatuses was known as Swedish gymnastics, which was seemingly a precursor to what is now rhythmic gymnastics. Men originally competed in this sport, and debates within the FIG at the beginning of the twentieth century show that there was competition between this school of gymnastics, and the school of Jahn's German gymnastics that relied on fixed, rather than handheld apparatuses.[12] In some ways, women's artistic gymnastics was a compromise between the two styles—particularly in the dance-based beam and floor exercises, the latter of which was performed to music.

Friedrich Ludwig Jahn and Turnen

Friedrich Ludwig Jahn, known in his native German as *Turnvater*, the father of gymnastics, began his work in the early nineteenth century around the same time as Ling. Employed as a teacher during Napoleon's occupation of German states, he designed a philosophy of movement called *Turnen* to improve German physical and moral strength.[13] In 1810, he began taking his schoolboy students to Hasenheide, a wooded park in Berlin, for twice weekly games and exercises.[14] As these activities became more popular, he moved from improvised vaulting horses made from tree trunks to creating fixed apparatuses, including balance beams, ropes, horizontal bars, and parallel bars.[15] Like Ling, he thus invented a number of apparatuses that are integral to the practice of contemporary gymnastics.

As Jahn's *Turnen* developed, the emphasis on games decreased as the students took an interest in developing new ways of using apparatuses and competing for excellence in performance. These are the fundamental aspects of competitive gymnastics that underpin the sport today. The methods for teaching the sport also rely on Jahn's original approach. Squads were organized by age and level, and participants were monitored for proficiency. Squad leaders took their athletes through the exercises that Jahn had prescribed in his writings, which outline the steps for progression toward more advanced and complex skills.[16] However, unlike modern gymnastics, Jahn's *Turnen* held that "the body was not supposed to be exercised for its own sake or because of some abstract achievement, but in view of its military usefulness."[17] Although sportive gymnasts do not have direct ties to the military, the sport still carries military associations when gymnasts march to music or salute the judges. Moreover, the use of athletes' bodies to represent national supremacy continues the sport's parallels with military.

Gymnastics clubs known as *Turnverein* spread quickly throughout Germany, adopting Jahn's formalized lesson outlines from Hasenheide. The physical benefit, comradery, and the patriotic ideas brought out in the songs and stories alongside the activities all contributed to the moral ideals of patriotism and solidarity that underpinned the movement. Jahn intentionally created a movement that prioritized nationalism over any concerns about social class or other barriers to participation. Children from schools and orphanages alike participated, and participants were encouraged to wear a linen uniform that would equalize students from different social backgrounds.[18]

But Jahn's political ambitions of uniting Germany led to his arrest in 1819. His Hasenheide gymnasium was closed because of the nationalist values it instilled, and all *Turnverein* in Prussia were closed by a government struggling to retain its power. Jahn lived in exile in Freyburg thereafter. Nonetheless, *Turnen* continued in other parts of Germany. As it became part of the school curriculum, gymnasiums became a space for adults and university students to practice *Turnen*, leading to an upward shift in age. By 1860, the practice had grown so much that a German gymnastics festival was held in Coburg with more than a thousand participants from 139 cities and villages. A year later, when the *Turnfest* was held in Hasenheide to celebrate the fiftieth anniversary, 2,812 participated from 262 municipalities.[19]

Other European Gymnastics

Shortly before Ling in Sweden, and Jahn in Germany, Franz Nachtegall was establishing a school of gymnastics in Copenhagen. Having read Guts-Muths's gymnastics manual, Nachtegall gave private gymnastics lessons before he established a private outdoor gymnasium. In 1799, he was invited to teach at the Vesterbro School, before King Frederik VI established an Institute of Military Gymnastics in 1804 in response to Denmark's defeat in the Napoleonic Wars. There, Nachtegall supervised the army and navy gymnastics programs. In 1814, gymnastics became a compulsory part of the elementary school curriculum, nearly thirty years before Prussia took similar action.[20]

In Czechoslovakia, the *Sokol* (falcon) movement was founded in 1862, following similar gymnastic exercises to Jahn's *Turnen* and also with nationalist aims.[21] Similarly, after the 1878 defeat of the Ottomans in the Russo-Turkish War, the *Yunak* (hero) gymnastics movement arose in Bulgaria, which was also based on *Turnen*.[22] In the nineteenth and particularly twentieth centuries, *Turnen* and *Sokol* were exported to the New World and colonies as immigrants arrived from Europe and established clubs.

Nationalism, Race, and Class

All of these gymnastics regimens sought to create unity among participants that would contribute to national pride and a base of well-trained military bodies. This was important when the Napoleonic Wars were causing the remapping of borders, but also at a time when European nations were looking to conquer the rest of the world. So, while these national forms of gymnastics were preparing military bodies, they were also fostering national ideals, which extended to racialized ideas about citizenship and belonging. They were about establishing shared understandings and cooperation between citizens who would all work together to bolster their nation. In an effort to promote national cohesion, Jahn and other educators intentionally removed social class as a barrier to participation. But race, on the other hand, was an identifier of national unity.

Indeed, nationalism and race were deeply entwined in the nineteenth century. Superiority in both was contested through war, conquest, and empire. The will to demonstrate racial superiority went beyond Europe too, as Europeans sought to justify the colonization and subjugation of other peoples throughout the rest of the world. Academic disciplines like physical anthropology, anthropometry, and phrenology (the study of skull measurements and intelligence) sought to use science to validate European superiority. In that respect, the national, racial, and militaristic links in each form of gymnastic was premised on the idea that it might contribute to a type of European supremacy. Racialized nationalist ideas were inherent in each of these forms of gymnastics. Gymnastics educators drew from the idealization of ancient Greece and notions of what a civilized society looked like to develop gymnastics. This supported ideas of Whiteness and White superiority. These gymnastics were seen as national and moral pursuits that would build better citizens and stronger nations, unlike the supposedly frivolous, disorganized, acrobatic pursuits of traditions of circus, martial arts, and dance around the world.

Gymnastics for Women

When GutsMuths, Ling, Jahn, and their contemporaries created gymnastics, they did so thinking predominantly of White men. This is not surprising given gymnastics' birth in the midst of Napoleonic wars and emerging nationalism. These gymnastics were to promote manliness and strong bodies, and they contributed to the construction and legitimization of a hierarchical gender order.[23] But as the nineteenth century wore on and gymnastics spread, women began practicing an adapted form of gymnastics.

Ling had advocated for women in gymnastics, but his Central Gymnastics Institute did not make space for them until 1864.[24] Its graduates then aided the incorporation of women into gymnastics elsewhere. For example, Swedish gymnastics exercise became a popular form of physical training for women in Victorian England, thanks in part to Martina Bergman-Österberg—an alumna of Ling's Royal Central Gymnastics Institute.[25] She developed gymnastics programs in England in 1882, designed to prepare middle-class girls to become teachers. These classes were supported by the British government.

Sociologist Natalie Barker-Ruchti argues that Swedish gymnastics' role in Victorian England was to improve the health of citizens experiencing pollution, population growth, and overwork from the Industrial Revolution. Gymnastics was a medical solution to offset poor health consistent with nineteenth-century notions of hygiene. Yet medical discourse held that women only had a finite amount of energy that must not be wasted on mental or physical activities. Women were expected to be "passive, delicate and dependent," so they could conserve energy for their duty of reproduction.

In this context, on both sides of the Atlantic, "the argument for physical activity had to be carefully constructed," according to historian Patricia Vertinsky.[26] Ideas about femininity, "menstrual disability," and a general sense of women's physical weakness had to be reconciled with a parallel logic that women must develop physical strength and health in order to be robust and productive mothers. In this sense, ideas about women's bodies not only limited their participation in physical activity but also dictated which physical activities were appropriate for women's delicate temperaments. Therefore, medical experts advocated an appropriate blend of rest and restorative exercise. Ling's Swedish gymnastics, and its origins in medicine, fit this remit.

Bergman-Österberg's Victorian gymnastics was a form of nationalism, demonstrated through public displays. Whereas men's gymnastics across Europe had been about preparing young men for military duty, Bergman-Österberg described her gymnastics for women as "the best training for motherhood."[27] The role of gymnastics in promoting women's roles as wives and mothers was also central to its development across the Atlantic. In the nineteenth-century United States, gymnastics for women was championed within schools and families to promote Republican motherhood and true womanhood.

US women were to serve the national interest via maternity and household management, molding the morality of their children to secure civic virtue.[28] This required them to be educated. An American writer from the time, Margaret Coxe, argued that "judicious, systematic, physical culture is needed for our daughters no less than for our sons. It is a requisite to promote the health, happiness, and moral excellence of both." Such arguments were framed as a Christian duty, which gymnastics could fulfill, according to contemporary educators like Catharine Beecher. Gymnastics was deemed appropriate for girls and was expected to teach them the performative dimensions of etiquette necessary for middle-class women. This light training would cultivate health and deportment characterized by "feminine grace, ease and elegance," proclaimed Coxe, ensuring women's bodies were "harmoniously developed."[29] There were not only educative, behavioral outcomes expected from gymnastics, but also an indication that the sport would produce healthy, aesthetic bodies. Performing femininity, through gait, grace, and good looks was fundamental to sanctioning females' practice of gymnastics.

To differentiate it from what males practiced, gymnastics for females was often referred to as calisthenics.[30] Calisthenics were part of a discourse that "sought to propagate a modern mode of disciplinary power that aimed to train and (re)form female bodies and behaviors in accordance with conceptions of (genuine) true womanhood."[31] By the 1850s, these forms of physical education for females pursued continuous improvement, implementing physical testing and measuring progress. This progress was charted toward the ideal of either the Venus de' Medici or the Venus de Milo, comprising a broad, full chest.[32]

Gymnastics for females, then, in both its European and American contexts, remained bound by Enlightenment ideals. It retained links to antiquity and the healthy bodies and societies of ancient Greece. Like the males' sport, it was also shaped by a person's duty to their nation. For women, this duty was to be a good Christian wife and mother, to embody femininity and adhere to social roles, to bear children for the nation, and to have robust and healthy bodies. These nineteenth-century forms of gymnastics for women were premised on tenets that would remain fundamental to women's artistic gymnastics in the twentieth century: feminine movement, idealized feminine bodies, and above all, demonstrating full control over one's body. In this space, there was no consideration of non-White bodies and what role they might play in physical education or nationhood. If nationalism was essential to the creation of gymnastics, so too were ideas about race and citizenship. When women began to participate in gymnastics as a sport, ideas about race did not change. Fundamentally, gymnastics practiced by either sex aimed to promote national feeling and unity. Racialized people did not fit into this framework, unless it was to prove national or European superiority. The prioritization of White, European values continued into the nineteenth century, as gymnastics federated and sportified around the ultimate homage to Greek ideals: the Olympic Games.

Sportifying Gymnastics

In 1881, Belgium, France, and the Netherlands joined together to establish a governing body for sportive gymnastics, the Fédération européenne de gymnastique (FEG).[33] Today, the international governing body for gymnastics points to this moment as evidence it is the oldest international sports federation in the world. This international collaboration was the first step in sportifying gymnastics. The purpose of the federation was twofold. First, it would facilitate and oversee gymnastics competitions between member nations, through standardizing both apparatuses and rules of competition. Second, it aimed to "encourage the institutionalization of gymnastics in schools across Europe."[34]

When the first modern Olympic Games were held in Athens in 1896, gymnastics was one of only nine sports to compete. This points to both its popularity at the time and its widespread appeal across Europe. It also aligned with Olympic founder Baron de Coubertin's desire to revive sports and events of ancient Greece. Women gymnasts, however, remained constrained by the local organizing committee that was in charge of the Olympic program and still considered competition for women to be inappropriate.

In 1896, the IOC recognized the FEG as the governing body for gymnastics. Despite this recognition, the FEG did not officially participate in those games. Rather, the local Olympic organizing committee (of the host city) was responsible for organizing the gymnastics competitions. Their success in doing so was enshrined in Greek law three years later, which proclaimed: "Concerning gymnastics and contests of gymnastics and sports [the IOC] shall be responsible for the continuation every four years of the Olympic Games, held in the year 1896."[35] Of course, as Pfister noted, the term "gymnastics" has had different meanings at different points in time. It is not clear whether this law was specifically about sportive gymnastics, or if it meant that an Olympic committee should preside over quadrennial Olympic sports competitions in general. Either way, it demonstrates that at the turn of the twentieth century, the Olympics were set up as the central forum for international sports.

Following the success of those games, the FEG was inspired to hold an International Tournament in 1903. Despite only four nations participating, the current governing body for gymnastics considers this event to have been the first "world championships." Not until 1908 did the FEG participate in the Olympic Games as the governing body for gymnastics "worldwide," and only in 1921 did the organization finally change its name to the Federation internationale de gymnastique (FIG), with sixteen member nations and nearly every continent represented.[36]

In 1933 the FIG created a committee to govern women's gymnastics. Countess Hedwig Zamoyska of Poland was appointed to chair the committee. Her father-in-law, Count Adam Zamoysky, was president of the FIG at the time.[37] While this personal relationship undoubtedly influenced Zamoyska's appointment, it was not necessarily the catalyst for the establishment of a women's committee. Shifts were already underway within the broader community of international sports to make space for women's participation.

Although women had participated in some sports at some Olympic Games before 1920, this was because the selection of sports and athletes had been largely left up to the local organizing committees. After World War I, the IOC changed the structure and membership of local organizing committees in order to regain some control over what would and would not be included in the Olympic Games.[38] Until (and including) 1924, gymnastics for women had never been included as a competitive sport. Instead, women gymnasts were only allowed to perform demonstration or exhibition exercises. They could show their routines at the Olympics, but there were no rules and results, as women were not allowed to compete. But in the 1920s, advocates for women's sports began pressuring the IOC to admit women's sports to the games.

In 1921 Frenchwoman Alice Milliat established the Fédération sportive féminine internationale. She did so in response to the IOC's and International Amateur Athletics Federation's (IAAF) refusal to let women compete internationally. Further, they had declined Milliat's request for the Fédération sportive féminine internationale to join the Olympic movement, so she instead took it upon herself to create opportunities for women's sports. In 1922, she organized the first Women's World Games, which continued every four years until 1934. This organization and its quadrennial event threatened the IOC's position as the supreme body of international sports, pressuring it to incorporate women's sports into its program. As her games became popular, the IOC encouraged international sports federations to take responsibility for women's participation in their sports (presumably so that they might become included in the Olympic movement). Thus, as historians Florence Carpentier and Jean-Pierre Lefèvre observe, the 1928 Olympic Games in Amsterdam were the first notable instance of women's participation in the games. The FIG authorized the participation of sixteen to eighteen women in the gymnastics competition at those games. But the FIG was censured at the subsequent IOC executive board meeting in 1933 for the fact that the ratio of the women's program to the men's was too favorable to women.[39] If women's sports were to be allowed, it must be only when they were lesser or subordinate to men's.

Carpentier and Lefèvre argue that the increase in women's participation across a number of sports in 1928 was "a means for male institutions to better control women in a changing social context." They also noted that the IAAF played a significant role in this shift, led by its Swedish president, Sigfried Edström, who had been an IOC executive committee member since 1920, and became vice president in 1931. It is, therefore, likely that formation of the FIG women's committee in 1933 was a response to broad pressure to include more women in the Olympics, and a need for the FIG to organize its women's events in a more structured way after their first event in 1928. Moreover, it is no coincidence that the FIG established a women's committee just as IOC instructed to international federations to incorporate, manage, and control women's sports in the early 1930s. However, unlike other sports, the FIG women's committee consisted exclusively of women. So, while the IOC wanted existing male institutions to incorporate women's sports to take control of them, the FIG uniquely created a space for women to control their own discipline.[40]

FIGURE 1.1. The Danish women's team works on the beam at the 1908 Olympic Games in London. The photographs in this chapter show the evolution of the balance beam in the first part of the twentieth century. © 1908 IOC—All rights reserved.

FIGURE 1.2. The Swedish women's team performs at the 1912 Olympics. © 1912 IOC—

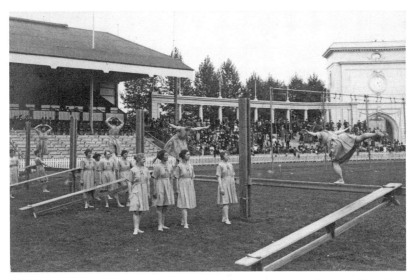

FIGURE 1.3. The Danish team performs another demonstration at the 1920 Olympic
Games in Antwerp.

Creating Women's Artistic Gymnastics

Although women's gymnastics was first contested at the Amsterdam Olympics in 1928, it actually had a much longer presence in the games as an exhibition sport. Photographic evidence indicates that women demonstrated team routines at the 1906 Olympics in Athens, 1908 in London, 1912 in Stockholm, and 1920 in Antwerp. But by the time it was accepted as a competitive sport for 1928, it still did not have a technical committee to govern it. The sport had not yet been standardized.

In 1928, women's gymnastics was a team event only. The competition consisted of the vault, "apparatuses" (it is unclear if these were handheld apparatuses, fixed, or both), and team drill.[41] Photographic evidence suggests that rope climbing was one of the apparatuses. Women's gymnastics was not included in the 1932 games, despite the moves afoot to incorporate women into sports more generally, and the FIG's will to establish a women's committee a year later. The following two Olympics, Berlin in 1936 and London in 1948, did include women's gymnastics, and each of these were a step toward the modern format of women's *artistic* gymnastics that would emerge in 1952.[42] In 1936, gymnasts performed compulsory and voluntary routines, which would be fundamental to the format of women's artistic gymnastics competition for the remainder of the century. They competed on vault, parallel bars, and balance beam, as is also consistent with contemporary apparatuses. But on the floor, they performed group exercises all at once, like they had in 1928. And like the competition at Amsterdam eight years earlier, the entire event was a team-only competition.[43] It remained a team-only event in 1948, and the group exercises on the floor persisted. But the apparatuses remained changeable. The women competed on rings instead of parallel bars, and the vault was referred to as a "side horse," referencing, for the first time, how that apparatus was modified for women's use.[44] Whereas men would vault over the horse longways, women would traverse only the width of the horse. Moreover, until the 1948 Games, both men's and women's gymnastics were outdoor sports. From the hills of Hasenheide to the Olympic Games, contests took place in the open air. But due to the rainy climate in London, the gymnasts' events were moved indoors in 1948, where they have stayed ever since.[45]

At the 1952 Olympics in Helsinki, women's gymnastics finally became "Women's Artistic Gymnastics." It consisted of the fixed apparatuses: vault, uneven bars, balance beam, and floor exercise—each of which was

FIGURE 1.4. The French gymnastics team competes on one of the apparatuses at the 1928 Olympics. © 1928 IOC—All rights reserved.

FIGURE 1.5. The Czechoslovakian women's team performs together on the floor with the handheld apparatuses at the 1936 Olympics. This kind of gymnastics would become a separate discipline known as rhythmic gymnastics by the mid-twentieth century. © 1936 IOC—All rights reserved.

performed individually. For the first time, medals were awarded individually for all-around and for each apparatus, and scores were compiled to formulate the team total. This can be considered the start of women's artistic gymnastics as it is now known. However, women's gymnastics in 1952 and 1956 was not entirely as it is now. The results from these two competitions show that gymnasts also still contested the "portable apparatuses" that would later become the separate discipline of rhythmic gymnastics.[46]

From its beginning, women's gymnastics was created as a space for women to be physically active within the realms of what was acceptable for women's bodies. Women's artistic gymnastics developed in this manner too, earning its acceptance into the Olympic movement on this basis. As the movement grew after World War I, the IOC steadily became preoccupied with "gigantism"—the idea that the Olympics were becoming too large and unruly, with too many sports, competitors, and medals. Discussion among IOC executive members on how to deal with this problem focused on only allowing women to compete in sports that were socially acceptable for them. IOC president Henri Baillet-Latour suggested in 1932 that swimming, gymnastics, tennis, and figure skating were appropriate for women, contrasting this with the proposed exclusion of all sports as being too energetic, aggressive, or not aesthetic.[47] Women's gymnastics' place in the Olympic movement was premised on the assumption that the sport must be consistent with beliefs about femininity—in particular, women's frailty, attractiveness, and ability to bear children. By its design, women's gymnastics set out to prove that women could compete in sports while maintaining their femininity. Although women's gymnastics operated within the confines of expected feminine behaviour, it also pushed those boundaries. Over the subsequent decades it quelled fears about the negative effects of sports for women, opening the door to women's participation in a wider range of sports. To this extent, it can be considered an ambitious, feminist sport.

At the 1950 IOC session, the IOC declared gymnastics a "compulsory sport" in the Olympic program.[48] The acceptance of women's artistic gymnastics into the Olympic program was strongly rooted in beliefs about what was appropriate for women and in concerns about appearing feminine. It required IOC and FIG leaders to cooperate and come to a shared understanding of femininity in sports and implement it in the rules of the sports. Women's movements were not to be seen as too strenuous for their weak bodies, so gymnasts performed light, graceful movements with minimal acrobatics and risk.[49] On the uneven bars, balance beam, and floor exercise, gymnasts demonstrated a series of poses to showcase their flexibility and passivity, moving softly and effortlessly between each position. Many of these gymnasts were former ballerinas, and the norm was for them to be in their twenties if not older. Hence, women's gymnastics came to have a dance component founded in ballet. Former Soviet ballerina Larisa Latynina was the reigning champion throughout most of this period, and her closest competitors from Czechoslovakia, Hungary, Germany, and Romania were similarly versed in dance, and came from countries with strong gymnastic traditions.[50] Women's artistic gymnastics had been considerably adapted from its educative, militaristic roots, to become a dance-like practice that was above all suitable for women's competition. Nonetheless, many countries maintained distinct styles from their own gymnastic and other cultural traditions and this had an indelible influence on the way they practiced the sport.

Women's Gymnastics in the Soviet Union and the United States

The Soviet Sports System

When the USSR joined the IOC in 1951, it had already spent the preceding years laying the groundwork for its acceptance into the Olympic movement. In 1948 it had joined the FIG.[51] Its influence was quickly apparent, when the 1952 games were the first in which gymnastics was now explicitly referred to as "artistic," per the Soviet style. As in Germany and Czechoslovakia, gymnastics had become popular in Russia for political reasons. Having also suffered military defeat in the Crimean war, Russia looked to gymnastics to regenerate its people and enhance national solidarity, morale, and preparedness. Although a gymnastics institute had existed in Russia since 1830, the first club arose in St. Petersburg in 1863, with more to follow a year later in five other cities. In 1868, the famous Dinamo Gymnastics club was formed in Moscow. Schools and colleges taught gymnastics too. Pytor Lesgaft introduced gymnastics to the army's physical education program, and by 1896 courses were available to civilians. By 1883, the Russian Gymnastics Society was established—the first national federation for any sport. Influenced by Lesgaft's teachings, Russian gymnastics favored a free style that encouraged will power and initiative—laying the foundations for the highly innovative nature of Soviet gymnastics that would characterize that nation's impact on the sport internationally.[52]

In the early twentieth century, Russian gymnastics was used as a form of national fitness to improve morale and cohesiveness. It was a means of diverting workers and students from their revolutionary impulses. After the October revolution of 1917, gymnastics retained its role in Soviet society because it was seen to discipline the population. Moreover, it had been sanctioned by Karl Marx himself. Physical education was to be part of the all-around education provided to citizens, "such as is given in the school of gymnastics."[53] Gymnastics became the foundation of Soviet physical culture, used to promote cooperation among the people.

By the 1940s, gymnastics was the fourth most popularly practiced sport in the Soviet Union for men and women. It had the support of the ruling communist party, which insisted that citizens acquire the dignity, grace, deportment, and bodily grandeur that people would derive from gymnastics. Moreover, it was used to promote a new Soviet culture, linking gymnastics to the Russian ballet and other forms of cultural expression. The aesthetic of gymnastics was a form of art, enriching cultural values.[54] The artistic values of international gymnastics and the emphasis on innovation can both be tied to the Soviet influence.

World War II reinforced a belief in the need for a population trained in physical education and sports. After the war, Soviet sports were predominantly structured around military sports clubs. Moreover, the postwar sense of pride in the nation's achievements during that war was redirected to pride in sports. From 1945 onward, athletes won cash prizes for "outstanding achievements," and some also received salaries and bonuses.[55] Since these measures conflicted with the concept of amateurism, on which international sports was built, the USSR needed to give the appearance of being amateur if it were to join the Olympic movement. So, in 1947, the Soviet Union reversed its earlier decree on monetary awards, declaring that there were no professionals in Soviet sports. Soviet athletes normally held one of three occupations: student, military service, or physical educator, under the sponsorship of their sports club. They were also provided expenses and leave to travel to high-level competition.[56] This structure allowed anyone achieving results to pursue elite sports, unlike the bourgeois amateur model that only allowed those with excess time and wealth to meet the costs of high-level sports. These support structures continued to support Soviet athletes throughout the century.

When the USSR joined the Olympic movement a year before the Helsinki Games, Soviet administrators promoted the Olympics as a mean of proving the superiority of the socialist sports system.[57] The need to dominate any contest it entered was essential to Soviet participation in international sports. "If you are not ready, then there's no need to participate," Stalin admonished sports officials after Soviet wrestlers finished second at the 1946 European Championships. Historian Jennifer Parks argues that the top Soviet sports official, Nikolai Romanov, learned from this exchange that "only a guarantee of first place would induce the Soviet leadership to send athletes to compete abroad."[58] The Soviet sports system was structured to support this ambition of international success. By 1962, the USSR established its first sports school and by 1970, there were twenty more. Talented young athletes could board at the schools, where they followed the standard Soviet curriculum and also received the highest level of training in Olympic sports. Gymnasts often spent upward of twenty hours a week practicing, in addition to their academic studies.[59] Talented athletes were funneled into the schools, and as adults, tertiary education institutions and military-affiliated clubs continued to support them. Between these organizations and the funding available to high-achieving athletes, the Soviet sports system facilitated, promoted, and incentivized excelling in international, Olympic sports.

The US Sports System

Sport in the United States similarly promoted national ideals and demonstrated the country's international standing. At home, it was part of a national program of well-being.[60] Internationally, US propagandists emphasized the voluntary nature of US sports, and the limited role of government in the lives of everyday people—a deliberate contrast with the Soviet sports structure. Sports in the twentieth-century United States were organized primarily around educational institutions (schools, colleges, universities), nonprofit community organizations like the YMCA, and health and fitness center businesses.[61] Male Olympic gymnasts in particular were sourced from collegiate athletic programs.[62] Unlike the Soviet Union, sports were organized at a local or regional level, not a national one.

The United States Olympic Committee, the Amateur Athletic Union (which governed a large number of sports, including gymnastics), and the National Collegiate Athletic Association (NCAA) operated on voluntary donations from private citizens and businesses.[63] Over the 1960s, the gymnastics community became increasingly upset with the Amateur Athletic Union's management of gymnastics, and by 1962 a group of coaches had broken off to form their own rival governing body, the US Gymnastics Federation (which changed its name to USA Gymnastics in 1993).[64] After nearly a decade of refusing to intervene in what was effectively a domestic governance dispute, the FIG finally withdrew its recognition of the Amateur

Athletic Union in 1970, instead recognizing the federation as the governing body for US gymnastics.[65] Until then, it had been difficult to coordinate a systematic response to the dominance of Soviet women gymnasts, as women's gymnastics had not been a focus for either the Amateur Athletic Union or NCAA.

At the dawn of the Cold War, discourse around US physical fitness centered on the "muscle gap," which worried that American bodies were weaker than their European counterparts. But US bodies were understood only as White, middle-class, and male. The USSR's early successes at the 1952 Olympic Games cemented these fears, in part because they had a broader view about who was doing sport. A response was clearly required to meet this challenge, but it could not be federally mandated, as that would go against the "American way." American liberalism had to contrast with the Soviet Union's totalitarian approach.[66] President Eisenhower created a council on youth and fitness and instituted a range of metrics to develop and test strength and fitness in schools, and students participated in sports in schools and recreation centers.

The muscle gap largely ignored women, and when it did think of them, women were still encouraged to avoid competition. While promoting intense training may have been the necessary answer to counter the Soviet sports structures, many were concerned about how such an approach would affect American women's femininity.[67] The Cold War thus prompted a wave of questions on how to deal with women's sports in the United States. It could no longer be ignored. So, in the 1950s, some colleges began offering women's sports competitions, under the supervision of physical educators. Then, in the 1960s, the US Olympic Committee formed a women's board to promote women's participation. Because concerns over appearing masculine were seen as an obstacle to women's participation, sports like gymnastics, which promoted feminine ideals, became popular choices.[68]

It is unclear which organization oversaw women's collegiate gymnastics when it began in the 1950s; the extent of competition it involved is also unclear.[69] By 1968, a collegiate gymnastics program existed under the American Association for Health, Physical Education and Recreation's Division for Girls' and Women's Sports. Then, in 1971 the Title 9 education amendments required schools and universities to offer athletic programs for both men and women. So, in 1972, the Association for Intercollegiate Athletics for Women was established, and it assumed control of collegiate women's gymnastics. In 1982, the NCAA became the governing body for collegiate women's gymnastics. All these institutions provided opportunities for women to practice gymnastics. But elite women gymnasts were rarely sourced from collegiate teams. Instead, US Olympians were almost always younger girls who had practiced in clubs and schools, not least in part due to a growing trend within the sport to link femininity with youth (see more on this in chapters 2 and 5).

Conclusion

Gymnastics was born in the fires of nineteenth- and twentieth-century European wars as a means of cultivating nationalism and preparing bodies to fight. It was all about instilling national cohesivity both in response to and in preparation for international conflict. The broadening of access to education, and the idea that physical education was important to learning, propagated the spread of gymnastics. Throughout Europe, national gymnastics traditions developed, but each focused on White men. When women began practicing gymnastics, their participation was also shaped by the patriotic duties they were expected to fulfill. It was to teach them etiquette and grace, as forms of femininity that would serve women as attractive wives and mothers, equipped to teach and raise their children. Gymnastics was equally to promote the health and robustness of women's bodies and their ability to bear children for the nation. As gymnastics developed for women, it was curated to promote feminine movement and feminine bodies. Despite the different national origins of women's gymnastics, they were united by a common goal of promoting women's health and serving the nation. And although the practice was born out of conflict, international collaboration enabled gymnastics to transform into a sport.

The process of sportification required international sports leaders to unite diverse national forms of gymnastics. They had to agree on how gymnastics would be contested, and this international cooperation was demonstrated when the FIG became the first international sports federation. But men remained the focus of these efforts. Competitive gymnastics was organized around the Olympics, and it was not until 1928 that women were allowed to compete at the games. This represented a kind of reluctant cooperation, as the IOC responded to pressure from activist Alice Milliat and her rival games. The FIG followed the IOC's request to create and control a women's gymnastics program, but it went further than required, uniquely establishing a governing committee consisting of only women. This committee designed women's gymnastics around the fundamental principle that gymnasts must demonstrate femininity. In doing so, the committee and the gymnasts quelled fears that women's sports would have negative societal consequences for health and femininity, which created further opportunities for women to compete in a wider range of sports. In this regard, women's gymnastics can be seen as a pioneering, feminist sport.

Women's gymnastics in 1928 was a hybrid of multiple styles of gymnastics, including apparatuses that are now divided into the distinct disciplines of artistic gymnastics and rhythmic gymnastics. The sport would not be standardized until 1952, when it also received a permanent place on the Olympic program. International collaboration within the FIG and the Olympic movement allowed this to happen. Leaders in both organizations had to agree on the aims and ideals of the sport, and in doing so, they promoted and perpetuated European values including ideas about gender. Discussions among IOC leaders reveal that women's gymnastics was accepted into the Olympic movement because the feminine ideals it promoted made the sport appropriate for women. Women performed light movements appropriate for their supposedly weak bodies, demonstrating passivity, softness, and grace. Their movements were designed to appear effortless, no threat to women's perceived fragility. Thus, in order to become accepted as an appropriate sport for women, gymnastics underwent several changes from its educative, militaristic roots.

A free, artistic form of gymnastics had attracted a large following in Russia and later in the Soviet Union. The Communist Party supported gymnastics and promoted its links with other Russian pastimes of cultural prestige, ballet and the circus. Soviet gymnastics then was seen to represent the values of the Soviet Union itself. And ideological ascendency was pivotal to this endeavor, so the USSR established a sports system designed to ensure sporting domination. Gymnasts attended specialized sports schools and were offered cash rewards and other incentives. Collaboration happened at the national level to create a system that would guarantee international success.

By contrast, gymnastics was popular in the United States but never approached status as a national sport. Moreover, the US sports system was designed to reflect American values of freedom and the absence of the state in everyday life. So, gymnastics was practiced in communities, often at schools or in private clubs. Women gymnasts had little place in this system until the domination of Soviet women athletes at the Olympic Games caused a reassessment of sports, femininity, and women in the United States.

2
FROM AMATEURISM TO PROFESSIONALISM

Under the leadership of American IOC president, Avery Brundage, from 1952 to 1972, the Olympic movement became consumed with the question of amateurism. It forbade athletes from receiving any economic benefit from sports, which not included not only financial support or sponsorship but even careers in coaching or sporting goods shops.[1] Many accused the Soviet Union of financially supporting and materially rewarding its athletes, making amateurism a major issue in Cold War sports. However, scholars have dismantled the idea that the USSR was unique in its assistance (medical, lifestyle, or financial) to athletes. "The practice of state funding," suggests historian Toby Rider, "had been in existence long before the Cold War, and countries that would commonly be called democratic partook in it."[2] As the century wore on, continued criticism of the amateur ideal proved inadequate to meeting the Soviet challenge. Moreover, it was impractical. By the 1970s, the IOC was suffering economically from its refusal to commercialize. Western athletes struggled to earn a living in paid employment while also training the full-time hours that had become necessary to reach Olympic level. In the 1980s, as the IOC moved toward professionalization, it was following the tide of public support. But true to the notion that the Cold War was also contested through the governance of sports, IOC members and the international federations were far from agreement on departing from amateurism.[3]

This chapter explores the shifting economic ideas about Olympic sports from amateur to professional, and what it meant for gymnastics. It argues that economic policy was a point of challenge, rather than collaboration, within the Olympic movement and its constituent federations like the FIG, as well as internationally. Initially, amateurism was used to discredit Soviet victories, but soon discourse shifted toward a desire to allow professional athletes in the games to truly level the playing field between vastly different sports systems. Gymnastics was not at the center of amateur debates, but it was still influenced by the economic policy. Amateurism contributed to the rise of child gymnasts and the pressures on them, and economic incentives were clearly linked to gymnastics success. When sports leaders around the world eventually agreed to professionalize and commercialize Olympic sports, it upset the existing order. US gymnasts began to challenge Soviet bloc athletes for victory. But while Olympic leaders could agree to abandon amateurism, the FIG—with its strong Soviet leadership—could not. It became a point of challenge between the FIG and the IOC, resulting in economically dire circumstances for the FIG. By the 1990s, the organization was barely remaining afloat and had to rely on IOC funding to survive. The chapter begins with a survey of the history of amateurism in the Olympic movement, before looking at how the Soviet entrance to the Olympics cast renewed interrogation of the issue. It then examines amateurism in gymnastics, and how the increasing professionalization of Olympic sports affected gymnasts, coaches, and the FIG.

The Origins of Olympic Amateurism

Originally, Baron de Coubertin's own ideas about sports as elite, noble pursuits helped shaped the IOC's economic policy. In the late nineteenth century, Coubertin had looked to British sports as the solution to securing the health of the French population. But his aspirations went beyond installing sports in education. His studies of ancient Greek sports inspired him to reinvigorate the Olympic Games for the modern era. In 1894, he gathered seventy-eight administrators from nine countries inside the Grand Auditorium of Sorbonne University. There, they voted in support of Coubertin's proposal to reestablish the Olympic Games and set up the International Olympic Committee (IOC) to govern them.[4]

In looking to Britain, the Olympic movement also adopted some of the class issues that underscored everyday life in that country. In late-1800s

Britain, commercialization and urbanization had opened up sports to the masses. "The growing influx of working-class players and teams posed a direct challenge to upper-middle-class hegemony," write historians Llewellyn and Gleaves.[5] Amateurism emerged as an answer to increasing meritocracy and democratization of society more generally, and sports specifically. Upper-class sports enthusiasts sought to avoid direct competition (and possible defeat) by lower classes, as well as trying to distance themselves from the working class that they perceived as unruly, violent and morally deficient. This is how amateur sports emerged.

Amateurism held that an athlete could not receive payment for their sporting pursuits. It was founded in ideas about keeping sports pure, asking athletes to engage in sports only for the love of sports, rather than for the prospect of monetary gain. The word has its roots in the Latin verb *amare*, "to love." However, amateurism also held that an athlete could not be compensated for time spent training or at competitions. It meant that only those who had enough money to be liberated from work commitments and enjoy leisure time could engage in high-level competition. It was thus used to exclude the working class from sports.[6] But like many aspects of Olympism, the amateur ideal was falsely attributed to and justified by what was presumed to be ancient Greek tradition.

Class exclusion was not the only goal of amateurism. Amateurism was also racist and sexist, "privileging Western (and masculine) values, principles, and beliefs."[7] In this vein, women and non-Whites were not considered to have the mental capacity to understand the selfless moral pursuit of sports for sport's sake. Coubertin, himself an aristocrat who had created the Olympic membership in his likeness of privately educated, upper-class men, demanded these values from the Olympic movement. However, this was a shrewd political move by Coubertin to ensure he gained the necessary support from his peers for the Olympic movement to be revived. Scholars have shown that Coubertin himself was ambivalent about amateurism.[8] Nonetheless, for the first half of the century, various nations held diverse interpretations of amateurism which were frequently debated and contested among IOC members, international federations, and officials. But amateurism had always been a minor issue until it was given a "Cold War flavor" when the Soviet Union entered the Olympic movement.[9]

Amateurism did not just concern payment for sports-related activities. It became an issue of sports systems and all the support athletes might get to devote themselves to athletic victory. It was not simply payments that were against the tenets of amateurism, it was also taking sports so seriously that training camps were used, supervised by teams of coaches, doctors, scientists, and other experts—this was more work than love. And these were the conditions in which Soviet athletes trained. Further, when Soviet athletes attended training camps, they received payments for "broken time"—time away from their regular jobs.[10]

The logic of amateurism excluding the working class, women, and non-Whites underpinned international sports by the mid-twentieth century. Amateurism was used to discredit the sporting victories of an entire nation that claimed to represent the working class and their many women athletes: the USSR. The Soviet Union's use of full-time "professional" athletes, whose sole employment was sports, prompted questions about that country's right to participate in the Olympics. But equally, the Eastern bloc challenged global ideas about amateurism, which were far from fixed or consistent. Indeed, soon amateurism in the West increasingly came under scrutiny because of the large numbers of student and military athletes representing the United States.

Amateurism and the Cold War Olympics

The Soviet entry into the games cast a spotlight on the IOC's enforcement of the amateur rule. Brundage was opposed to Soviet participation because of its state-run sports system, supported by material rewards. At the same time, though, if the IOC was to live up to its peacekeeping aims and grow its global appeal, it could not exclude a nation as large as the Soviet Union. In preparation for its bid for Olympic membership, the USSR ceased awarding cash prizes, and in 1951, formed a national Olympic committee. Its leader, Konstantin Andrianov, assured the IOC that the Soviet Union would cooperate with IOC ideals.[11] After visiting the Soviet Union in 1954 and seeing for himself the joyous group displays celebrating sports for their own sake, Brundage was convinced of the Soviet Union's pure intentions.[12] This conclusion is, however, unsurprising given the Soviets' expertise at supervising foreign visitors, allowing them to see only what their handlers desired.[13]

Nonetheless, Brundage remained cautious. During his 1954 visit to the USSR, he challenged the head of Soviet sports, Nikolai Romanov, to respond to US press clippings alleging Soviet professionalism. When Romanov insisted that "Russian athletes must place their education and their jobs ahead of sports," there was little more Brundage could do—he had to take representatives at their word.[14] This pattern consistently appears in documents in the IOC archives. Whenever allegations of Soviet professionalism arose, Brundage took them to the Soviet National Olympic Committee, which assured Brundage that the USSR believed in and practiced amateurism. The IOC had no investigative powers or procedures, and indeed, amateurism was to be enforced by the national Olympic committees. "We obtain three signatures to the Olympic oath, that of the competitor, the federation and the National Olympic Committee," Brundage commented in 1968. He also admitted the limitations of the IOC's enforcement of amateurism: "If any of these three people have lied, what can we do? The Olympic Games operate on an honor system."[15]

Meanwhile, the *New York Times* consoled readers that Soviet victory in the Olympic Games could only be achieved because they cheated. "How can nations . . . which draw a line of demarcation between professional and amateur sports . . . hope to compete on anything like even terms with such subsidized athletes?" asked journalist Allision Danzig.[16] This told US readers of the unfair advantages afforded to Soviet athletes because of their immoral, dishonest ways. It supplied American readers with an excuse for why the Soviet Union was doing so well in the Olympics, as well as a reason to dismiss this success—it was achieved by cheating. Another article declared that the Soviet Union's "strange notions of amateurism" were no longer acceptable now that it was "winning practically everything entered."[17] At the 1952 games, the Soviet Union had been just behind the United States in medal count, but at international events for several sports in the following two years, the Soviets started winning more. By 1956, the USSR pulled ahead in the medal count. Western critics saw this as the product of intense training in a full-time, government-funded sports system, which clearly contravened the amateur rule. Such stories reassured Americans that their athletes—and the entire ideological, political, and economic society they represented—would have won had they been on equal footing, and moreover, that they were morally superior to the Soviets. Further, it put pressure on Olympic leaders to enforce amateurism and, in particular, to crack down on so-called state amateurs, or amateurs receiving support from their nation.

But while the *New York Times* quoted international officials berating the acceptance of "Russian state amateurs," Australian media commented on the hypocrisy of US sports officials and commentators.[18] "Don't let anyone from the States—Avery Brundage . . . included—try to kid you about a small

matter of amateurism in American athletics," warned Melbourne reporter
Ken Moses in the lead-up to the 1956 Olympics. "These great stalwarts of
amateurism wear specially constructed long-range spectacles with their
line of vision guaranteed not to drop short anywhere within Uncle Sam's
territories."[19] Moses was highlighting the dubious nature of the many army-
employed and college-scholarship winning athletes on the US Olympic
team. Indeed, propaganda experts in the US State Department had purposefully avoided raising the questionable status of such US athletes.[20] Yet the
hypocrisy was not lost on foreign commentators. In fact, behind the closed
doors of the IOC, the British IOC member, Lord Burghley, collaborated with
the Eastern bloc to lobby against the "shamateurism" of US Olympians who
were also collegiate athletes.[21]

Brundage responded to these arguments with an amendment to the
Olympic oath, taken by all athletes, in 1956. They had to promise not only
that they were amateur, but that they would remain so *after* their participation in the Olympics.[22] While athletes were prepared to abstain from commercial contracts while they were competing, around the world they were
opposed to promising that they would never work in the field they loved.
Four years later, Brundage doubled down on his commitment to amateurism, with a new decree banning "state amateurs subsidized by their governments and college athletes receiving scholarships based mainly on athletic
ability." The ban on state amateurs was predominantly aimed at Eastern-bloc
countries; the ban of athletes on college scholarships was directed at US
athletes. Significantly, Brundage believed that the rule would "disqualify
about half of the American Olympic team." This policy was a direct reaction
to international condemnation of professional athletes directed increasingly toward the United States. "Eighty-five per cent of the criticism," said
Brundage, "deals with 'state amateurs'—boys taken away from their work
and studies to train. The other criticism has been our paid and subsidized
athletes. In international circles we [Americans] are considered worse than
the Communists."[23]

On this issue, neither Brundage nor the media made much mention
of women. Although some women leveraged their athletic success in the
interwar period, by and large, sports leaders rarely contemplated women
when amateurism was being debated, contested, and shaped.[24] This may
be due to the intermittent acceptability of women's work outside the home
until World War II and to women's limited participation in Olympic sports.[25]
But, after World War II, the lack of attention to women in discussion of

amateurism is striking. In the 1950s, women's participation in the Olympics was still highly controversial, with repeated calls throughout the decade to ban all women athletes. Yet, the combination of women as worker and women as athlete was so inconceivable that women did not feature the discourse around amateurism. It is little surprise that an organization like the IOC, known to be an old boys' club, paid little attention to a minority demographic like women in sports.

Amateur Gymnasts

Gymnastics had been missing from discussion of amateurism, including in the media coverage. (For its part, the FIG didn't appear to think amateurism was an issue in gymnastics: amateurism did not appear in the IOC's correspondence to the FIG or in the FIG's own records.) One reason for this absence is gymnastics' status as a "minor sport" in America. "Russia's overwhelming supremacy in competitions that the United States ignores, and for which it enters teams that are little more than token representation, carried her to the top," reported the *New York Times*. Two of these "token sports" were identified as Greco-Roman wrestling and gymnastics. The latter saw the Soviet Union come away with eleven medals to the United States' zero.[26] Not only does this evidence gymnastics' standing in US sports culture, reportage like this also served to minimize Soviet athletic victories by implying that the United States was not really trying to win in sports deemed to be unimportant.

In gymnastics, amateurism did not prevent the best athletes from competing because there were no alternative professional leagues. Gymnastics had been founded on principles of mass participation in order to meet its military and educative aims. The Olympic Games had always been the pinnacle of gymnastics competition. American male gymnasts came from a strong collegiate system that prepared the best for the Olympics. These were some of the athletes considered "shamateurs" by other countries, who saw the system of sports scholarships as akin to the Soviet Union's state support. But women Olympians were not coming from college teams. Although collegiate gymnastics for women existed from the 1950s onward, these were not necessarily competitions for advanced athletes. Indeed, there were no serious qualification procedures for collegiate competition until the NCAA championships began in 1982.[27] By the 1980s, there were 2,063 women gymnasts in NCAA gymnastics.[28] Yet, college gymnasts were still not entering Olympic competition. Although this issue is entwined with ideas of femininity and age, the amateur rule also influenced a preference toward teenage athletes in women's gymnastics internationally (see chapters 5 and 6).

The United States pioneered the use of young female gymnasts as a way of circumventing amateur rules. US women's artistic gymnastics drew on those who had all the trappings of professional athletes: young athletes with no work or family commitments, who were supported to sleep and train, whose every meal and every need was taken care of. Only, it was the parents who were the sponsors. While male gymnasts scored college scholarships to support their training as adults, no such support was available for women (until the 1980s), who were additionally burdened with the social expectation that they marry, bear children, and stay at home. The way around the amateur rules for women's artistic gymnastics in the United States was to rely on child athletes. This trend only developed further in the 1970s and 1980s with changes to rules, equipment, and coaching styles (see chapter 5). Longtime international gymnastics official Hardy Fink explains: "What does professional mean? All your needs are taken care of, you maybe get a salary, maybe not. But you're completely taken care of for everything. . . . So, there are your girls. Most of the gymnasts are young teenage girls. . . . Their parents pay for their room, their housing, their school, they drive them back and forth to the gym, they pay for their fees."[29]

While the United States and the USSR debuted their Olympic gymnasts in 1952 with an average age of almost 28, the average American age quickly declined to under 20 from 1956 onward. Meanwhile, the USSR also saw a decrease in age, although much slower, with the average age remaining in the mid-20s until the end of the 1960s. The average (mean) age for gymnasts from the United States was 18.3 in 1960, decreasing to 17.5 by 1976. By comparison, gymnasts from the USSR averaged 24.5 years of age in 1960, dropping only to 19.5 in 1976.[30] Throughout this period, several US gymnasts were aged fifteen in the Olympic year, and by 1980, two thirteen-year-olds and two fourteen-year-olds had been selected for the Olympic team. While the smaller pool of US gymnasts might mean that one could ascend to the top quicker, resulting in younger gymnasts, it cannot fully account for this US-led trend. The economic context of amateurism and parental sponsorship were crucial to the United States' early adoption of child gymnasts. However, around the world, the average age of gymnasts was declining at a steady pace—it was not only the United States.

The ages of Eastern-bloc gymnasts decreased only when the style of women's artistic gymnastics changed as a result of male coaches beginning to work with women (see chapters 5 and 6). These coaches favored the

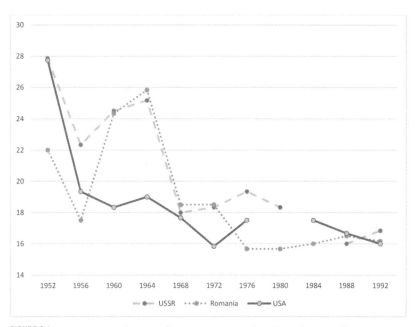

FIGURE 2.1. Average ages of women's artistic gymnastics Olympic teams between 1952 and 1992.

FIGURE 2.2. Maria Filatova was the second Soviet Olympic gymnast younger than fifteen. She competed at the 1976 games. © 1976 IOC—All rights reserved.

prepubescent bodies of younger women, as they resembled the boys with whom they were accustomed to working.[31] The worldwide drop in age in the late 1960s also coincided with changes to the style of gymnastics being performed, and modifications to equipment (see chapter 5). Older women with families, jobs, and little time were unable to meet the increasing training demands of elite gymnastics. This difficulty was exacerbated in the 1970s as the complexity of the sport increased and Olympic champion Nadia Comăneci's coaches, Béla Károlyi and Márta Károlyi, advocated training over five hours per day. Their success spurred many to adopt this regimen, both in terms of hours and the recruitment of children.[32] Eastern-bloc countries could meet these demands through the system of state amateurs or student athletes financially supported to concentrate on training. As a result, age and gendered domestic responsibilities bore less influence on a gymnast's ability to train and Soviet athletes remained older than their Western counterparts. Centralized support was largely unavailable in most Western nations before the 1980s, while private sponsorship would disqualify women for professionalism. The answer for Western nations was to work with athletes already supported outside the gym, with no other work or familial responsibilities: children. While amateurism was not the sole cause of the abundance of teenagers in women's gymnastics, it was certainly one of the early contributing factors to the United States' steep decline in average age, which was echoed elsewhere in the West. Around the world, these young athletes supported the employment of their coaches, officials, and other support staff, who also could win material and financial rewards for their gymnasts' successes.

Despite amateurism's looming presence, gymnasts were not immune to the commercial encroachment into the Olympic movement. Since 1956, Adidas had sought ways to get its shoes on Olympians, whose images were then broadcast around the world as free advertising for the company. Competition with Puma only amplified efforts to have athletes seen in company attire. Sportswear companies turned their attention to national federations as a way to achieve this publicity, outfitting Olympic teams. After the 1968 Olympics, Adidas became the official sportswear supplier to the Olympic teams of the Soviet Union, East Germany, and other countries.[33] Images from the 1976 Olympics testify to Adidas's success in this endeavor, despite gymnasts not wearing sneakers while doing their sport. Ludmilla Tourischeva of the Soviet Union graced the competition in her red leotard ornamented with Adidas's trademark three stripes running under the arms and down the body, while Nadia Comăneci stood on the medal podium

FIGURE 2.3. Nadia Comăneci wears an Adidas leotard during the 1976 games, demonstrating the commercial encroachment into gymnastics despite the amateur rule. © 1976 IOC—All rights reserved.

sporting the same style leotard in white with three stripes down each side in the Romanian national colors: red, yellow, and blue. Because the athletes did not personally profit from this—their attire having been supplied by their national federations—it did not break the amateur rule. Rather, it demonstrates a double standard: national federations were allowed to accept such commercial sponsorship, but athletes could not.

Toward Professionalization

As it became clear that Eastern-bloc athletes were virtually unstoppable, discourse shifted from denouncing Soviet cheating and toward openly accepting professionalism. This allowed US athletes to compete on equal footing. "The Soviet Union gives athletes sinecure jobs and other rewards as the athletes are subsidized by the state. Can Americans sneer at the Soviet and feel superior?" asked the *New York Times*'s Arthur Daley. "They had better not. We do that same thing but use a different system." The collegiate sports system was the particular target of this analysis. Colleges awarded athletic scholarships under the auspices of the NCAA, which, "no matter how you shave it," Daley announced, "is capitalization of athletic fame and therefore professionalism of the boys involved."[34] It is perhaps strange that capitalizing on athletic success was so vehemently denounced by a country that prided its capitalist ideology over that of its communist enemy. Such a paradox was bound to bend under the stress of interrogation.

The US and Australian public came to see amateurism as unrealistic, in terms both of enforcement and the demands of contemporary sports. Daley was among the columnists voicing their concerns that the modern sporting world could no longer be held to the aristocratic English ideal from which amateurism arose. "The toffs could afford to work at their play because they didn't deign to work at work," he said in 1967. "But a changing world has eroded pure amateurism so completely that only the dilettantes are true amateurs." Four years later, US Olympic swimming gold medalist Don Schollander and *New York Times* writer Duke Savage added their support to the increasingly loud rhetoric for an official policy move away from amateurism. "[Amateurism] ignores radical changes in sport—both economic and competitive—and important changes in worldwide attitudes toward them. The fact is that amateurism is dead." Concurrent to these shifting perspectives, vilification of "professionals" was displaced by the rise of anti-doping rhetoric.[35] These views challenged the IOC's position.

By the 1970s, Olympic sports were becoming ever more popular thanks to increased leisure time, televised broadcasts of Olympic competition, and government promotion of sports participation for health. With a greater number of athletes came tougher competition, and in order to contend for medals many athletes trained four hours per day, six days per week.[36] In an amateur system, not only were training and competing unpaid, but they came at a cost to athletes, through coach fees, club fees, travel expenses, and broken time. With so many pressures on athletes, many concluded that the amateurism rule, ostensibly in place to promote practicing sports for its own sake, was obsolete. "In sports, no one can become the best only for money," remarked Schollander and Savage. "An athlete, paid or not, can survive today's pressure and competition only out of love for his sport."

By the end of the 1970s, journalist Dave Anderson announced that "the world has outgrown the Olympics amateur concept." Llewellyn and Gleaves situate this change in public opinion in the counterculture movement that challenged existing social norms and highlighted social inequalities in the 1960s and 1970s.[37] Amateurism entered its decline. But an official departure from amateurism during Brundage's long term as IOC president was seen by commentators as impossible. Despite this groundswell of support for professionalization, it would be another two decades before it finally came to fruition.

Before athletes were allowed to professionalize, the IOC experimented with its own commercialization. Brundage set the precedent for selling television broadcasting rights, which formed the bulk of the IOC's income to the 1980s, and his successor, Irishman Lord Killanin, demanded that local organizing committees share responsibility for negotiating the sale of broadcasting rights with the IOC.[38] Throughout the 1970s and 1980s, the games continued to commercialize. The IOC took on McDonald's and Coca-Cola as major sponsors, turning a profit at the 1984 games thanks to the new economic model that maximized television revenue and demanded higher sums from exclusive sponsors.[39] Then IOC president Juan Antonio Samaranch sought a way to establish the Olympics as the pinnacle of sports while attracting more spectators and thus more revenue. The most obvious solution was to allow professional athletes. If such changes had been a long time coming, there were certainly strengthened by the economic recession of the early 1980s. Host cities, athletes, federations, and governments needed a reason to invest in the Olympics. They needed participation in the games not to come at a loss to them. The games had to adapt to their economic potential, or risk being deemed superfluous in a time of economic austerity.

When Samaranch became Olympic president in 1981, he announced his intention to guide the Olympic movement into a new epoch, shifting the economic landscape of elite sports. "The Olympic movement must forget the word 'amateur' and open its doors to the world's best athletes," he announced. "The Olympic Games are now the major sports event in the world, and we must allow the best athletes to take part." Over the next decade, he oversaw the IOC shift from an organization barely staying afloat to one of the most lucrative international corporations.[40] But while public support to professionalize the Olympics had been building over the last decade, there was far from consensus among the ranks of international sports administrators.

The Olympic Congress needed to vote on any official changes to the rules. At the Baden-Baden Congress of 1981, athlete representatives appeared for the first time and the IOC amended its rules to allow the international sports federations to create their own eligibility criteria. This resulted in wide-ranging approaches to defining amateurism.[41] After tennis first allowed professionals under the age of twenty to compete at the 1984 Olympics, the next step was to expand professionalism into more sports.[42] In February 1985, the IOC executive voted to allow professional tennis, ice hockey, and soccer players into the 1988 games at the request of those federations, as long as the athletes had not reached the age of twenty-three.[43] The "experimental" rule was to apply to the 1988 games only, as a trial toward wider professionalization in the Olympics. It came as a result of pressure from those international federations, combined with Samaranch's ambition to professionalize the games. The IOC indicated that if international federations requested it, more sports might also professionalize.

Despite these efforts to cooperate with the wishes of the public, athletes, and federations, in 1986 Samaranch had to placate Olympic leaders' concerns over the haste of professionalization. After the eleven-member executive board of the IOC "endorsed a plan to give professional and State athletes the same opportunity," the Olympic General Assembly were to vote on the idea in November. The decision would have superseded the 1981 decision to leave the question of eligibility to the international federations for each sport. But by October, meetings of the national Olympic committees that would be voting at the Olympic General Assembly indicated little support for the move. By November 1986, the only two supporters of Samaranch's push for professionalization were New Zealand's Lance Cross and Britain's Charles Palmer, "who called for an end to 'hypocrisy' and for the Olympic movement to face the 'reality' that professionals had already participated in the Games." Much of the resistance came from the Eastern bloc, which would undoubtedly be disadvantaged by inclusion of the West's top paid athletes. As Samaranch observed, there was "no difference between professionals and Soviet-bloc State-supported athletes."[44]

Professional Gymnastics?

While the IOC leadership was open to professionalization, the FIG was not. Instead, it challenged the IOC on its shifting policy. Noting the inclusion of football, tennis, and hockey in the games, in his 1986 report FIG president

Yuri Titov questioned how sports with major professional branches could include paid athletes at Olympic Games.[45] It appeared that the FIG was unaware of the shift of eligibility rules from the IOC to the international federations. They decided to refer the question of professional participation from soccer, tennis, and hockey to the IOC for clarification.

A year later, and no longer ignorant of the shifts underway in the wider Olympic movement, the FIG reiterated its position that amateurism would remain firmly intact in both men's and women's gymnastics. Although international federations could now set their own rules, the FIG's reluctance to professionalize was an attempt to align the FIG with the IOC's historic values. Moreover, the FIG's agenda was being set by its Soviet leader, Yuri Titov. A former Olympic gymnast himself, the policy he set for the FIG also adhered to his nation's stance on amateurism, opposing any shift toward professionalizing the games. The FIG thus refused to contemplate a shift in its own amateurism rules: "As far as the FIG is concerned, our statutory dispositions and Rule 26 [the amateur rule] of the Olympic Charter are still both applicable and applied," declared Titov in 1986.[46]

The FIG refused to entertain the idea of professionalization for the remainder of the decade. Although it expressed concerns over athlete safety and the quality of the sport, its fears also echoed the elitist, antiquarian discourse that had birthed the modern Olympic Games and given gymnastics its name. "Professionalism in gymnastics would rapidly lead us on a downward path," suggested Titov, with coaches "replaced by 'publicity agents' or, worse, by 'impresarios'."[47] Such comments also adhered to the Brundage era of Olympic politics, echoing rhetoric about purity and love of sports being incompatible with financial investment and reward. In this sense, the FIG could be seen as a highly conservative federation, loyal to the IOC of old, rather than to the modernizing movement. The FIG's discourse consistently sought to assert gymnastics as pure, one of the original Olympic sports, and still aligned to the original values of the modern games. In this perspective, the FIG upheld the traditional Olympic values as the IOC itself departed from them.

By 1988, as the IOC diverged further from its amateur roots, the FIG wrote its own rule on eligibility. Gymnasts were allowed to be financially supported by their national federation, receiving "pocket money" and having their lodging and coaching taken care of. But gymnasts must also refuse to claim "professional" status, must not appear in advertising (unless it was under the directive of the national federation or Olympic committee), and were prohibited in taking part in any competition for money.[48] Yet, despite its opposition to professional athletes, the FIG had entered one of its first financial partnerships in 1985, "collaborating" with Longines, a Swiss timekeeping company.[49] While the language used in the FIG's announcement suggests it was more of a quid pro quo arrangement than an income-generating sponsorship deal, it was nonetheless one of the FIG's first forays into the emerging modern economic framework for sports. The FIG adopted the commercial aspects of Samaranch's IOC but refused to abandon Brundage's amateurism.

The FIG was probably not alone among international federations in its misgivings about professionalization, but its reluctance to abandon amateurism disadvantaged gymnastics in an era of emerging commercialization. Gymnastics was increasingly invisible even as the quadrennial Olympics became its main source of revenue, compared with other sports that enriched themselves through the income and publicity attached to frequent global contests and major leagues. Both interest and financial investment in women's artistic gymnastics suffered as a result.[50] For example, the IAAF hosted regular world championships, for which it sold sponsorship and television rights. The financial benefits wrought by this model allowed the IAAF to become more powerful in sports politics.[51] The same cannot be said for the FIG. The slow establishment of its own revenue streams meant that it remained dependent on the IOC into the twenty-first century.

Despite the FIG's languishing economic policy, its gymnasts were not necessarily so slow off the mark to reap the rewards that professionalization promised. While gymnasts were not allowed to become professional, there was no limitation on enjoying professional opportunities after an Olympic success if a gymnast never intended to compete internationally again. The potential income from private sponsors opened a profitable and typical career trajectory for many successful US Olympic gymnasts. As potential income from gymnastics rose, so did the rankings of US gymnastics.

Following their historic successes at Los Angeles, the 1984 US team was swamped with lucrative offers from companies interested in the rising popularity of the sport. All-around champion Mary Lou Retton appealed to audiences and sponsors alike in her stars-and-stripes leotard, exuding energy from atop the medal podium. She became the first female spokesperson for Wheaties (a General Mills cereal); signed a contract with hair product manufacturer Vidal Sassoon; and agreed to be a worldwide representative for youth sports programs for McDonald's fast-food chain. Meanwhile,

FIGURE 2.4. Despite the FIG's amateurism policy, the professionalization of Olympic sport more generally provided new opportunities for Mary Lou Retton (pictured here at the 1984 Olympics closing ceremony) and other gymnasts. © 1984 IOC—All rights reserved.

several of the successful male and female gymnasts at the 1984 games won acting opportunities as a direct result of their athletic success.[52] Despite FIG rules rendering them ineligible for further Olympic competition, the victorious US gymnasts readily renounced their amateur status to reap the rewards of their Los Angeles success.

A number of gymnasts who represented the United States in the Olympics later followed in Retton's footsteps. Kathy Johnson also pursued a career in television, as did Julianne McNamara, Betty Okino, Dominique Dawes, Tasha Schwikert, Shawn Johnson, Nastia Liukin, Gabby Douglas, McKayla Maroney, and Laurie Hernandez. Others pursued different careers in entertainment: in singing, stunts, and the post-Olympic gymnastics and ice-skating tours. More recently, others forwent show business for other sponsorship deals. Jordyn Weiber accepted a deal with Adidas, Aly Raisman had a number of sponsorship deals across fashion and leisure, and Simone Biles has lucrative contracts with Nike and other firms. In 1996, the "Magnificent Seven" Olympic team appeared on Wheaties boxes too, followed by Olympic all-around champions Carly Patterson and then Nastia Liukin. Additionally, since the 1990s many US Olympians (and many former Eastern-bloc gymnasts who relocated to the West) have published their autobiographies. Many US gymnasts also created leotard lines with gymnastic apparel manufacturer GK Elite Sportswear. Others have leveraged their success to attract business to their own gymnastics clubs. To add to these incentives, from 1993, the US Olympic Committee awarded medal bonuses of up to $15,000.[53]

While some male gymnasts like Kurt Thomas similarly used their gymnastics success to launch entertainment careers, and many elite gymnasts now perform for Cirque du Soleil, the international circus, male gymnasts' commercial opportunities have generally been fewer. To some extent this can be explained by the US men's relatively sparser successes, winning team gold 1984, silver in 2004, and bronze in 2008. Paul Hamm's win of the all-around gold in 2004 was shrouded in controversy after the judges upgraded the score of the runner-up after the competition, which put Hamm's victory in question. As a result, Hamm allegedly lost a pending appearance on the Wheaties box. It is also possible that gendered perceptions of gymnastics as a women's sport meant male gymnasts had fewer commercial opportunities (see chapter 5).

It should be noted, though, that many gymnasts have had to decline professional opportunities. The NCAA awards scholarships or tuition waivers only to amateur athletes. Gymnastics is one of the well-supported programs for women college athletes. While the retention of amateurism in college sports poses little problems to athletes in sports like football, where athletes can get their education on a scholarship then go on to pursue professional football careers, gymnastics is another story. There is immense pressure on female gymnasts to peak around sixteen, which means professional opportunities come their way much sooner—before college. There is no physiological reason that women gymnasts cannot continue to compete internationally after college age—as Oksana Chusovitina, Vasiliki Millousi, Mai Murakami, Marta Pihan-Kulesza, Chellsie Memmel, and others have proven to be true. But the pressure to peak so early can mean that burnout and physical injury leave female gymnasts' bodies so fatigued by their twenties that pursuing gymnastic professionally after college is out of the question. So, despite the rise in professional opportunities for US gymnasts after the 1980s, gymnasts have had to gamble on which path is more lucrative: retaining amateur status for a funded college education or revoking amateur status for professional contracts. A relaxation of the collegiate sports amateur rules was only announced in October 2019.

The notion that economic opportunity has incentivized gymnastic success goes beyond the US victories that coincided with the emergence of professionalism. From the 1950s to the 1970s, Soviet and Romanian gymnasts raised both their incomes and standards of living through international victories. FIG official Hardy Fink reflected that they were the real capitalists in gymnastics.[54] Successful gymnasts like Tourischeva were offered positions within the Communist Party, and athlete and coach salaries, cars, and apartments were tied to their competition results.[55] The situation was similar in Romania, where the government covered training and equipment costs, and poorer families saw gymnastics as a way of attaining accommodation, education, and a better life. Meanwhile, until the 1980s their Western counterparts, relying on private funding for training and competition, had little opportunity to improve their economic fortunes through gymnastics, no matter how successful they were. But when the IOC relaxed enforcement of the amateur rule in the 1980s, it changed the economic potential of gymnastics for Western athletes. At this point, US gymnastics champions began to emerge. Although improved training systems, better networking, and the 1984 boycott also played a part in creating a more favorable environment for Western gymnasts, the new economic situation was also crucial to changing the power balance of international gymnastics. Moreover, at the same time as sponsorship opportunities opened up in the United States, Eastern-bloc fortunes shrank under the glasnost and perestroika of the 1980s. Centralized support for sports decreased, while visibility of the quality of life and opportunities abroad increased. The emigrations this prompted in the 1980s and 1990s are further discussed in chapter 6.

While Western athletes had been enjoying the new prosperity of professional sports (and the impacts of Eastern bloc decline were yet to be fully felt), the FIG was suffering from its refusal to commit fully to commercialization and professionalization. In its 1992 report, President Titov indicated that the federation was barely staying afloat. Competition costs for the world championships nearly exceeded income, yet competitions were the main source of revenue for the FIG.[56] In the 1990s, the organization thus began an overhaul of its economic policy, modeled on the IOC's recent history. First, it allowed advertising on leotards. Yet, a 2019 FIG report noted that this has not been such a successful endeavor because "the space has been too small for advertisements to be recognized."[57] Then, in 1996, it followed the IOC's lead, partnering with International Sport and

Leisure (ISL)—a sports marketing company—that had previously worked with the IOC. ISL brought television contracts worth over $2 million US to the FIG, along with $2 million of sponsorship deals.[58] In addition to these private commercial ventures, ISL also secured $4.6 million from the IOC and a grant to pay for the 1997 world championships in Lausanne, reaping the benefits of the IOC's earlier professionalization. "Since the FIG engaged in collaboration with the world-known agent ISL, its financial state has recovered well," concluded Titov.[59] Two decades later, his successor, Bruno Grandi, offered further insight into the FIG's economic situation at that time. Grandi said that when he began his presidency in 1996, the FIG's entire financial situation had been at stake and he had had to ask the IOC for help to stage the artistic gymnastics world championships.[60] Indeed, it is difficult to know just how much financial independence ISL brought to the FIG, as the company collapsed in 2001, with executives accused of fraud and embezzlement. Whatever the case with ISL, it is certain that the IOC had financially sustained the FIG well until the 1990s because of the FIG's own refusal to commercialize.

When Grandi replaced Titov in 1996, he continued seeking opportunities to increase revenue beyond the IOC. He emphasized not just competition but televised competition coverage. This policy was more attuned to the direction the IOC was taking. "We must realize that financial stability is not possible until we offer the television market a technical presentation of gymnastics more in keeping with the expectations of the public and competitive vis-à-vis other sports," wrote Grandi in 2000.[61] Moreover, the FIG realized the need for it to modernize if it were to remain favored within the Olympic family. Grandi was conscious that gymnasts needed to compete with X sports that rivaled gymnastics' previous monopoly over aerial sports. To attract viewers, it decreased the length of competitions by removing the "compulsory" routines where gymnasts all performed the same exercises. It was also at this time that discussions of the post-10 code of points seriously took hold, as a way to increase the objectivity of the sport, and in doing so attract viewers and win the approval of the IOC (see chapter 4 for more on the post-10 code). To further incentivize gymnasts to perform awe-inspiring, boundary-pushing feats, the FIG started awarding cash prizes to medal winners in the new millennium. Grandi's goal was to make gymnastics "top-level sporting entertainment," so it would receive the associated financial rewards from the IOC, which distributed Olympic revenue to federations based on viewership. In this endeavor, the FIG was successful. Gymnastics has since become one of the most popular Olympic sports, which has in turn led to financial rewards for the federation. In 2013 the IOC awarded gymnastics tier 1 level, which means that, alongside track and field and swimming, gymnastics nets the most IOC funding.[62] After the 2016 Rio de Janeiro Olympic Games, revenue distributed to international federations totaled $540 million.[63]

Yet, even by 2019, it was clear that the FIG had few commercial contracts. A summary of the 2016 and 2017 accounts indicates that the FIG used its quadrennial payment from the IOC to fund its operations for the next four years.[64] According to Morinari Watanabe (of Japan), the FIG president as of this writing, the FIG's only sponsors have been VTB (a Russian bank), Longines, and Cirque du Soleil.[65] However, this statement was made to cast light on the president's achievements in securing two new agreements in 2018: one with Fujitsu (a Japanese technology company) and one with Pasona (a Japanese human resources company). The FIG has had a number of further "partners" over the past two decades, but the extent to which these organizations made financial contributions or donated their services in kind is unclear. The organization is thus still bound to the IOC and reliant on its revenue distribution. While its top athletes can now seek professional contracts, doing gymnastics to pay the bills remains viable only for a select few.

Conclusion

The FIG's resolute commitment to amateurism throughout the Cold War shaped the financial situation in which the FIG and many of its gymnasts find themselves today. Economic policy was a place of challenge in Cold War gymnastics, rather than cooperation. Fans and media long pressured the IOC to relax amateur rules to allow more parity in training conditions between East and West. The amateur rule contributed to a decline in average age for female gymnasts in the West as a way to gain the financial and domestic support required to be able to train full-time. However, when the IOC finally began making changes in the 1980s, the FIG remained devoted to amateurism. Even so, gymnasts began to accept increasing professional opportunities from the 1980s onward, which reshaped the landscape of medalists from then on. It is clear that the economic incentives offered to gymnasts have been directly proportional to their success in the sport. As the United States embraced commercial possibilities in gymnastics, it began climbing the medal rankings. By contrast, economic downturn in the Eastern bloc, leading to funding cuts and removal of incentives, coincided with the beginning of a decline in Soviet domination.

The FIG's commitment to amateurism despite global change caused economic strife for the organization. It struggled to cover its operating costs, and the profile of gymnastics diminished as other sports established professional leagues and attracted a lot of attention. The FIG was not working with the IOC or other international federations, and in fact it was doing the opposite of what they were doing. The FIG's opposition to professionalization made the FIG reliant on IOC funding. Its failure to cooperate with wishes of other international sporting bodies, gymnasts, and officials ultimately caused the organization financial pain and weakened the position of the sport in comparison to others.

3

DIPLOMACY IN GYMNASTICS
AND THE OLYMPIC MOVEMENT

In the 1970s, teams of the Soviet Union's best gymnasts toured the West performing gymnastics displays. Their mission: to share the values and ideals of the Soviet Union with the rest of the world. This chapter argues that such tours were examples of international cooperation during the Cold War, in which gymnastics was used for diplomatic purposes. The tours capitalized on the sport's popularity while also reaffirming its values of femininity, diminutiveness, and compliance. But at the same time, these star-spangled spectacles also increased the pressure on the young girls as they became responsible for earning acclaim not only for themselves and their coaches but for their nations too. A form of citizen diplomacy, the tours were designed to win Western hearts and minds. They communicated their regimes' cultural values through the gymnasts' bodily movements, which drew on various national traditions like circus and ballet. The gymnasts' movements were intended to communicate broader ideas like the freedom with which they moved. These bodily discourses were a crucial form of messaging Western audiences. While US gymnasts did not have the celebrity appeal necessary to engage in similar tours to the Eastern bloc, their political leaders nonetheless saw value in this sports diplomacy, taking the opportunity to meet with the touring Soviet gymnastics troupes. Notwithstanding the Olympic movement's avowed apoliticism, such engagements went to the heart of Olympic values, forging international cooperation through sports, despite the Cold War.

The latter part of this chapter situates gymnastics diplomacy in the context of broader Olympic diplomacy. As détente froze over by the end of the decade, sports were no longer a cause for global celebration. If the 1970s proved the value of sports as a form of soft power, by 1980 this power was being harnessed in the form of Olympic boycotts in an attempt to influence geopolitical tensions. Without overstating the centrality of women's artistic gymnastics to this trajectory, it is clear that sports tours like the Soviet gymnasts' 1970s tours of the United States demonstrated the utility of sports as a form of soft power, which lead to the Olympic boycotts of the 1980s. While the boycotts, as public forms of diplomacy, played out on the world stage, they also had significant impacts on the makeup of sports' governing bodies. And while the Olympic boycotts might seem, on the surface, to show a lack of international cooperation, this chapter shows that they actually resulted in newfound collaboration. It was as a result of these boycotts that the Goodwill Games were born, aiming to bring Soviet and American sports back together. The boycotts also caused the IOC to become more deeply engaged with United Nations (UN) initiatives to foster Soviet-US collaboration through sports. This chapter begins with a discussion of forms of diplomacy in sports, then explores the Soviet and Romanian gymnastics tours of the 1970s, before turning to the 1980s Olympic boycotts and the IOC's response to them.

Sports Diplomacy

Why would international sports be relevant to statecraft? How does a leisure activity assume importance in international relations? The answer is: by many of the same processes in which gymnastics had developed as a patriotic practice, promoting nationalism through an "imagined community." Historian Barbara Keys shows that international sports can be seen as the construction of an "imagined world"—governed by distinctive and transnational laws and practices, sharing symbols, traditions, ideals and values. "Through international sport, belonging to the world was mediated by belonging to a nation." More than half the world's nations participate in the Olympic Games, with billions of people across more than two hundred countries watching television broadcasts of the event.[1] The state and its relationship to foreign states have always been central to international sports.

Many scholars have linked the popularity of international sports to their potential as a political tool. The toils of sporting contest align with the fundamental aim of public diplomacy, winning hearts and minds. Sports create narratives of winner and losers, underdogs and nobodies challenging dominant powers, villains and heroes. In the Cold War context, athletic rivalry between the Soviet Union and the United States underpinned the quadrennial games. Adding to the arms race and the space race, in sports, the Cold War meant an Olympic medal race.[2] But more than a race to accumulate the most Olympic medals, sports, as a form of entertainment, was also the subject of a push to win over public opinion. People who did not speak the same language or grow up in the same cultural, social, or political conditions could share in an understanding of sports and their internationally agreed upon values and ideals. Feats of athleticism cross gender, religious, and economic boundaries; witnessing the awe of human achievement is understandable to anybody. For these reasons, observe historians Heather Dichter and Andrew Johns, "sport is especially suitable as a vehicle to build bridges between governments and peoples."[3]

As a practice of leisure and a form of entertainment, sports have never carried the esteem given to matters of statecraft. They generate great interest and carry multiple nationalist meanings, but at the same time, they are not seen as a serious matter that could pose a risk to foreign relations. This is precisely why sports have been so well employed as a form of soft power. The scholar who coined the term, Joseph Nye, explains that soft power is "the ability to get what you want through attraction," (attractiveness of culture, credibility of political ideals) in contrast with using military or economic coercion to get others to change their position.[4] Soft power is about influence rather than force, and in this sense it can be seen as an instrument of diplomacy, aimed at preserving peace between nations. Because it is about influence, soft power is primarily communicated through public media.[5]

Soft power is fundamental to the forms of diplomacy seen in gymnastics and the Olympic movement. Between the tours of the 1970s and the boycotts of the 1980s, gymnastics and the Olympic Games were sites of public diplomacy, cultural diplomacy, and citizen diplomacy. Public diplomacy influences international relations through communications with the general public. Hence, for the historian it reveals what a state tells its people about relations with other countries. A stellar example of this is Rider's analysis of how US government agencies utilized sports during the Cold War to influence public opinion and to put pressure on communist regimes abroad. He shows how *Sports Illustrated* worked with the Central Intelligence Agency to aid the extraction and defection of Hungarian refugees from the 1956 Olympic Games.[6]

Rider's example is additionally significant because it shows that diplomacy is not always limited to state actors. It can rely on individuals and private organizations too. This goes beyond the (traditional) realist understanding of diplomacy as being limited to actors of the state.[7] International nongovernment organizations, like the IOC and international federations, are central to understanding sports diplomacy too.[8] They create many of the circumstances and sites for sports diplomacy to happen, both publicly and behind closed doors. These opportunities are created by individual citizens taking part in a global network of exchange. In sports, this happens not only in the competition arena but also within the governance of international federations, where people across ideological divides nonetheless connect and collaborate.[9] After the 1980 Olympic boycott, such citizen diplomacy took place out of the public eye and behind the closed doors of sports' governing bodies.

Sports, as entertainment, provided a space for public diplomacy, where nations seek to "cultivate" foreign publics, through cultural diplomacy and exchange.[10] Soviet athletes went to the United States to dispel American propaganda about the communist regime. But while they were visiting, their hosts encouraged them to adopt American practices and values. Known as cultural infiltration, this informed diplomatic policy on all sides of the Cold War.[11] The United States and the Soviet Union had already established something of a cultural exchange program during the thaw years of the 1950s and 1960s. The 1958 Lacy-Zarubi agreement enabled exchange between Soviet and American scholars, cinema, science, dance, and sports.[12] But scholars have given less attention to cultural exchange during détente in the 1970s, when the Soviet gymnastic tours took place.[13] The relaxation of East-West tensions under détente created opportunities for more public displays of bilateral cooperation. Indeed, the 1970s gymnastics tours were designed solely to be seen in public. Rather than exchanges of coaches, sports scientists, or choreographers—gymnastics exchanges were a platform of spectacle and propaganda, where the athletes represented the state and its values through public displays.

Citizen diplomacy was essential to the tours and relations within international federations. It affirmed the role of non-state actors in navigating difficult interstate relations, as precursors to official state involvement.[14] That is, people who would not usually be given an officially recognized diplomatic role were still able to represent the state, and in some cases, their unofficial status allowed them to do things an official diplomat might not. At the heart of citizen diplomacy are people-to-people exchanges, everyday citizens contributing to improving foreign relations and aiding the state's agenda. Such diplomacy happened in sports organizations, where officials acted away from the public eye, and also in public, where famous athletes drew media attention.

Athletes already occupy a position as state representatives without the connotation that they are political actors. The pageantry of international sports—with athletes adorned in their national colors, the flags on their uniform echoing those decorating the arena, anthems playing before games or during medal ceremonies—makes it clear which countries the athletes represent. The possibility of athletes as diplomats becomes even clearer when athletes are sent on missions off the field meeting with other athletes in front of the press, or even meeting with foreign leaders. Their actions—as every day, nonpolitical citizens—pose little threat to international relations between states.

The potential of athletes for citizen diplomacy had been well established by the 1970s. A decade earlier, the US State Department had sent professional basketballers to tour the African continent, teaching their sport and countering Soviet propaganda about racial inequality in the United States.[15] More famously, in 1971, Chairman Mao Zedong invited the US table-tennis team to a series of exhibition matches in China in what became known as Ping-Pong diplomacy.[16] The links formed between the athletes from each country foreshadowed the warming relations between China and the United States, one year ahead of President Nixon's first visit to the communist state. In both examples, citizen diplomacy offered the benefit of being both high-profile and well-publicized, with little risk of political fallout because none of the actors held official political roles. Athletes could be used in lieu of more official diplomatic channels.

While the Eastern bloc sent male and female gymnasts to tour the West and perform in exhibition shows, there is scant evidence of gymnastics tours occurring from West to East. US gymnasts certainly encountered Eastern-bloc athletes at international competitions and occasionally at dual meets, though they do not appear to have traveled to Eastern Europe for exhibition performances. The tours were not competitions but public-facing spectacles designed to showcase gymnastics and gymnast personalities to adoring fans. Most Western countries simply did not have many gymnasts, and the top national athletes had no special social status either at home or abroad. More-over, since the Soviet Union was already home to the world's best gymnasts, what interest would Soviet audiences have in watching inferior performers from abroad? Western gymnasts captured little attention overseas with their relatively unremarkable competition results, so they did not have the public appeal that underpinned this mode of diplomacy. But, as this chapter shows, the US hosts of Eastern-bloc athletes also used the tours to further their own forms of diplomacy. For countries on both sides of the Iron Curtain, popular appeal was central to the use of gymnasts in cultural diplomacy.

To garner the attention of the media and public, the athletes involved in this cultural, citizen diplomacy had to be highly credible and popular. Such a public form of diplomacy was meaningless without public interest in the athletes conducting it. Newspapers additionally contributed as much as the athletes did to setting the tone of these meetings and garnering enough support for them to have political impact. When the USSR employed gym-nasts to improve US perceptions of Soviet life, and Americans used this opportunity to showcase Soviets embracing US values, it contributed to the thaw in Cold War relations while laying the groundwork for high-level political meetings. Flic-flac diplomacy—a play on Ping-Pong diplomacy that a refers to a common gymnastic skill—can be understood as the use of gymnasts to serve diplomatic interests.

Flic-Flac Diplomacy

The rise of the celebrity athlete in gymnastics was a critical foundation for the development of flic-flac diplomacy. This happened in 1972 at the Mu-nich Olympics, where Soviet gymnast Olga Korbut introduced the general public to a new risky brand of gymnastics, distinct from the balletic style that had previously characterized the sport. She performed somersaults in her bar routine and tumbled on the beam. She was the poster girl for the sport's new acrobatic direction, and audiences loved it. Scholars Roslyn Kerr and Natalie Barker-Ruchti observe that such performances transformed the sport into a spectacle, while Wendy Varney notes that it was easy for audiences untrained in gymnastics to appreciate Korbut's skill.[17] But just as important to her impact was her personality. Western audiences, accus-tomed to the poker-face norm of Soviet athletes, empathized with her joy as she took the lead in several events, and her devastation on making an elementary error that snatched the gold from her reach. If she appeared to show unrehearsed emotion as she laughed and smiled in her performances, Korbut herself eventually acknowledged she had been coached to smile at all the correct times in order to provide an entertainment package.[18] Korbut had dramatized women's artistic gymnastics, while cultivating an image of youthfulness.

Meanwhile, in the Romanian town of Oneşti, a husband and wife coaching team selected children from local elementary schools to take part in an experimental gymnastics school, based on the state-controlled Soviet training system. One coach was an expert in gymnastics, while the other brought psychological, strategic, and strength and conditioning notions from a range of sports, including track and field, handball, rugby, and boxing.[19] Together, Béla Károlyi and Márta Károlyi added a high standard of execution and enormous consistency to the mixture of difficulty, risk, spectacle, and youth. While there had been glimpses of this program's success before 1976, at the Montreal Olympics the rest of the world learned of gymnastics' new prodigy, fourteen-year-old Nadia Comăneci.[20]

FIGURE 3.1. Olga Korbut projected a childlike image that appealed to audiences and positioned her as a nonthreatening actor for diplomatic purposes. Here she performs her beam routine at the 1976 Olympics. © 1976 IOC—All rights reserved.

FIGURE 3.2. Part of Korbut's appeal to Western audiences came from her emotional range. At the 1972 games, Korbut wept after making a simple mistake that cost her the gold medal on uneven bars (pictured here next to Coach Polina Astakhova).

FIGURE 3.3. Nadia Comăneci of Romania became an international celebrity after her record-breaking performances at the 1976 games. Here she has received a gold medal for one of her performances.

FIGURE 3.4. Comăneci performs her signature skill on the bars. She received a perfect score seven times during the Montreal Olympics. © 1976 IOC—All rights reserved.

Korbut and Comăneci were not simply astounding the gymnastics community, they captured the interest of a larger audience than women's artistic gymnastics had previously enjoyed. One *Sports Illustrated* article from 1976 claimed a fivefold increase in participation at US gymnastics clubs due to Korbut's and Comăneci's popularity.[21] Seizing on the publicity women's artistic gymnastics was attracting, the Eastern bloc began using gymnasts to improve their relationships with the West. This relationship between Western fans and Eastern-bloc gymnasts can be seen as a kind of collaboration between citizens who would otherwise be Cold War adversaries.

The Soviet and Romanian gymnasts and their acrobatics can be seen as embodied, stylized cultural exports promoted by the state to demonstrate ideological superiority.[22] The continual success of Soviet athletes demonstrated the general fitness and athletic abilities of their people, but more so the efficacy of the systematic production of elite athletes. At the same time, aesthetic innovation promoted through circus and ballet influences in women's artistic gymnastics paid homage to important Russian cultural traditions.[23] The gymnastics performances were, therefore, bodily discourses that transcended linguistic barriers, offering alternative forms of communication with Western audiences.

Korbut embodied the new style of difficult, acrobatic elements combined with traditional ballet techniques, and this, plus her popularity in the West, made her central to Soviet flic-flac diplomacy. Historian Sylvain Dufraisse found that the need to include her in the tours was a source of concern for the Soviet sports authorities, who could not trust her unruly, unpredictable personality and were displeased by her behavior abroad.[24] They knew that athletes' visibility could work both for and against regimes.[25] Yet her celebrity status made Korbut an essential Soviet sports ambassador. When she was later left off a US tour, the American organizers canceled the whole event.[26] As the Soviet daily sports newspaper, *Sovetsky Sport*, declared in 1973, "the foreign policy of our Party and government is reflected in international sports relations which must play their part in establishing firm foundations of mutual understanding and friendship between our peoples."[27] So shortly after her Olympic success in 1972, Korbut and the Soviet women's artistic gymnastics team toured several Western nations, including the United States, Australia, and Great Britain, performing and raising money for the government at home, as well as engaging in public relations appearances to bolster the political image of the USSR.[28]

Following the Soviet gymnasts' successes at the 1972 Olympics and Korbut's newfound celebrity, the US public was excited for the gymnasts to visit and tour in 1973, or as one article put it, when the "pixies invaded the US."[29] This phrasing epitomized the contradiction of the gymnastic tour for Western audiences. Since the athletes hailed from enemy territory, the tour was labeled an "invasion," yet the invaders were slight youngsters— nonthreatening, childlike, "pixies." The touring athletes that year included Korbut, Ludmilla Tourischeva, Tamara Lazakovich, Antonina Koshel, Lubov Bogdanova, and Rusiko (Rusudan) Sikharulidze. The seven-city tour beginning in Houston sold out performances in Los Angeles and College Park, Maryland, ending at New York's Madison Square Garden, where an audience of twenty thousand tossed roses to their Soviet "idols."[30] A year later, nineteen thousand came to see Korbut's return to Madison Square Garden, where she and her teammates raised over $150,000.[31] The Soviet government continuously employed Korbut and various teammates to continue the US tours in 1975 and 1976.[32]

The demands of this grueling program did not sit well with Korbut. She felt touring left her little time to train, as her skills slipped below par internationally. "I was exhausted before '76," she recalled in a 2012 interview. "I can tell you the government used me for money. It's not good."[33] A former Soviet coach, Vladimir Zaglada, also recalled in his autobiography how the government used the tours to raise money for the State Committee for Sport and the Soviet Gymnastics Federation. He further noted that coaches and gymnasts selected for the tours were tempted by the prospect of getting access to hard currency themselves, which was rare in the Soviet Union.[34]

Yet Korbut's testimony calls into question how much that money from the tours really reached the athletes. A running theme in her reflections was of being overtaxed with little benefit to herself or to her ability to compete at the Olympic level. Instead of Korbut seeing any monetary reward for her work, tour proceeds were going to what she called the "fat big-shots on the Sports Committee" back home.[35] To this end, when Soviet ambassador to the United States, Anatoly Dobrynin, set up a meeting for the Soviet touring athletes with President Nixon, Korbut refused to participate until Soviet officials promised that she could train after the appointment.[36] The exhausting schedule did little to help her prepare for the next Olympics in Montreal in 1976. Only the best gymnasts and coaches, or the most well connected, were chosen for the tours.[37] But despite their exclusivity, those grueling experiences could diminish gymnasts' competition results by reducing training time. The tours provided a more positive experience for lesser-known gymnasts at the time, such as Nelli Kim, who likely benefited from the international exposure before their Olympic debuts.

While the tours drew crowds largely thanks to Korbut's popularity, several newspaper articles and spectator interviews indicated awareness that Korbut was not the top gymnast on the team—something that was commonly understood in the gymnastics community. Although the audience appreciated the skills of superior gymnasts like 1972 Olympic champion Tourischeva, Korbut ignited the greatest enthusiasm from the crowds.[38] This highlights the importance of Korbut as a charismatic individual of interest to Westerners.

Media coverage of the gymnastic tours and the athletes' daily experiences as they traveled around the United States helped make Korbut a relatable figure to US audiences. For instance, in 1973, she was asked personal questions such as what her favorite fruit was (answer: all fruits, from watermelon to grapes) and who her favorite singer was (Tom Jones).[39] She appeared in a *Sports Illustrated* article wearing a cowboy hat, with accompanying text marveling at the Soviet gymnasts' love of ketchup and cartoons.[40] Further commentary on the gymnasts' gradual Westernization over their years of tours included recalling the Soviets' excitement during their early tours, when they bought several years' supply of jeans.[41] Keen to report on the Americanization of the group, in 1976 the *New York Times* reported their enjoyment of a "beer and pizza party," dancing at a disco, watching a professional football game, seeing movies like *Carrie* and *King Kong*, and visiting Disney World.[42]

This reporting and the staged experiences offered to the Soviet visitors reveal US diplomatic efforts. They were a sign of American cultural infiltration, in which the Soviet visitors were exposed to new ideas, American values, and American culture while touring to promote the Soviet regime. Keys argues that this kind of cultural infiltration contributed to the erosion of communist authority that ultimately undermined the entire regime.[43]

In the short term, though, the tours bolstered Soviet prestige through sports and international relations. Korbut's reported Americanization in the media also enhanced the impression that East and West were growing closer. It highlighted the similarities between the people of the Soviet Union and the United States and presented the public with the prospect of a thaw in the Cold War. Scholar Ann Kordas observes, "if any one Soviet citizen was responsible for convincing Americans that not all Soviets posed a threat to the American way of life, it was the eighty-four-pound 'soldier' Olga Korbut."[44] Indeed, seen as feminine and diminutive, with hair in pigtails and playful demeanors on the competition floor, the female gymnasts were seen as nonthreatening. This perception not only helped them appeal to the public, but it ultimately steered the group toward a 1973 meeting at the White House.[45]

After Korbut and her teammates met President Nixon at the White House on the 1973 tour, she told the press, "Yes I met the President—He's a nice guy!"[46] In the Oval Office on March 21, Nixon spoke of the United States' appreciation of the gymnasts, as well as US ideas for future relations between the United States and the USSR.[47] This encounter demonstrated the use of these young female athletes in Cold War diplomatic efforts toward détente. Following some banter about the one-foot height disparity between himself and Korbut, Nixon commented on the gymnasts'

FIGURE 3.5. The Soviet gymnastics team met with President Richard Nixon during their 1973 tour, contributing to both countries' perceptions détente. Meetings between athletes and politicians often preceded higher-level diplomatic talks. Photograph courtesy of the Richard Nixon Presidential Library and Museum (National Archives and Records Administration).

remarkable ability always to land on their feet, despite their complicated aerial maneuvers. He joked that politicians would be lucky to have this catlike skill. Amid the gymnasts' laughter, he focused on the crux of their meeting: "I welcome you not only for your achievements but for what you represent. As I meet with your leaders, we will be talking about the future, the young people. Whatever differences there are between leaders, we want a world in which the young people can live in peace."[48]

Interviewed years later, Korbut recalled Ambassador Dobrynin saying to her after the Oval Office meeting, "Thank you very much. You did for one visit what we [top diplomats] could do for five years."[49] She claimed to have no idea until then that she was "kind of melting the ice between the countries."[50] The Soviet policy of using gymnasts to facilitate détente was working.

The meeting between the president and the gymnasts was designed, on both sides, to demonstrate to the public Soviet-American cooperation. This was a high-profile, relatively low-risk tactical maneuver to break the ice before political leaders met to pursue high-level diplomacy. The White

House encounter was a precursor to the Brezhnev-Nixon meeting in the United States in June 1973, where they signed nine accords, including the Agreement on the Prevention of Nuclear Arms.[51] While the Soviet gymnasts were unquestionably used as tools, their foray into sports diplomacy was not unusual. International visibility for top athletes was a fundamental tenet of Soviet sports. As James Riordan observed in 1977: "The Soviet Union is not slow to capitalize on international sporting success by using its outstanding sportsmen as 'ambassadors of goodwill,' not infrequently as a 'try-out' for political initiatives."[52]

Romanian Gymnastics Tours

While Korbut reached the highest echelons of sporting ambassadorship in the United States, Comăneci was more detached from her adoring public. Like Korbut, Comăneci's US tours followed her stellar performances at the Olympic Games, touted by Romanian leader Nicolae Ceaușescu as representative of the communist regime's supremacy.[53] A US tour was planned within days of her first appearances at Montreal.[54] However, there is much less reportage about these tours than about Korbut's, probably due to the smaller scale and lesser frequency of the Romanian tours.

Another reason Comăneci's presence in the United States might not have saturated press reports was her "serious" personality. "Comăneci never smiled, never flirted with the crowd as Korbut always had," observed one *Sports Illustrated* article. "There was fervent applause for her brilliance, but no love affair." A letter to the editor of the *New York Times* reflected similar perceptions of Comăneci among the general public: "One of the most incredible phenomena of recent years in sports is the barrage of criticism directed at Comăneci for possessing a normal, rather pleasant personality rather than satisfying the insatiable demands of the press and public by being 'cute,' 'charming,' 'lovable,' or hyperemotional."[55] There was respect for her athleticism, awe over her performances, but no emotional attachment to the athlete.

Certainly, when Comăneci finally made it to the United States for exhibitions at the end of 1977, after her earlier appearances that year had been canceled due to illness, coverage of these events focused on her changed appearance and failure to engage the audience. Disappointed that "this was not the Nadia of fifteen months ago," *New York Times* journalist Robin Herman was sharply critical of the maturing Comăneci. "Her shiny ponytail had been cropped in favor of a shaggy haircut in need of a shampoo, and her formerly slim muscular form had turned almost hefty." Herman was equally uninspired by the show, calling her Madison Square Garden performance "decidedly mundane and brief." "It was almost an hour into the program before Miss Comăneci had the floor to herself, running through a comfortable balance-beam routine that featured only a forward somersault as the most daring move." Moreover, the exhibition being outside competition format, and devoid of any particularly spectacular routines or breathtaking skills, "there was a severe lack of drama in the presentation."[56] This reportage reinforces the idea that audiences wanted to see young women, behaving childlike, in the sport of gymnastics. It also shows that these gendered expectations could be led by women: Robin Herman was the first woman journalist to be permanently appointed to the *New York Times* sports section.[57]

Notwithstanding Comăneci's relative lack of charisma, her tours may have also received less coverage because they were worse orchestrated than the Soviets'. First, Comăneci fell ill, forcing the March 1977 shows to be canceled across five cities.[58] Then an earthquake in Romania prevented the gymnasts from visiting New York, where Comăneci was to collect a $10,000 prize for the Pinch Woman Athlete of the World.[59] When Comăneci and her cohort finally managed their first US tour in October 1977, the media had little access to the gymnasts. "A stern group of Rumanian federation officials that attended yesterday's performances at the Garden . . . forbid any interviews of Miss Comăneci or the rest of the young Rumanians by American journalists."[60] Then again in 1978, a six-city Romanian tour was "abruptly cancelled without notice."[61]

Given the mediocre contribution to public-relations outcomes of the Romanian tours, no political meetings were organized and the Romanian gymnasts' contribution to détente was negligible. The gymnasts' strictly limited engagement with fans and media also made it harder for the United States to influence or Americanize the gymnasts as part of its cultural infiltration program. With Korbut, this Americanization had been the focus of much of the news coverage. Comăneci's celebrity was rooted in her extraordinary feats in Montreal. Neither at the Olympics nor on tour did Comăneci challenge ideas about the Eastern bloc, nor did she appear a relatable, Americanized gymnast. It is likely that this less-than-warm relationship with the public contributed to the lack of interest in and commentary on her tours. At the same time, the Romanian gymnasts and coaches may not have appeared so friendly because they were subject to their own stresses during the tours. While the exhibitions provided little benefit for the gymnasts, distracting them from their training and competition preparations, they also put the team under immense pressure from their own government. As did the Soviets, Romanian government officials closely monitored the teams on their trips abroad, fearing that they might subvert the regimes they were meant to be promoting. This relationship soured in the years following Comăneci's 1976 victory, and the government's fears proved correct when, in 1981, the Károlyis defected to the United States during one of these tours.[62]

Implications of Flic-Flac Diplomacy

While sending gymnasts abroad to promote an Eastern-bloc way of life was the main reason for initiating the tours, other factors were at play. In particular, the tours raised revenue for Eastern-bloc governments and officials, as well as the US Gymnastics Federation and the companies that organized the events. The tours also reveal collaboration between national governing bodies for gymnastics, with the US Gymnastics Federation cosponsoring the 1978 Romanian tour.[63] For the gymnasts, the tours may have undermined the training of some, like Korbut, who nonetheless cooperated with their country's aims. For others, like Kim, the tours provided an opportunity for international exposure before important competitions. In all cases, the athletes selected for Western tours were expected to advance their government regime, but the Károlyis' defection illustrates how the program sometimes backfired. The US government and the public that hosted the gymnasts were able to share American cultural values and ideas with the gymnasts, as part of a wider program of cultural infiltration. The cultural popularity of the Olympic gymnasts abroad enabled them to be used as political emissaries. While the Romanian government was less strategic with its tours, the Soviet Union deployed Korbut as a symbol of goodwill preceding official talks, which strengthened East-West ties and helped facilitate détente. This was gymnastics being used to demonstrate, and even facilitate, bilateral cooperation.

The tours proved the popular appeal of Olympic sports, even outside the quadrennial games. But they also solidified the expectation that gymnasts be feminine and young. And they showed how valuable girls were to their coaches and nations, both of whom demonstrated their ascendancy on the basis of their gymnasts' success. Korbut's testimony suggests that the priorities of the adults around her outweighed any consideration of the impact on her and of her own desires to rest and train.

But the tours also showed that if a sport like gymnastics could be used to engender affection and common understandings between foreign nations, it could also later be used to demonstrate hostility. As the Cold War retreated into a deep freeze over the winter of 1979, government leaders looked to the 1970s' demonstrations of sports as a form of soft power to inform their foreign policy in the new decade. This context of sports diplomacy in the 1970s helps explain the Olympic boycotts of the 1980s.

The Olympic Boycotts

In March 1980, President Jimmy Carter announced the US decision to boycott the Moscow Games in protest of the Soviet Union's invasion of Afghanistan some months earlier.[64] The Olympic boycott was an attempt to increase pressure on the Eastern bloc after a grain embargo yielded no change to the Soviet position. It was not the first time the Olympic Games had been used for political protest. Four years earlier, thirteen African nations had withdrawn from the Montreal Games only forty-eight hours before their commencement, demanding that the IOC exclude New Zealand for its relations with the South African rugby team during apartheid.[65] Twenty years earlier, several nations had boycotted the Melbourne Olympics to protest the Soviet Union invading Hungary. With these precedents, plus both the Soviet Union and the United States' newfound appreciation for sports diplomacy after the tours of the 1970s, it was almost inevitable that the Olympic Games become a pivotal part of government-led public diplomacy. As the largest global sporting event with lavish media attention, the Olympics were eminently suitable for protests that attempted to sway public opinion.

Historians' analyses of the 1980 and 1984 boycotts abound. "An Olympic boycott is obviously a weak and ineffectual weapon," concluded historian Allen Guttman in the 1980s, "but it was attractively available and relatively inexpensive in political as well as economic terms."[66] Thirty years later, historian Nicolas Sarantakes agreed that the Olympics were a weak tool for diplomacy, but he concluded nonetheless that it was not the Soviet invasion of Afghanistan that ended détente, it was the Olympic boycott.[67] Swiss historian Jérôme Gygax argued that the invasion of Afghanistan provided the necessary pretext for the United States to boycott the games in order to denounce the human rights situation in the USSR.[68] Few scholars, however, have examined what either of these boycotts meant for international connection, collaboration, and politics in the governance of Olympic sports.

The United States called on its allies to join the 1980 boycott and pressured other national Olympic committees not to attend the Moscow Games. Many of these allies called for the IOC to change the venue to another country, but the IOC resolved both to hold the games in Moscow and to remain committed to the separation of sports and politics. The Soviet Union used the IOC's continued support for the Moscow Games as evidence that a superior authority recognized the Soviet commitment to the friendship and peace—the fundamental tenets of Olympic ideology.[69] Soviet rhetoric cast the Americans and their boycotting allies as anti-Olympic in contrast with the exemplary Soviet behavior, a position that enhanced Soviet authority within the IOC and international federations. The 1980 Moscow Games went ahead without the United States and sixty-one other nations.[70]

The US boycott had little effect on the gymnastics competitions, where the contest had always been between Eastern-bloc nations or among the Soviet gymnasts themselves.[71] US gymnasts had made only occasional challenges to this standing at various world championships. In 1970 Cathy Rigby won a silver medal on the beam, followed in 1978 by Marcia Frederick winning a gold medal on uneven bars. But by and large, US women gymnasts were not considered a serious threat to Soviet domination, and indeed, their absence had little bearing on the competition. The FIG women's technical committee (the group of judges who governed women's artistic gymnastics internationally) reported little concern about the boycott's impact on the quality of gymnastics at the games. "Although the gymnasts of some countries were unable to participate because of the decision to boycott the Games taken by their governments," wrote chairwoman Ellen Berger, "the gymnastics competitions were characterized by a high standard of performance and were representative of the international level of women's gymnastics."[72] But FIG executives made no mention of the boycotts, nor did they appear to be a concern in FIG and IOC correspondence. This reflected both organizations' continued commitment to the separation of sports and politics.

However, the absence of US officials at the 1980 Olympics had a greater impact on the makeup of governing bodies and committees in both the IOC and the FIG. Historian Jennifer Parks shows how the Soviet Union tried to democratize the Olympic movement to gain power and influence within the IOC and international federations.[73] If the United States and its allies were absent from the games, the Soviet goal of attaining such power would become even easier. The boycott meant Western nations lost representation and thus influence within international sporting governance. In May 1980, President Carter and his advisors met with Lord Killanin and Monique Berlioux, executive director of the IOC, at the White House. A confidential report on the meeting revealed Lord Killanin had warned Carter about potential repercussions for sports governance if the United States went ahead with the boycott: "Firstly, [Americans] had taken no action when the Eastern representatives were taking over the international federations. Now, it would be difficult to oppose many of their actions. They should be careful regarding the Congresses to be held at the time of the Games."[74]

The Olympic Games were an important networking event for leading sports administrators in international federations. There, they elected members to executive positions during various congresses held during the games, and they discussed policy and formed agreements using their international networks. To achieve political gain from sports, officials needed not only to work with international federations but to be embedded within them. Eastern "Bloc leaders realized that they needed to demonstrate their commitment to the sports bodies' ideals, and therefore work with them, in order to use international sports arenas for political gain," wrote historian Johanna Mellis. "Sport diplomacy in the Cold War thus required competition and cooperation."[75]

While competition happened in the arena, cooperation and diplomacy happened within sports organizations. In gymnastics, the Soviet Union sought influence in governance as soon as possible, culminating in Yuri Titov's ascension to the FIG presidency in 1977—a position he held until 1996. There was also the executive committee, and technical committees for each discipline that offered opportunities to influence the governance of gymnastics. American Frank Bare was elected to the executive committee in 1972, and Jackie Fie made it onto the women's technical committee in 1976 after nearly a decade of judging internationally.[76] Fie had to learn the working language of the FIG, German, in order to slowly gain more influence in the organization.[77] But elections to these roles happened at the congresses that were often attached to each quadrennial Olympic Games. Killanin believed that US absence from the 1980 games would result in US officials being removed from their positions.

Although Carter eventually agreed to permit officials (judges and committee members) to attend the games and the corresponding international federation congresses, many patriotic officials did not go to Russia. In the letters to the IOC from July 1980, there are many instances of US officials declining to come to Moscow (e.g., Los Angeles Olympic Organizing Committee representatives and IOC medical commission members), and in turn, the IOC insisting that US representatives attend or be removed from their posts.[78] As Killanin had feared, "by their action, Americans were playing into the hands of the East."[79]

Sports diplomacy happened in private. In the negotiations, power and authority were fought for within the membership of international sports federations. Diplomacy in sports governance was built on networks between individuals; friendships forged and nurtured through social events. Béla Károlyi, famed Romanian-turned-US gymnastics coach, commented on this being one his biggest hurdles to advancing US gymnastics. "You Americans are so far behind in sports politics. The Americans go to world championships or congresses and, quick, want to go home," he explained. "The officials from the Eastern countries go to all the parties, mix together, make friends. So when it is time to vote, they know where they can find help."[80] Oral histories confirmed the importance of social networking at international events. Liz Chetkovich, an international coach and commentator, noted that international competitions were often friendly reunions and celebrations for the diaspora of coaches working around the world. Diplomatic activities in sports governance relied on friendly relations between the individual actors involved, echoing the hosting, feeding, gossiping, entertaining roles that have long been integral to mainstream diplomacy.[81]

The US boycott of the 1980 games further entrenched the problem of diplomatic influence across several more Olympic positions and sports. No Americans served on the IOC executive committee after the 1980 Congress. Leadership shifts in swimming resulted in the Eastern bloc moving to limit the number of medals that could be won in swimming—a US stronghold sport.[82] At the FIG General Assembly, no American ran for election to the FIG executive committee, reinforcing the Eastern European dominance of gymnastics governance.[83] Although Fie was able to attend the 1980 FIG congress and retain her position on the women's technical committee, it took another two decades for her to secure the influence the United States needed in the FIG.

Four years later, on May 9, 1984, the Soviet Union announced its intention not to compete at the Los Angeles Olympics, citing fears for its athletes' welfare and "anti-Soviet hysteria."[84] But it refused to term its absence a boycott, instead couching its nonattendance in US failure to adhere to the

Olympic charter.[85] Historian Allen Guttmann suggests that threats to Soviet safety were in fact negligible, as anti-Soviet demonstrations had drawn fewer than a hundred people.[86] He concluded that the Soviet absence was revenge for the 1980 boycott. However, historian Robert Edelman argued that despite the small size of the group, Soviet leadership was genuinely troubled by the protesters and the US government's failure to silence them. "The Soviets' understanding of US politics was so distorted that they could not comprehend why the US government could not simply throw a group of ardent anti-Communist protesters into prison for the duration of the Games."[87] Indeed, the generally accepted historical consensus is now that the Soviet Union did not immediately intend to boycott the Los Angeles Games in retaliation for the US boycott of Moscow.[88]

The Soviet absence from one of gymnastics' most prestigious international competitions only months earlier should have foreshadowed the Olympic boycott that was to come. In March 1984, only one month after the new Soviet general secretary, Konstantin Chernenko, took office, the Soviet and East German gymnasts withdrew from the American Cup at the last minute.[89] In a telegram to the US Gymnastics Federation, the Soviet Union announced: "Due to the intensification of anti-Soviet campaign jeopardizing security of Soviet sportsmen in USA, we regret we have to decline participation in American Cup." East Germany stayed home apparently due to the "illness of their athletes."[90] Both countries were supposed to compete in the weekend, and they sent this message only on the Monday of that week. The timing and reasoning of this withdrawal from the competition are strikingly similar to what would happen months later at the Los Angeles Olympics. By the time of the 1984 Los Angeles Olympic Games in July, the USSR, fifteen of its allies, and Afghanistan had declared their intention not to participate. The absence of many world-class Eastern-bloc athletes enabled the West to dominate the medal tally. This was especially important in subjective sports like women's artistic gymnastics, because it provided Western countries the opportunity to break into the medal tally and establish the recognition and reputation necessary for continued success.

The women's technical committee was more concerned about the Eastern-bloc absence from the 1984 games than it had been when the United States and allies boycotted four years earlier. But it was not concerned about mixing sports and politics. Their anxiety was for the reduced quality of gymnastics.[91] The FIG leadership made no comment to the IOC addressing the 1984 absence, which is consistent with how Soviet FIG president Titov had responded to the US boycott in 1980. In his annual report for 1984, his only allusion to the boycott was a few words about "all the difficulties encountered within the Olympic movement and world sport in general."[92] This vaguely echoed the Soviet propaganda line: boycotts arose when nations failed to uphold the Olympic chapter.[93] But aligning himself with the traditional views of international sports leaders who desired to maintain a separation between sports and politics, Titov added, "it is hardly within our power to change the structures of world sport and we must, perforce, live with our times, advancing with the existing ideas and problems."[94]

A Newly Diplomatic IOC

The absence of the world's two superpowers at the 1980 and then the 1984 Olympics dealt a massive blow to the credibility of the Olympic movement. The IOC worried that instead of the Olympic Games imparting peace and goodwill to the world, governments were hijacking the games to promote their own political purposes. As one IOC report put it, the Olympics were "in danger of becoming a mere object of international politics, rather than playing an active role itself."[95] These two occasions of boycott became the catalyst for increased international collaboration thereafter.

In 1981, the IOC presidency went to Juan Antonio Samaranch—a Spaniard who had formerly served as a diplomat to the Soviet Union. In the wake of the boycotts, Samaranch sought to reestablish the IOC at the top of the international sports hierarchy, above even the governments that the athletes represented.[96] He campaigned for the United Nations General Assembly to declare a protection of the Olympic Games, committing governments to participate in the games regardless of international politics. In effect, he tried to persuade the UN to step in to ensure governments would not boycott the games again. The irony in Samaranch's effort to depoliticize the games by appealing to the world's most politicized body has not been lost on scholars.[97] But few governments were willing to support the IOC's initiative in the UN General Assembly. As New Zealand prime minister David Lange explained, "I have real doubts about the wisdom of the IOC's opening itself up to UN involvement—some might say meddling—in its affairs, even if only in indirect ways."[98] But actually, this was something of a two-way street between the IOC and the UN. The IOC was not only asking for the UN to protect the games from international politics and conflict: it also began positioning itself as an active member of the diplomatic community through official involvement with government leaders, trying to broker world peace through sports.

When the United States announced its intention to boycott the 1980 Olympics and showed no signs of changing its mind as the games drew closer, IOC president Lord Killanin set up a meeting between Carter and Brezhnev. Killanin offered to act as mediator between the two, hoping to help them resolve their differences enough for the games to proceed with full attendance.[99] Although neither party proceeded with Killanin's proposed meeting, it demonstrated the IOC's first foray into actively trying to broker peace between nations.[100] Such efforts increased under Samaranch's leadership.

The new leaders of the USSR and the United States, Mikhail Gorbachev and Ronald Reagan, met for the first time at the end of 1985.[101] Ahead of their November meeting in Geneva, Samaranch offered the IOC's best wishes to Reagan, urging him to forge new, amicable relations with the Soviet Union: "On behalf of all the members of the IOC, International Sports Federations and National Olympic Committees, as well as the hundreds of millions of people throughout the world which share the Olympic ideals of brotherhood, mutual understanding and respect, friendship and peace, I would like to express to both of you the most ardent and sincere wishes for success."[102] Trying to protect Olympic interests—the continued full attendance of the games and more generally, world peace—Samaranch had asked the national Olympic committees of both countries to meet and decide on the development of cultural links through sports.[103] The IOC would oversee this program, elevating its diplomatic credibility. The IOC justified its entry into Cold War diplomacy: "The Olympic movement fosters, and is intended to foster, goodwill, mutual understanding among nations and youth of this world."[104] The two national Olympic committees agreed with the IOC that they would encourage their national sports federations to expand exchanges through bilateral and multilateral competitions and joint training camps. This cooperation was also "to extend to the exchange of coaches, officials, referees, researchers and other sport experts and their participation, upon invitation of the host country, in seminars, clinics and meetings of common interest."[105] That is, the IOC was organizing forms of citizen diplomacy to strengthen links between its constituent countries. A protocol following the meeting gave specific instances of exchange. Soviet swimming, synchronized swimming, and track-and-field experts would go to the United States to share their knowledge, and US coaches would supply the USSR with track and field as well as synchronized swimming advice.[106]

While some coaches from other Western countries like Australia and Great Britain had been allowed to observe Soviet coaching, few Americans had been welcome until the 1980s, so great was the rivalry between the two superpowers. Oral histories from inside and outside the Soviet Union concur on this point, although one US doctoral student was allowed to observe the Soviet women's program in the late 1970s.[107] Only in the 1980s did the Soviet Union relax its secretive policy toward Americans. Under the new policy of glasnost, combined with the protocol of exchange agreed on between the national Olympic committees of the Soviet Union and the United States, US gymnasts and coaches began visiting the Soviet Union. These exchanges still focused on lower-level gymnastics, rather than elite, although future Olympic champion Shannon Miller was part of one such exchange six years before her Olympic debut.[108]

While the IOC busied itself with stretching its diplomatic credentials, or perhaps even as a result of the cooperation it had encouraged between the US and Soviet national Olympic committees, a rival, global multisport festival arose in the late 1980s. The Goodwill Games were a symbol of cooperation between East and West, led by US media mogul Ted Turner.[109] And with seventy-nine countries from every continent represented, the Goodwill Games was a sizeable event attracting proportionate media attention.

A document in the IOC archives professes the purpose of the Goodwill Games: "to promote strengthening of cooperation and mutual understanding among the countries."[110] Encompassing many of the same sports and athletes, the Goodwill Games were certainly a rival to the Olympic Games. Yet their purpose must have been music to the Olympic movement's idealistic ears. Here was rhetoric of mutual cooperation, even peace, through sports—two of the very principles around which Olympism is based. Indeed, Samaranch cooed this mantra to the press when questioned about the Goodwill Games: "Without doubt, the competitions held in the Soviet capital open a new chapter in the development of sport. It is conducive to friendship, mutual understanding and the ideals of the international Olympic movement as a whole."[111]

In this light, it is not surprising the Goodwill Games earned some support from the IOC. However, it seems the IOC was not approached for permission or endorsement of the Goodwill Games. After the US and Soviet national Olympic committees signed an agreement of mutual cooperation, both seemingly organized their national contingents for the first Goodwill Games, even though it was not an Olympic, or Olympic-related event. Moreover, they did so without any official communication with the IOC—much to Samaranch's annoyance.[112] "The position of the IOC regarding the Goodwill

Games is very special because we don't know a single word officially," he complained in an IOC executive board meeting. "Nothing. Not a telex, not a letter, not an invitation. Nothing. Nothing." However, US Olympic Committee president Robert Helmick was feeding information about the establishment of the Goodwill Games to the IOC. "We know what is going on only because you report to me privately and so we have read many things in the papers, radio and television," Samaranch bristled in an executive board meeting with Canadian IOC member Richard Pound and Helmick. "You know that, in principle, we the IOC, have nothing against sports organizations, sport events. But, we are surprised with this kind of thing. We are surprised that one side of the Games are managed by the Soviet Olympic Committee and the other side, the US Olympic Committee."[113]

Despite the Goodwill Games' unsanctioned leveraging of the IOC's international structures, the IOC publicly supported the Goodwill Games. It had to if its claims to peace through sports were to stand up to scrutiny. The Goodwill Games were organized as a result of the 1980 and 1984 Olympic boycotts and the subsequent push for collaboration through sports. They continued quadrennially in the middle of Olympic cycles until 2001. Although the Goodwill Games were not under the leadership of the IOC, the participating nations (including the largest Olympic players) were represented by their national Olympic committees. If the IOC wanted to be a world mediator and sports a tool for world peace, then it had to lead by example with its handling of the Goodwill Games.

For gymnastics, the Goodwill Games became an important competition in the international calendar in the years between Olympic Games. The Goodwill Games took place in the middle year of each Olympic cycle—a year for which the FIG did not have a world championship scheduled. Participating nations, including the United States, the USSR (and later Russia), Romania, and China sent their very best gymnasts. It became an important competition providing an opportunity to those gymnasts who peaked two years early or two years late to make an Olympic team. If gymnasts could remain at the top of their sport for long enough, then the Goodwill Games provided an important debut for young athletes to gain experience on the world stage before competing at the Olympics.

Conclusion

Over the 1970s and 1980s, the value of Olympic sports as a diplomatic tool became clear. Building on the cultural exchanges of the 1960s, the Soviet

Union sent its most popular gymnasts to tour the West, promoting the Soviet way of life. These tours were founded on the celebrity status of the touring gymnasts, aimed at winning public approval. Their gymnastics and extracurricular activities explained to audiences that East and West were really not so different. They also directly countered accusations that other Soviet female athletes were too masculine. More than that, they cemented an expectation that female gymnasts be young and act childlike. This was the source of gymnasts' spectator appeal, and also their reputation as non-threatening. The gymnasts' bodily discourses also shared with audiences Soviet values like ballet and circus, and showed them how well-trained and supported Soviet athletes were. The young gymnasts became very valuable to their coaches and nations for their ability to bring public recognition of their training in these values. But the interests of the coaches and the nation were put before those of the gymnasts, like Korbut, for whom the schedule was grueling. When Romanian gymnasts surpassed the popularity of Olga Korbut in 1976, they too undertook Western tours, although theirs were not as organized and not as warmly received.

On tour, the Eastern-bloc gymnasts were subject to a form of cultural infiltration, as they were exposed to American cultural values and ideas, and US media almost gleefully reported the gymnasts' Americanization. The tours were a hybrid of public, cultural, citizen diplomacy that drew on the value of sports as a form of soft power. They were suitable for communicating with foreign audiences and more importantly, influencing what citizens thought of each other's governments. As diplomatic efforts, the tours showcased collaboration between citizens from East and West, and they preceded political cooperation that resulted in bilateral agreements.

The use of gymnastics for propaganda in these ways, outside the Olympic roster, elevated awareness of sports' value as a diplomatic tool. It makes sense then, that when Cold War relations turned at the end of 1979, sports were once again commandeered for diplomatic purposes. US president Jimmy Carter sought to take advantage of the popularity of the Olympic Games to pressure the Soviet Union to retreat from Afghanistan and draw attention to its human rights record. He hoped that sports could influence public opinion and provide a nonviolent way to advance the US foreign agenda. Despite the efforts of the IOC, the boycott went ahead, with dismal consequences for US influence within sports federations. Absent from the international congresses at Moscow, the United States lost leadership positions in sports governance, deteriorating its diplomatic abilities within said organizations. Commentators were not surprised though. The United States had never been particularly engaged with the social networks that supported international sports. But US absence from Moscow prompted a new commitment to diplomacy within international federations thereafter, and this relied on international collaboration. Indeed, Jackie Fie—already an FIG member—would slowly rise to the ranks of FIG leadership over the following years, where she could influence the direction in which women's artistic gymnastics developed.

After the Eastern-bloc absence from the 1984 games, combined with the appointment of Samaranch, a former diplomat, as IOC president, the organization adopted a more active role in global diplomacy. While it stayed committed to its goals of world peace and committed to the separation of sports and politics, it also engaged with the UN and the Soviet and US governments in an effort to protect the Olympic movement. The boycotts of the early 1980s ultimately fostered greater collaboration through sports. Through collaboration with the national Olympic committees of the Soviet Union and the United States, the IOC brokered a bilateral sporting exchange program based on citizen diplomacy. Like the gymnastics tours had a decade earlier, such meetings preceded talks between higher-level government leaders. Their purpose was to warm cultural relations so that official meetings were more amicable and effective.

But these efforts at getting the two superpowers to work better together had the unintended consequence of aiding the establishment of a rival sports mega-event, the Goodwill Games. Both the US and Soviet National Olympic Committees were deeply involved in organizing these events, but they failed to keep the IOC officially informed about them. Still, the IOC could hardly challenge an event that had the same peace-promoting, anti-political aims as its own. Instead, it led by example, allowing the Goodwill Games to continue and to draw on Olympic sports and structures, all in the name of world peace. Sports have always been an important instrument of soft power. In the 1970s and 1980s, this became increasingly visible as various nations, individuals, and even nongovernment organizations like the IOC harnessed sports to pursue diplomatic ends. And despite the boycotts of the early 1980s, ultimately these efforts enhanced international collaboration.

4

MAKING AND BREAKING THE RULES

Olympic founder Coubertin included gymnastics in the first modern Olympic Games in 1896 because the sport appealed to his idealization of the ancient Greeks. While various national forms of gymnastics were centered around military drill, Coubertin's gymnastics was an idealistic, beauty sport, finding its place within the burgeoning Olympic movement as part of "a program of moral beauty," and "immaterial aesthetics."[1] By 1903, the FIG (then the FEG) organized its first international tournament, inspired by the success of those first Olympic Games. The FIG set about creating the rules that would govern gymnastics, which was part of a process of rationalization and global standardization of competitive sports. Only in 1933 did it begin organizing women's competitions, prompted by IOC pressure on international federations to take control of women's sports. But as this chapter shows, Olympic pressure was behind many more rules that shaped gymnastics as the century continued.

Although the quadrennial games provided the impetus for the FIG to mobilize, expand, and organize its own competitions, the Olympic Games remained gymnastics' pinnacle event. Considering that travel for much of the early twentieth century was both costly and slow, it makes sense that a four-yearly multisport festival might have more significance than any gymnastics-only event. The first world championships for gymnastics were held in 1931, while a World Cup circuit was not introduced until 1975. In this context, the role, visibility, and significance of the Olympic Games as the ultimate competition in gymnastics grew in the absence of any alternatives. This early history formed the basis of the hierarchy established between the IOC and the international sports federations, including the FIG. The IOC established the terms of international competition and the standards required for inclusion in the Olympic movement, and the federations shaped their sports to please the IOC. But while FIG leaders were working within the parameters set out by the IOC, gymnasts, judges and officials worked to break the gymnastics' rules, putting the sport's inclusion in the Olympic Games in jeopardy.

This chapter demonstrates how the dynamic between the IOC and the FIG influenced the rules of gymnastics. It argues that cooperation and collaboration occurred both within the FIG and in its relationship with the IOC, and when officials conspired to break the rules. But too often, these rules were made and broken without input from the gymnasts themselves. For decades, coaches and officials have prioritized their own and their national interests ahead of the gymnasts'. This chapter begins with a discussion of how the FIG rationalized and standardized gymnastics through the creation of a rulebook, known as the Code of Points. It then examines the IOC's skepticism about the sportive merits of gymnastics, both in terms of its questionable status as a team sport, and the suspiciously concentrated medal distribution. These issues, the IOC argued, contributed to gymnastics' outsize presence in the games. As the IOC grappled with gigantism, the FIG made various amendments and concessions to its program to remain in the games. But score fixing and the high number of *ex aequo* (tied) scores threatened gymnastics credibility. By the early twenty-first century, the FIG abandoned the perfect 10 system and introduced an entirely new code of points in an effort to reclaim some legitimacy for the sport. However, score fixing was not the only form of cheating. While gymnastics had the occasional incident of doping, a larger problem was age falsification from the 1980s onward.

Rationalizing Gymnastics

Sociologist Max Weber described rationalization as the transformation from disorganized, spontaneous social phenomena to carefully devised rules and procedures aimed at maximizing efficiency.[2] Some scholars have used this understanding of rationalization in sports to look at how athletes strategize to achieve faster, higher, stronger in sports, through the use of expert coaches, game plans, growing fan bases.[3] Rationalization can also explain the emergence of modern sports. As sports scholar Allen Guttman explains, the intellectual discoveries of the eighteenth century began a quest of measurement and comparison. These were the roots of quantification in modern sports and, thus, the pursuit of records.[4] By the early twentieth century, "participation was no longer an end in itself, but was directed to the production of concrete, quantifiable results: goals, inches, seconds," argues Barbara Keys.[5] However, while competitive gymnastics was premised on the quantification of performance through numerically judged routines, it was also limited in that once the perfect 10 had been reached, there were few further records to attain. Hence, records in gymnastics became determined in terms of the number of rotations and twists a gymnast could perform. The first gymnast to perform a new feat would be recorded in the Code of Points with a new element bearing their name. For instance, Nelli Kim was the first woman to perform a "double back," two backward tucked somersaults in the air, on the floor exercise in 1976. The skill is officially recorded in the Code of Points as a "Kim." Two years later, her teammate Elena Mukhina added a full twist to the first rotation, creating the "full in," recorded in the Code of Points as a "Mukhina." Speaking the language of gymnastics is therefore speaking its history and invoking its pursuit of records.

Anthropologist Sebastian Darbon's notion of the sports system explains how measurement structures sports.[6] It does this first through universal rules, which in gymnastics are outlined in the Code of Points. Second, there must be institutions to apply those rules. For gymnastics, this is the FIG, which operates in the larger context under the IOC. Third, the sports system operates under the principle of equality of competition. This principle underpins the design, contest, and fairness of gymnastics. The fourth aspect of the sports system is a sports-specific space, such as the unique apparatuses that define gymnastics competition. And the final element of the sports system is the determination of time that outlines the duration of contest—in gymnastics this could be the time limits on routines as well as the overall structure of competitions, in which gymnasts perform one by one on the apparatuses, with all apparatuses going at once. Together, this structure of measurement was the foundation for establishing a system of judging in gymnastics. Unlike sports where objective measurement was clear, aided by stopwatches to determine speed or rulers, rods and measuring wheels to determine heights and distances, the mode of measurement in gymnastics was less well-defined.

Thus, the Code of Points created in 1949 set out an agreed-upon transnational standard of gymnastics performance.[7] It outlined what skills a gymnast should perform (e.g., cartwheels), how they should perform them (e.g., the body should pass through an inverted vertical position during the cartwheel), and the deductions they would receive if they failed to meet these criteria. Gymnasts would start from 10 points if they showed all the required skills, from which tenths would be deducted for execution faults. Later, the starting score would be lower than 10, and gymnasts would have to get "bonus" points to build their start value up to 10 points. The Code of Points outlined the rules for each element on each apparatus. Over time, gymnastics elements were assigned different levels of difficulty that would accrue more points for the gymnast, and new skills were added to the code, named after their originators. Until the mid-1990s, the Code of Points also prescribed compulsory routines the gymnasts must perform in one round of competition, while for the other round, they could create their own routines that sampled different elements from each required category. Gymnasts were to perform all of their routines according to the code, and judges were to award and deduct points according to the code. After each Olympic Games, the content of the code was amended. The FIG would change the value of skills in response to how gymnasts had performed them over the last four years, or it would change which elements were required in an effort to drive performance in a certain direction (e.g., more leaps, or tumbling). This was the rationalization of gymnastics.

Notwithstanding the irony of associating fast food with a sport known for slight athletes and eating disorders, George Ritzer's theory of rationalization, known as McDonaldization, is highly applicable to gymnastics. He argues that the key aspects of rationalization in the fast-food industry have been calculability, efficiency, predictability, and control.[8] These notions can explain the way gymnastics has been designed for competition. First, the calculability of gymnastics lies in the assignment of scores for performances. This measurement quantifies performances in an effort to remove subjectivity. Every action is specified, and scores are determined by how closely a gymnast's movement align with that specified ideal. Gymnastics ideals were defined through efficiency of movement. The optimal method for accomplishing a skill would attract the most points, while superfluous movements like steps on landing or wobbling the arms would attract deductions. Efficiency was mediated through scores, and scores quantified gymnastics. This led to predictability. Gymnasts wore leotards with pre-scribed length and coverage, they performed on standardized apparatuses, and the FIG's classification of skills ensured that gymnasts performed what the FIG wanted to see.[9] Of course, a degree of unpredictability was equally fundamental to maintain its appeal. The risk of a fall, a mistimed takeoff, a step on landing all contribute to drama and thrill of competition. Lastly, throughout the twentieth century, the FIG attempted to control contests, particularly for human error (or intentional subjectivity) through the use of technology. Computerized judging aids developed over the course of the twentieth century testify to the FIG's ceaseless search for the infallible judge. While the FIG may have pursued these elements of rationalization of its own accord, the IOC pressured the FIG, like other federations, to make its sport credible and fair. As the IOC grappled with gigantism, the FIG had to update the code and even the format of competition in order to demonstrate its value to the IOC and appeal to audiences.

Elected volunteer judges from around the world serving on the FIG tech-nical committees collaborated to develop these rules and create a globally standardized sport. They often made these judgments in response to what gymnasts and coaches were doing, representing both cooperation and chal-lenge. They also created their rules in response to directives from the execu-tive committee, like introducing new judging controls. There was a technical committee for each discipline, and at least one member from each technical committee was also on the executive board of the FIG, which governed the sport more broadly. These groups had to work together within the FIG, in harmony with the gymnasts, coaches, and judges they were governing, and entirely within the parameters of the IOC.

The Threat of Gigantism

The sports program of the IOC grew over the first half of the twentieth century, as more sports sought an Olympic berth and host nations added their preferred sports to the Olympic roster. By the first Cold War Olympics of 1952, the IOC was facing an increased number of athlete participants too, as more countries were ready to join the competition. Further—and to the ire of many conservative members—the inclusion of women from many of these new nations (the Soviet Union in particular) only added to the ballooning size of the games. In this context, Olympic leaders came to see gigantism as a significant concern and looked to make cuts to the Olympic program to combat it. The IOC identified gymnastics as a sport that was taking up too much space in the games, through its large contingent of male and female gymnasts and the length of competition.[10]

The IOC became critical of "artificial team" sports, forming a commission in 1953 to assess gymnastics, equestrian events, and fencing.[11] It could reduce the number of athletes at the games by eliminating such artificial teams and restricting these sports to individual contests only. As all the gymnasts comprising a team did not compete together at the same time, IOC leaders believed that the "team" aspect of competition was forced and false: these were individual sports masquerading as team sports. "If I am not mistaken," IOC president Brundage wrote to the FIG president in 1954, "in the 1912 Games in which I participated, there were only gymnastic demonstrations, no competitions."[12] Brundage was mistaken. Gymnastics had been a competition event for men since 1896, and the team competition had always been a major component. Moreover, in the early twentieth century, teams had competed in unison, performing group routines. Nonetheless, Brundage continued to outline why he saw the gymnastics competition as unduly large in the Olympic Games. "In 1920 there were only individual events (no teams). . . . As a matter of fact, in recent years, although [the FIG]

FIGURE 4.1. The Danish men's team competes on the floor demonstrating the "free system" exercises at the 1920 games. Teams had over ten members and all athletes competed at once. © 1920 IOC—All rights reserved.

FIGURE 4.2. The Danish women's team performs together on the floor in 1920. Women teams performed exhibition exercises as gymnastics had not yet been accepted as a competitive sport for women. © 1920 IOC—All rights reserved.

permitted teams of 8 men, most countries have sent only 5 or 6." Brundage's recollection was again inaccurate. In 1920 it had been a male-only team event, with teams of as many as twenty-seven gymnasts. Although the FIG must have been aware of these inaccuracies, it nonetheless agreed to reduce its team size from eight to six gymnasts in order to help reduce the number of athletes at the games.

The IOC's satisfaction, however, was short-lived. Four years later, in 1958, the IOC again attempted to decrease team size, this time to five. The IOC had made this decision without consulting the FIG, whose leaders in turn sent several furious letters to Brundage. FIG president Charles Thoeni wrote: "In reducing again our participants from 6 to 5 we would have a suppression of 40% of the number of our gymnasts, which is far beyond the goal we wish to attain, a sacrifice which you would never ask any other federation to accept."[13] Brundage told Thoeni he was surprised to receive such a letter; he thought Thoeni should be thanking him for saving the gymnastics team competitions from being cut altogether.[14] Moreover, Brundage said that he had been able to save the team competition only because of the support he received from the Soviet IOC members. It makes sense that the Soviet IOC members, Alexei Romanov and Konstantin Andrianov, would protect the team competition—not only was gymnastics culturally important to the Soviet Union, but it was also a sport in which a large number of medals could be won, and indeed, *had* been won by the Soviet Union. A year later, though it is unclear how, the FIG negotiated its position back to six team members, preventing cuts to gymnastics for the time being.[15]

Although the FIG had initially cooperated with the IOC's requests to downsize the sport, the FIG pushed back on continued attempts. For instance, in 1961 Thoeni complained to the IOC chancellor that "gymnastics is not a minor sport . . . To what do we owe these restrictive tendencies toward our sport?" Thoeni thought that the IOC was being particularly scrutinous of gymnastics, despite the FIG's cooperation. "For a number of years now the gymnastics sport found itself perpetually compelled to struggle in order to maintain the place at the bosom of Olympism to which it deems itself entitled." Only days earlier, he had penned a letter with the leaders of the men's and women's technical committees to Brundage, explaining how upset members of the gymnastics community were threatening to leave the Olympic movement and replace the games with biennial world championships. At the leadership level, though, the FIG remained cooperative with the IOC, concluding the letter with the assurance: "However, we of the head of the FIG have grown firmly attached to the Olympic ideal and we refused to consider this alternative." In response, Brundage affirmed the value of gymnastics in the Olympic movement, noting that he considered gymnastics "fundamental in any national sports program" and his view that its minor status in the United States was a "national misfortune."[16]

Little over a decade later, the status of gymnastics teams came up again in response to the FIG's request to add rhythmic gymnastics to the Olympic program. Rhythmic gymnastics had become its own discipline shortly after the handheld apparatuses were removed from women's artistic gymnastics in the early 1960s. The discipline was based on music, choreography, and rhythm and was designed to promote a more traditional idea of femininity.[17] As women's artistic gymnastics became increasingly acrobatic in the 1970s, FIG leaders wanted to add rhythmic gymnastics to the Olympic program to reestablish gymnastics as feminine and appropriate for women (see chapter 5).[18] But the IOC rejected the FIG's request—due to "the necessity of combatting gigantism"—and countered it by suggesting a reduction in the number of gymnasts per team in the artistic disciplines.[19] The IOC then submitted a formal proposal to limit the number of teams in the women's artistic gymnastics competition to twelve. As a compromise, the FIG agreed to a reduced number of teams on the condition that the team size remain at six.[20] In acceding to the IOC request, the new FIG president, Arthur Gander, made sure to emphasize the "substantial opposition" from member nations, but how the FIG nonetheless cooperated with the IOC. Gander observed that the FIG made the decision in "goodwill and understanding in view of the IOC's good intentions and mutual collaboration between the IOC, international federations, and National Olympic Committees in the interests of the future Olympic Games."[21] This reflected the FIG's continued ambition to remain at the heart of the Olympic movement.

The practical need to address gigantism was easily appropriated to fulfill Cold War rhetoric about what was considered fair in sports. This was part of a broader dialogue about what sports really mattered and who was practicing them. After the 1956 games, in which the Soviet Union surpassed the United States in medal count, media commentators suggested that a good number of those medals were in sports that had little value. US journalists argued that the Soviet Union's success was due to its participation in sports for which the United States only had perfunctory participation, including gymnastics. But in addition to being portrayed as unimportant to the United States, such sports were also perceived as unfair because so many medals could be won. "Avery Brundage was asked whether it was an equitable distribution of rewards for the effort expended to give three gold medals to one person for gymnastics," noted *New York Times* journalist Allison Danzig, "when the decathlon goes through exhausting tests in ten sports from morning to night on two consecutive days and receives only one medal."[22]

The IOC was alert to these issues. In 1956, it created a new rule declaring that an athlete could only receive one medal per performance. This would have serious ramifications for gymnastics competitions, which yielded the potential of several medals per gymnast. Without such a rule change, it would be like a 400-meter runner having their race time eligible for the 100-meter, 200-meter, and 400-meter medals. Before this rule was implemented, gymnasts performed a compulsory and voluntary routine on each apparatus. The scores for the eight performances in women's artistic gymnastics (or twelve in men's artistic gymnastics) were tallied to determine the winner of the team competition, the individual all-around competition, and the winner on each of the apparatuses. This policy would not contribute to reducing the size of the games, but rather redistribute medal potential, which was all-important in the Cold War–era games.

This edict would also affect several other sports that did not yet have separate qualification and final competition rounds, such as cycling, fencing, and equestrian events.[23] But the Fédération equestre internationale had proceeded with the 1956 Melbourne Olympic competition without enforcing this new rule. Because Australia's strict biosecurity laws made it difficult to get horses into the country, the equestrian competitions of the 1956 games had been held some months earlier in Stockholm. The change in medal policy had been missed by the organizers, and subsequently, competitors had won several medals from single performances. The FIG successfully managed to argue that it would be unjust for the IOC to then apply the rule to other sports.[24]

As these debates continued after the Melbourne Games, the Soviet IOC members suggested a solution that would become the first step toward the current format of gymnastics.[25] In the first days of competition, gymnasts would compete for the team and all-around medals based on their compulsory and voluntary routines. From this competition, athletes would be selected for the apparatus finals. In the decades to follow, this would continue to evolve into separate team and all-around competitions as well. This proposal retained the number of medals available in gymnastics but solved the problem of disproportionate reward for only one performance.

However, this new format had little impact on the number of medals that one athlete could win. A few gymnasts, mostly from the Eastern bloc, continued to win most of the medals, and the IOC noticed. Soviet champion Boris Shakhlin is seen in one photo draped in Olympic medals (fig. 4.3); a note from IOC officials accompanying the photo describes Shakhlin as looking like "a prize bull at a market." "If one man can win eight medals in an international set of Games, the events must be altogether too simple," Avery Brundage accusingly wrote to the FIG president in 1971. "And it certainly detracts from the importance of the sport."[26] So, in 1973, the IOC demanded that the FIG "limit the number of entries per country [in the] final competition [to] two gymnasts (men or women)."[27] This would create greater diversity in the finals and ensure that medals were more widely distributed. The FIG again cooperated with the IOC. With strong support from the Soviet FIG members, it introduced a new rule to this effect for the apparatus finals.[28] However, it refused the IOC's suggestion of two gymnasts per country in the individual all-around as well, and instead

FIGURE 4.3. Soviet gymnast Boris Shakhlin poses for media wearing the six medals he won at the 1960 Olympic Games. Such images drew criticism from the IOC that one gymnast could win so many medals. © 1960 IOC—All rights reserved.

suggested it could bear reducing the number to three.[29] The IOC accepted this compromise.

The Soviet Union's support for diversifying the playing field is unsurprising. It would have little effect on their position at the top of the sport, and it would contribute to Soviet aims in sports diplomacy. Historian Jennifer Parks shows how Soviet leadership promoted their sports officials as "leaders in the development and cultivation of their sports."[30] This imperative demanded cooperation among the international federations. The Soviet Union wanted to democratize the IOC and international federations by breaking down the old boys' networks within international sports and creating a more egalitarian leadership consistent with the egalitarianism that underpinned Soviet society. They envisioned this would be achieved by increasing representation from around the world (particularly the Third World and those who might be sympathetic to the Soviet Union). This initiative elevated their status in international federations and gave credibility to the Soviet's commitment to Olympic ideals, including the internationalization of sports. Such acts enabled the Soviet Union to gain allies who could then vote in support of Soviet initiatives in international federations or promote the ascension of Soviet members to the leadership of those organizations. This is certainly apparent in gymnastics, where Yuri Titov was promoted to president of the FIG only four years after the rule to diversify finalists was introduced, in 1977.

These compromises to the format and size of gymnastics enabled the FIG to forestall the IOC's consistent pleading to reduce the team size from six to five. It appears this was the FIG's purposeful strategy in dealing with its Olympic overseer. "We would like to point out that with a reduction in the number of teams . . . as well as a limitation on the possibility of one gymnast winning too many medals, our sport has made the absolute maximum of sacrifices in the Olympics Games according to its characteristics," Gander told IOC technical director Henry Banks in 1973.[31]

Nonetheless, the medals awarded in gymnastics tended to be concentrated among Eastern-bloc countries for most of the century. In an effort to make the sport more globally diverse, the FIG voted to discontinue an entire component of competition: the compulsory routines. Until the 1990s, gymnastics competitions ran over several days and sessions. In the first competition, all gymnasts performed set routines developed, choreographed, and prescribed by the FIG technical committees. As these were not extremely difficult, the margin of error between gymnasts was small. The competition relied on perfect execution and was judged very strictly. Moreover, by seeing the same routines performed all day, the judges could easily make comparative assessments, driving the expected standard high and the competition close. In the second competition, gymnasts could perform "optional" routines, created entirely by the gymnasts and their coaches. When the executive committee voted to drop the compulsory exercises in 1993, it declared that the decision would come into effect after the 1996 games, in fairness to the gymnasts already preparing for that competition.[32] The women's technical committee heavily opposed this divisive initiative.[33] But when the FIG leadership put the question to the general assembly a year later, the vast majority voted in favor of abolishing the compulsories.[34]

The FIG abolished the compulsories because of IOC pressure to increase gymnastics' spectator appeal and create more opportunities for athletes from other countries. The lack of diversity in gymnastics medal distribution had long been a concern for the IOC, but by the 1990s the Olympic Games were also facing shrinking spectatorship as X sports, or extreme sports, became increasingly popular. The IOC thus put pressure on sports like gymnastics to make its competitions more television friendly and globally attractive. The abolition of compulsories is now almost unanimously seen as the turning point for diversifying women's artistic gymnastics. "[It] leveled the playing field, because compulsories had really kept the lower countries from even playing the game," remarked Australian gymnastics commentator and longtime international coach, Liz Chetkovich. "By taking [compulsories] out new people could come in. Before, if you couldn't do the compulsories you couldn't even get to optionals."[35] So, finally, after nearly half a century of complaint from the IOC that too few nations—and indeed, too few gymnasts—dominated gymnastics, the FIG had found a solution in the removal of compulsories.

From Subjective Judging to Score Fixing

Implicit in the IOC's concern about few gymnasts winning so many medals was a suspicion that either something was wrong with the format of gymnastics or someone was cheating. Both diving and figure skating had been subject to allegations of score fixing.[36] As another judged sport in which the Eastern bloc excelled, gymnastics also came under scrutiny in the mid-1970s. While no major gymnastic scandals erupted in the public eye during the Cold War, the judging system in gymnastics was anything but fair.

No matter the FIG's attempts at rationalizing the sport, there has always been a subjective element. From at least the 1960s onward, the FIG held intercontinental judging courses to educate and qualify judges to become brevet international judges.[37] Before reaching this level, judges received domestic judge education, administered by the national governing body. Nonetheless, subjectivity remained. A 1974 FIG report reflected: "We rely on the more or less subjective assessment of experienced judges who more or less consciously compare the performances with some stereotyped perfect performance that is presumably accepted and known by all concerned."[38] The nature of the 10 system required rating gymnasts based on comparative impressions. The entire scoring system of women's artistic gymnastics was based on an assumption that all judges held a single, unified vision of an ideal performance. But this report demonstrated the problem that judges' understandings of the ideal were not always uniform. Efficiency of movement through alignment of limbs in relation to the apparatus was theoretically sound, but the human eye could not catch everything. Moreover, concepts like "virtuosity" attracted points yet eluded definition, so judges invariably held differing opinions of what constituted "virtuosity" and consequently awarded different scores.

The difficulty in judging went beyond finding an orthodox understanding of ideal performance and how points were given and awarded. It was complicated further because judges inevitably judged gymnasts at least in part according to their reputation. "The socio-psychological literature is replete with studies showing that a judge's beliefs about the personal characteristics of a gymnast (race, personality, attitude, etc.) will affect his rating," observed the same 1974 FIG report.[39] Throughout the twentieth century, judges awarded higher scores to certain gymnasts because they anticipated that those gymnasts would excel, in a self-confirming cycle.[40]

So, despite the FIG having demarcated deductions for, say, a small wobble on the beam (minus one-tenth) versus a large wobble (minus three-tenths) versus a fall (minus half a point), what constitutes a small wobble and what constitutes a large one is still a subjective matter.[41] Cognitive confirmation is higher in such circumstances, when gymnasts may be given the benefit of the doubt when they or their country already have a strong reputation based on previous results. Unconscious (or conscious) bias can go beyond nationality too. Gymnasts who have different body types or skin colors can be disadvantaged because they do not conform to traditional expectations of what excellent gymnasts look like. This kind of bias reinforces the dominance of the nations at the top, which goes some way to explaining the ascendancy of Soviet gymnastics for such a long time.

There was indeed conscious cheating alongside these underlying biases. Eastern-bloc officials collaborated to fix scores. They made agreements to exchange higher scores with sympathetic partners in order to share the medal podium. As one international judge recalled, many international judges in the 1970s "did what they did for the Eastern bloc, and they shared among themselves."[42] While gymnasts were merely pawns in these arrangements, cheating was not limited to judges. It extended to the FIG leadership. A technical expert for the 1976 Olympic Games recalled that only after being appointed to the technical committee did they realize the extent of cheating: "They [the technical committee] arranged the scores and they arranged the results. We ran the test event in Montreal in '75, and the technical president actually said to me: 'Do you want to do a proper draw, or do you want to make it interesting?' I was so idealistic!"[43]

With the Soviet Union dominating women's artistic gymnastics for so long, it was an advantage for other countries to cooperate with its judging.

For example, if the members of the technical committee agreed to give a Soviet gymnast the top score on beam, then an East German could take the gold on vault. It was worthwhile for smaller nations to cooperate with their large neighbor. Reciprocally, the Soviet Union looked after its bloc. "They made all their little Soviet countries happy," commented one judge.[44] But it was difficult for countries outside the Eastern bloc to break into these circles. Speaking from Montreal in 1976, US Gymnastics Federation founder and executive director Frank Bare observed, "Who the hell are we going to make a deal with? There are two judges from the US, two from Canada and you know where the other 48 are from."[45] Bare spoke of the men's competition, and although the situation was likely similar in women's artistic gymnastics, further exploration is needed to confirm. In her autobiography, Olga Korbut believed Western judges were difficult to bribe but also indicated that Eastern-bloc officials may not have tried, as it would have required allowing some Western victories in return and "it was important that there be a Socialist victory over capitalism."[46]

Korbut recalled her own experience with score fixing at the 1974 world championships in Varna, Bulgaria. There, she thought she had performed an excellent routine—enough to put her in first place. But her score was not the best of the day. When she asked her delegation leader to file a protest, Yuri Titov remained unmoved. "Each of the winners had been selected before we even set foot on the podium," claims Korbut. She alleges that the Soviet Union had arranged for the uneven bars medal to be given to an East German, in exchange for Soviet star Ludmilla Tourischeva's guaranteed victory on floor. "The adults who ran the sport treated us like pawns on a chessboard, deciding who would win or lose for their own selfish reasons," she claims. Indeed, the East German judge was reprimanded for her judging at this event but was back judging again within the next two years. Meanwhile, no Soviet was punished, and Titov went on to become president of the FIG two years later. Although some might question the credibility of Korbut's charge, her claims echo others' concerns over score fixing.

Béla Károlyi also alleged cheating in the 1970s, implicating Ellen Berger (she and Károlyi had a long-standing enmity) several times throughout his autobiography. Discussing the 1977 European championships, he claimed "Ellen Berger, once the East German gymnastics coach and now part of the judging committee, was pulling strings for the East Germans."[47] While like Korbut's, these words should be read with caution given their appearance in an autobiography and Károlyi's reputation for self-promotion, they nonetheless add to the growing number of allegations of score fixing. "The Russians were using dirty tricks to win the gold on the vault. Nothing unusual," purported Károlyi, referring to an incident at the same competition, discussed later in this chapter. Citing another example at the 1980 Olympics, Károlyi suspected that the judges had delayed Comăneci's final performance on the beam until rival Elena Davydova of the Soviet Union had completed her bar routine and "until they had figured out what score should be given to make Davydova the winner." The US Olympic Committee's report on those games alleged score fixing in this incident too. However, the US report indicated that Romania, not the USSR, was at fault. The head judge on beam was Romania's Maria Simionescu, who, knowing the 9.85 was too low, refused to enter it into the system. After thirty minutes of arguing, Berger stepped in and did it for her.[48] When Károlyi complained to Titov, the FIG leader appeared upset and worked to amend the situation, in keeping with sentiments from peers about his integrity as president. But when Titov's efforts failed to move Comăneci into first place, Károlyi

FIGURE 4.4. Elena Davydova of the Soviet Union competes at the 1980 Olympic Games. Károlyi alleged that the judges refused to post Comăneci's score until they had decided Davydova's. © 1980 IOC—All rights reserved.

was infuriated. "This is a disgusting cheating game, and you [Titov] were the orchestrator."[49] However, Károlyi's anger appears to have colored his accusations: historical evidence and comment from his contemporaries agree that after ascending to the FIG presidency, Titov made a number of changes to improve judging.[50]

Documents show that the sport had been plagued with purposeful bias in judging since just after World War II. American Frank Cumiskey recalled his experience at the 1948 London Olympics: "The judging was very bad in this meet, not because the judges did not know gymnastics or the rules at that time, but because they were cheating. . . . It was disgusting to watch."[51] The Eastern bloc was able to manipulate scores in the decades that followed only because the conditions already existed in the sport—not through its inherent nature but due to the way those in power were running it. Throughout the 1970s, the women's technical committee was led first by Frenchwoman Berthe Villancher, subsequently by Hungarian Valerie Nagy; Ellen Berger of East Germany took over in 1976. Through much of this time, the president of the FIG was not a Soviet, but the Swiss Arthur Gander. Cumiskey accused Gander himself of being involved in the score fixing at the 1948 games, saving the best scores for last. "I approached Arthur Gander who was a judge [in 1948] and asked why [I only received] a 9.00—his answer was that the good teams had not performed yet! Mr Gander was later to head FIG and I always hoped that I had misunderstood him."[52]

Putting the best performers last in the lineup became a strategy for gymnastics teams because it is believed that judges save higher scores for later performances—and studies support this theory.[53] If judges award high scores early then see better performances later in the competition, they are unable to make ample differentiation between the better performers—per Gander's response to Cumiskey's allegations of cheating. "You must judge according to the first routine," explained British judge Ursel Baer in 1976. "There may be slight imperfections but you may have to go to a 10 (perfect score) because it's better than anything that's been before."[54] That 10 ceiling limited the gap in score between pioneers like Comăneci, who mastered and surpassed the requirements of the day, and her competitors. Deliberate manipulation of this concept skewed the competition at the Montreal Olympics.

Many sports fans are familiar with Comăneci's historic feat in 1976: the first perfect 10 in Olympic competition. It was gymnastics' four-minute mile, a score that had never been reached, a record that had never been broken. Although, it was not in fact the first 10 ever. Comăneci herself had scored a perfect 10 some months earlier at the 1976 American Cup, and before that, Czechoslovakian gymnast Věra Čáslavská had scored a perfect 10 at the 1967 European Championships. Nonetheless, it was Comăneci's 10 that captured the world's imagination.[55] Gymnastics fans watching her routines may ask how she received a perfect score not once but seven times. They see a one-tenth deduction for a hop on landing here or a slightly bent leg there. Of course, her routines were superb, but they were not perfect. However, perfect is relative. The scores of that competition had been artificially inflated to reduce the margin between Comăneci and her nearest rivals.

Blatant score fixing was not possible. Comăneci was clearly the best gymnast present, and it would have raised serious questions if this superiority were not reflected in her scores. But it could be arranged to keep her scores within a tenth of a point of her competitors, making sure she had no margin for error. "I wouldn't say her 10s were orchestrated so much as all the 9.9s below her were," observed one longtime official. The slightest fault would put the Soviet gymnasts back in gold medal contention. "She was so far ahead, and there was no way they were going to beat her. And even with a fall she had a margin. So, they took the margin away. . . . All the top gymnasts were getting 9.9. OK, Nadia was getting 10s, but if she ever fell, she was out."[56] This certainly limited the distance between Comăneci and her closest competitors. Days after Comăneci's first 10, Soviet gymnast Nelli Kim became the first person to score a perfect 10 on the remaining apparatuses, vault and floor.

Bare alleged that Valerie Nagy of the women's technical committee—and Hungary, a nation closely controlled by the Soviet Union—"tried to change the judges in the floor exercise illegally . . . to hurt Romanian star Nadia Comăneci's chances in that event."[57] Nagy attempted to replace the Western judges on the floor exercise with East German and Russian judges, until a protest from Bare blocked the move. These incidents reinforce the idea that a select group of judges, extending to the highest positions of power in the FIG, was responsible for manipulating the scores of this monumental competition.

Most judges were probably not involved in this plan, but few had reason to question the scores. Lowly ranked nations were happy to be suddenly scoring higher than ever. Many judges also unknowingly contributed to the inflated scores due to peer pressure. If one judge's marks were significantly different from the others, it might reflect poorly on their judging, as they were under pressure to keep within range of their peers. One official suggested that "the judges cheerfully go along because they don't even realize what's happening. If everyone gives 9.9 are you going to give 9.1?"[58]

An elite cadre of judges with positions of power within the FIG technical committees were largely responsible for the score fixing, and their practices influenced many other judges. They had the power to realize competition results, while the gymnasts—even after the most awesome performances of their life—were at their mercy, the interests of nations put ahead of their own. "We would call it corruption," explained one North American judge. "They would call it the way of doing business." Often these judges simply did not understand that this was cheating: they simply saw it as "working for their country."[59] Many of the FIG judges, particularly those in high positions or on committees, were in salaried positions working for their governments, including President Titov. Certainly, the IOC addressed telegrams to his Moscow address, at the Soviet Sports Committee.[60] Indeed, after ten years work at the FIG, Titov was promoted to secretary general of the Soviet National Olympic Committee.[61] This points to his particularly skillful leadership. Without alienating the country he worked for, he took steps toward reforming the sport's judging. At the 1977 European Championships, he introduced an initiative to draw lots for which apparatus each judge would preside over, and to broadcast the lottery on television to promote transparency and objectivity.[62] Titov also introduced video referencing to further promote accountability and transparency at the FIG, warning that "the judges should therefore be aware their work can be checked up on."[63]

Despite these efforts, at the same 1977 European Championships, allegations of biased judging prompted the Romanian team to storm out mid-competition. At the time, the championships were one of the most important competitions on the gymnastics calendar, featuring the strongest nations in women's artistic gymnastics. This competition was also the first major event following Comăneci's Montreal victory, which had been used as testimony to the success of Romanian dictator Ceauşescu's regime. With a new interest in gymnastics, Romania had arranged for televised coverage at home. Ceauşescu demanded success for Romania, but the rest of the Eastern bloc was reluctant to agree. The FIG described the incident: "The Romanian Delegation left the competition before the end and this we could not understand. This behavior is regrettable."[64] The reasons behind Romania's impromptu boycott, and the FIG's alleged part in it, are notably absent from this report.

Other sources claimed that, during the first event of apparatus finals, the scores were changed to enable a Soviet victory. Comăneci had the highest mark on vault, with Kim coming second. The Soviet Union then protested Kim's score in light of her having performed a vault of greater difficulty. The protest was accepted, and Kim's score upgraded so that the two gymnasts tied. Yet when the medal ceremony began (after the first of four rotations during the competition), Kim was given the gold and Comăneci took second place.[65] While Comăneci went on to perform on the bars and then the beam, back home in Romania Ceaușescu became so indignant over the score adjustment that he ordered the Romanian team to leave the arena immediately.[66] "The entire country of Romania had been watching the championships, and the people were infuriated by the unfairness of the judges," Comăneci recalled in her autobiography. "For the first time in our country's history, the event had been on television, and when they'd seen Béla [behaving as usual] carrying on and shaking his fists against the judges they demanded that the Romanian team be saved from injustice."[67] Yet again, allegations of cheating come from those whose preferred winner was not winning. Notwithstanding the veracity to claims of score fixing—Comăneci had scored two perfect 10s on the bars and beam while Ceaușescu watched it all, enraged—Ceaușescu sent the Romanian ambassador to withdraw the Romanian team from the competition immediately. The statement was meant to be heard loud and clear: Romania would not tolerate unfair, biased judging. The Soviets, in particular, received special vitriol, with the US ambassador to Romania reporting that the incident did little to serve Soviet-Romanian friendship: "No one will convince the Romanian public that it has not once again been discriminated against by its Russian neighbor." The ambassador accused Titov of doing little to ease tensions by accusing the Romanians of walking out because they could not accept that Comăneci was simply not the best.[68]

Following this incident, Romania proposed to the FIG a new rule that each judge show their score, to ensure accountability.[69] The highest and lower scores were excluded, and the average of the remaining scores determined the final result. But only the judges were privy to the mathematics behind this formula, meaning they could adjust their scores to influence the final outcome. The FIG took nine years to approve Romania's proposal. In light of what happened with Comăneci at the Montreal Games, this suggests that Romania was not in the select group of allied, score-fixing judges. US proposals also point to the Americans' exclusion

FIGURE 4.5. Nelli Kim and Nadia Comăneci shake hands during a medal ceremony at the 1976 Olympic Games. A year later, the Romanian team would walk out of the 1977 European championships in protest of alleged score-fixing affecting the results of these two gymnasts. © 1976 IOC / United Archives—All rights reserved.

and disadvantage in the judging system. In 1975, they had proposed that judges for finals be from "neutral" countries only, those "not having any gymnasts in the final competition in that event."[70] But the FIG's records contain no further discussion of these ideas, and no changes were made to the Olympic format until both countries gained more influence on the technical committees.

On the FIG Executive Committee, President Titov continued to persevere in solving the judging problem, through increased numbers of judges, better supervision of judges, and the use of digital technology to aid judging. At the 1985 world championships, the FIG pioneered six-person judging panels. The women's technical committee was thrilled with this development, claiming that "a new standard of differentiation and objectivity was achieved in the evaluation of the exercise." Gymnastics officials from other countries seemed pleased too, with one Australian judge telling her compatriots that "judging also appeared fairer and less political . . . with six judges."[71]

But Titov remained convinced there was more to be done. He was reluctant to attribute scoring controversies to judging incompetence. Rather, he saw "a subjective attitude in the evaluation of the real value of the exercises," or in other words, biased judging. The abundance of perfect 10s being awarded underscored this point. Subjective judging was not only a problem within gymnastics, but as Titov alluded, also had implications for gymnastics' inclusion in the Olympics. "This situation can be in favor of a persistence of a certain corruption which would be very dangerous for our sport, even a vital danger."[72]

In 1986, the FIG introduced what it called the Superior Jury to check the work of the judges on each apparatus. The FIG also partnered with Longines, the Swiss watchmaker, to develop a computerized control system that promoted transparency and accountability. Each judge had to input their score, which was immediately displayed. Viewers could see every score, rather than just the average.[73] An incident at the 1980 Olympics helped prompt the above reforms. During the floor-exercise finals at the Moscow Olympics, Comăneci's score had been upgraded from 9.00 to 9.50. Chair of the women's technical committee, Ellen Berger of East Germany, said the British judge had mistakenly entered her score as 9.50 instead of 10. The upgraded score was a correct recalculation. A British judge, however, insisted that Berger had changed the score following a protest from the Romanian team. In any event, the scores resulted in a tie for gold between Comăneci and Kim.[74] Combined with the earlier allegations of score fixing, and Titov's concern that the sport was in danger, the FIG was under pressure to refurbish gymnastics' reputation.

Both in response to these concerns about score fixing, and wanting to make the sport more attractive to spectators, in 1989 the FIG introduced a new rule that reset a gymnast's score to zero for each round of competition.[75] This new rule applied to both men's and women's artistic gymnastics. Previously, the points a gymnast had accrued in the qualification round would carry over into the finals, effectively giving some athletes a head start. Under the "new life" rule, once a gymnast had made it through to finals, their previous scores did not matter, everyone started from zero. The new rule raised suspense, added drama, and also meant that audiences could tune in for the final, rather than having to watch days of competition. Combined with geopolitical shifts as the Cold War drew to a close, the "new life" rule not only reduced tedium but also made gymnastics victories more accessible to a wider range of countries.

From 1984 onward, judging problems involved the United States, which was by then a growing threat to the powers of world gymnastics. At the 1984 Olympics, the US gymnastics team was on home ground. After Mary Lou Retton performed one of her best routines, her coach, Béla Károlyi, jumped over the press barricade to congratulate her. But only official team coaches—which he was not—were allowed on the competition floor. Ellen Berger, head of the jury and in charge of the competition for those games, warned Károlyi she would impose the 0.50 penalty if it happened again. But knowing the rule was unlikely to be enforced in front of a large US crowd, the next day he did it again. Berger did not follow through to enforce the penalty, and Retton went on to win the competition with less than a half-point margin. The head coach of the 1984 US team was Don Peters (since disgraced following allegations of pedophilia). He alleged that Berger's "prestige was wounded, but she chickened out, because it would have taken the medal away from Mary Lou here in Los Angeles."[76] While home-ground advantage may have enabled the women's technical committee to turn a blind eye to the US infringement in 1984, it aggravated East-West tensions, which came to the fore at the following Olympics.

At the Seoul Games in 1988, the US team missed out on the bronze medal due to a similar technical penalty enforced by FIG chiefs Titov and Berger. As Kelly Garrison-Steves performed her bar routine, teammate Rhonda Faehn mounted the podium to remove a springboard out of the way.[77] While this assistance is permitted, the teammate is required to dismount the podium as soon as the equipment is in place. Faehn, however, merely moved to the side of the podium to watch Garrison-Steves finish her routine. Titov claimed that several nations had reported the infraction.[78] After reviewing the video footage, the bars judges, along with Titov and Berger, voted to penalize the US team, taking half a point from their team total, thereby relegating them to fourth place behind the Eastern European powers: the USSR, Romania, and East Germany. US coach Peters decried the penalty as invoked by an "obscure" rule that he had never seen enforced in his twenty years' experience. He also blamed his rival Károlyi for the incident. Berger's intention may have been "to gain back the prestige she lost at the 1984 Games . . . when she failed to impose a penalty on the US team that would have cost its prize student, Mary Lou Retton, the gold medal in all-around competition."[79] Károlyi, however, called it foul play. "That's dirty, and that's sick. What does it matter, even if the kid is on the podium? What change is there in the routine? It doesn't disturb anything. I've never seen that before."[80]

FIGURE 4.6. Kelly Garrison-Steves performs her beam routine at the 1988 games. © 1988 IOC / Richard Harbus—All rights reserved.

US newspapers seized on the controversy as a sign of political maneuvering in women's artistic gymnastics, arguing that the US team had been persecuted to increase East Germany's chance of taking the bronze medal. "It's obvious the East German judge wanted to keep the scores down," Károlyi claimed. "They're fighting desperately to keep their place."[81] Indeed, the results of the Seoul judging and the 0.50 penalty enabled East Germany to clutch the bronze with less than a 0.475 margin over the US team. Károlyi and Peters did have significant motives to be making such complaints. Under their watch, the US team narrowly missed out on its first team medal at a fully attended Olympics, because of a simple mistake unrelated to performance. But on the other hand, there is some merit to suggestions of political judging, which has a long history in gymnastics. For example, when asked how Cold War tensions have affected gymnastics, a long-time international coach immediately mentioned "deals behind the scenes." "There's definite blocs of judging. When the Americans started to come through . . . a lot of unfair judging happened!"[82]

After its leaders had been embroiled in so many of these allegations, the 1990 FIG Congress decided that technical committee members could no longer serve as chief judges on the apparatus panels. Moreover, the chair, first vice chair, and secretary would not serve on any apparatus panel, but would instead form an appeals jury in the case of unfair scoring from the apparatus panels. The remaining members of the women's technical committee formed a "control brigade," appointed to supervise the work of judging panels on each apparatus "to prevent manipulation of any kind."[83] But equally, the FIG's mission to rationalize the sport is clearly visible in such decisions. "The tendencies of weak or biased judging had to be stopped," wrote Titov in his 1992 report, "and this is why we introduced the new system [of removing] our technical committee members from active judging and using them to control the activity and the standard of judging."[84] Titov was both removing some of the most influential score fixers from judging positions while repositioning them to limit their involvement to instances of appeal or other problems.

By the 1990s, gymnasts and their coaches were playing to the crowd who in turn would pressure the judges. Such a tactic was not cheating, but it certainly reduced the FIG's control over its judges. For instance, at the 1991 Indianapolis world championships, "the local press—apparently in association with the US trainer, Károlyi—attempted to exercise open psychological pressure by directing gross attacks, abuse and insults towards all judges," Berger accused in an official report.[85] Presumably she was referring to booing and yelling from the audience when they were unhappy with a score, although there is little evidence of this in media coverage of the event. When US judge Jackie Fie became chair of the Women's Technical Committee in 1992 these problems did not stop. Although she introduced a new computerized system that measured judges' adherence to the Code of Points and benchmarked their scores against their peers, biased judging continued. At the 1996 Olympic Games alone, three sanctions were issued in women's artistic gymnastics to deal with unethical judges.[86]

At this point, the IOC stepped in. After the 1996 games in Atlanta, it compelled the FIG to introduce a rule to break any ties in Olympic competition.[87] It did not make this demand of any other sport. As of this writing, swimming and track and field retain ties, as do other sports, although ties are rarer there. In the IOC's view, gymnastics should have had fewer ties than other sports because subjective judgment comes into play. Gymnastics is not limited by timekeeping or other forms of measurement in the way other sports were, ergo, it should have been possible to use judgment and make decisions to avoid ties in gymnastics. The judging problems at the 1996 games prompted the IOC to make this change, but in fact the IOC had been asking the FIG to reduce the number of *ex aequo* (tied) scores for years. The number of ties across many sports in the games had first come to attention after the IOC Baden-Baden Congress of 1981.[88] But gymnastics was quickly identified as one of the main sources of ties.

In 1983, IOC sports director Csanádi asked that the FIG avoid "the situation of having more than one athlete gaining the same placing (*ex aequo*) . . . in future Olympic Games."[89] The IOC demanded that the FIG devise a system to break ties.[90] Unable to agree on such a system, the executive committee of the FIG wrote to the IOC that ties were allowed in other sports, and thus should be maintained in gymnastics.[91] Csanádi responded

FIGURE 4.7. Shannon Miller was involved in two ties at the 1992 Olympic Games. © 1992 IOC—All rights reserved.

that because gymnastics was one of the most notorious sports for ties, the IOC would no longer allow it *any* ties, in order to rehabilitate gymnastics' credibility. "Although ties are theoretically possible in a few sports other than gymnastics, no cases occurred at the last winter and summer Olympic Games. The only case on record is the men's relay at the last cross-country skiing championship," explained Csanádi. "On the contrary, *ex aequo* cases in gymnastics occurred repeatedly at past Olympic Games and World Championships." In the ten years between 1972 and 1982, the FIG awarded twenty-two ties—eight at the three Olympics in that period, including six in women's artistic gymnastics.[92] Unlike sports that use objective measurements like distance, speed, or points, the IOC saw gymnastics as highly subjective. Its view was that the ties in gymnastics were entirely created by poor judging. But equally, because judging was the mode of measurement, the IOC determined that ties could be more easily avoided in gymnastics than in other sports, as gymnastics judges had more tools at their disposal to distinguish between performances. Nonetheless, after this correspondence, there were no further letters or decisions on the matter, and *ex aequo* rankings continued.[93] Perhaps this was because the IOC was preoccupied with issues such as the boycotts and the role of the Olympics in sports diplomacy. But by the 1990s, *ex aequo* scores were back on the IOC's radar.

The fall of the Soviet Union exacerbated the *ex aequo* issue. When the Soviet Union collapsed, the block of judges willing to fix scores fractured. There were now more countries trying to fix scores to attain Olympic victory. This worsened in the coming years when former Soviet coaches and judges fled to other nations around the globe. "Suddenly there were 10 or 15 of [countries willing to fix scores] and if anyone wanted to collaborate then there was a whole bunch more to collaborate with," recalled one official. "It worked for a short while perhaps, but then there were so many created ties. So suddenly we had tie breaking at the Olympics."[94] There were eight ties at the 1992 Olympics, across fourteen events.[95] This meant that almost half of the competitions across men's and women's artistic gymnastics at those Games resulted in a tie. Of the forty-two medals available, 20 percent were jointly awarded due to *ex aequo* rankings. Further, sometimes those ties were split between three people. For women's artistic gymnastics, gymnasts were tied for a medal in three out of the four apparatus finals. At the 1996 games, there were four ties across fourteen events. Even this lower number showed that ties remained a problem in gymnastics, across both the men's and women's artistic disciplines. Hence, the IOC demanded change.

Table 4.1: Ties in artistic gymnastics at the 1992 Olympics

	Gold	Silver	Bronze
		Men's Artistic Gymnastics	
Floor exercise		Yukio Iketani (Japan) Grigory Misutin (Unified Team)	
Pommel horse	Vitaly Scherbo (Unified Team) Pae Gil-Su (North Korea)		
Rings			Andreas Wecker (Germany) Li Xiaoshuang (China)
Parallel bars			Igor Korobchinski (Unified Team) Guo Linyao (China) Masayuki Matsunaga (Japan)
Horizontal bar		Grigory Misutin (Unified Team) Andreas Wecker (Germany)	
		Women's Artistic Gymnastics	
Vault	Lavinia Miloşovici (Romania) Henrietta Ónodi (Hungary)		
Balance beam		Lu Li (China) Shannon Miller (USA)	
Floor exercise			Cristina Bontaş (Romania) Shannon Miller (USA) Tatiana Gutsu (Unified Team)

Since its introduction after 1996, the gymnastics tie-breaking rule has undergone a number of incarnations. For example, in the event of a tie in the all-around competition, the tie could be broken by ascertaining who had the highest score over their best three events (instead of four). Since 2006, the FIG has looked at breaking ties by comparing the execution scores and excluding difficulty. Whatever iteration the tiebreaker rule is in, it has only

Table 4.2: Ties in artistic gymnastics at the 1996 Olympics

	Gold	Silver	Bronze
		Men's Artistic Gymnastics	
Rings		Szilveszter Csollány (Hungary) Dan Burincă (Romania)	
Horizontal bar			Fan Bin (China) Alexei Nemov (Russia) Vitaly Scherbo (Belarus)
		Women's Artistic Gymnastics	
All-around			Simona Amânar (Romania) Lavinia Miloşovici (Romania)
Uneven bars		Amy Chow (USA) Bi Wenjing (China)	

ever been employed at the Olympic Games. The FIG continues to allow ties at all competitions except the Olympics, confirming that the rule was created to cooperate with the IOC's demands. The Olympic tie-break rule continues to be a source of frustration for gymnastics fans, who as Titov already pointed out, cannot see why gymnastics is unable to consider two athletes perfectly matched if the same can also be true of sprinters, swimmers, and most other athletes whose achievements are quantitatively measured. FIG president Grandi agreed with that perception in 2012: "I believe it's correct to have two gold medals. But this is my modest opinion. The IOC is different."[96] And clearly, the FIG cooperated with the IOC, adapting gymnastics' rules at the games. The IOC, for its part, insisted that it is precisely because gymnastics is judged that performances can and should be differentiated.

Abandoning the Perfect 10

Before the IOC stepped in to resolve the *ex aequo* issue, FIG member Hardy Fink had been working on a solution to the broader cause of ties: subjective, biased judging and score fixing. In the early 1990s, he began designing an open-ended scoring system that would decentralize the judging panel's control over outcomes. Instead of a judging panel awarding their average score for a routine, Fink's system saw two panels on each apparatus, each responsible for a different part of the final score. The first panel would control the score for the difficulty, building it up from zero based on the elements performed. And the second would control the score for the execution, making deductions from 10 points based on faults in performance. The final score would be determined by combining the two scores from these separate panels. This system would make it harder for judges to manipulate the final score. But more than loosening cheating judges' grip on final scores, Fink was designing a system for gymnastics where athletes perpetually strove to break records. Until 1976, the unattainable record had been the perfect 10. But once Comăneci achieved this score, athletes could only match, not exceed, that perfect 10. Fink's idea was that removing the limit of 10 points would also be a way to create distance between exceptional gymnasts and the rest of the field. With no upper score limit, this system would also allow athletes to pursue new records.

But while the FIG had been prepared to modify its judging panels and provide computerized judging aids, forsaking the 10 was a step too far. It would be another decade before the FIG's hand was forced, in the face of IOC pressure and public distrust of gymnastics judging.[97] At the 2004 Athens Games, a number of scoring controversies arose, including a calculation error in the men's all-around that relegated the winner into third place. Then, the crowd could not make sense of the scores given in the men's high bar final. Fan favorite Alexei Nemov of Russia had to ask the crowd to stop booing the judges for the score they had given him so that the remaining gymnasts could compete. The crowd thought the score was too low and could only see fault with the judges. With its credibility exhausted, the FIG returned to Fink for help with rewriting the rules. "The men's scandals from the 2004 Olympics had a huge effect. That resulted in the forced change of the Code of Points that I'd been trying to promote for the 20 years before—at least in the separation of execution and difficulty," he recounted. "The men's judging scandal gave the excuse to suddenly impose it, so the judges couldn't control both parts of the score."[98]

When the FIG first discussed Fink's work on developing a new code in the 1990s, it was in the context of needing to improve gymnastics' viewership. The Olympics were suffering a drop in popularity, and X sports threatened gymnastics' monopoly on aerial feats. Score fixing was also undermining gymnastics' credibility. These issues put gymnastics' inclusion in the games at risk if it failed to modernize. President Titov thought a new, simplified scoring system might help with popularity, as well his goals for more objective judging. He envisioned a permanent, universal code with difficulty values assigned to every element performed or possible in future, and consistent across both the men's and women's disciplines.[99] His successor, Bruno Grandi, shared this vision. He wanted to make the competitions more attractive to "full television coverage" while also converging the Codes for men's and women's gymnastics and "guaranteeing sports fairness."[100] So, contrary to the complaints of modern fans that the post-10 code is too complicated for viewers, it actually had its origins in trying to achieve a fairer sport in a more spectator-friendly format.

Titov asked the men's and women's technical committees to collaborate in February 1995 to align their respective codes, making the judging of the two disciplines "as similar as possible." Titov wanted the committees to observe the scoring systems of diving and trampolining, which already divided scores into difficulty and execution, and apply those principles to their own disciplines. To promote more creativity and originality, he wanted the number of requirements reduced so that gymnasts had opportunity within the time limit to "show what they can do and be rewarded for it."[101] Titov's challenge to the committees became the key characteristics of the new code: separate difficulty and execution, fewer requirements, and more points for the best elements.

When Grandi took over as president in 1998, he reaffirmed these challenges and asked that the two technical committees continue collaborating to develop the new code.[102] They decided to create an A panel to assess the difficulty of routines, and a B panel to evaluate the execution, as Fink had mooted. But the committees remained devoted to the idea of a perfect 10. They decided that the way to retain the 10 would be to use a formula: Double the B score for execution, add it to A score for difficulty, and divide by three.[103] The division by three, commented Fink, was not really necessary but was included to maintain the illusion of the perfect 10, pacifying opposition to the new system.[104] The formula would not only retain the 10 but also resolve the question of how difficulty should be weighed against execution. Execution was worth twice as much as difficulty. The executive committee was happy with the proposal, announcing, "This formula assures that the important factors of perfect execution and artistry take precedence over difficulty. The display of unmastered difficulty will result in large deductions as well as no credit for the difficulty of the element."[105]

However, the women's technical committee was frustrated with the new direction, despite their cooperation in developing it. Following an October 1998 meeting with the men's technical committee, it held its own separate meeting to discuss its qualms with the new system. They decided to tell the executive committee that the proposed code was not simpler, would not be easily understood by spectators, and would thus only worsen the marketability of the sport "with unfamiliar and untraditional scores unrelated to 10."[106] They also cited general safety, stress, and injury concerns. Moreover, they thought the executive committee was rushing the introduction of the new code without appropriate testing. It was already the end of 1998, meaning everyone would only have twenty-four months to adapt to the idea and come up with new rules and values before the code came into force at the end of the year 2000.

Fie, who had recently seen her country achieve its best results with an Olympic team gold in 1996, led the opposition, sending the FIG into frantic negotiations as the deadline of 2000 approached. Grandi sent a representative to the next women's technical committee meeting in March 1999 to persuade them to adopt the changes. "Hans Jurgen [Grandi's ambassador] explained that it is okay to have different opinions, but we must accept and follow the decisions of the executive committee," recalled Fie in her summary of the minutes. But in response, she told the executive committee that "the women's technical committee feels they have been completely left out of the decision making process."[107] She was ignoring the several joint meetings with the men's committee at which the new system was discussed. And as Jurgen told her, the executive committee wanted the women's technical committee to test the new code as it saw fit. But the women's technical committee maintained that there was simply not enough time to test it before the Sydney Olympics, and there would be only a few months after the games before the code came into force. Fie claimed that the executive committee had listened only to Fink, not to the individual members of the technical committees.

However, Fink recalled that opposition to the new code only came from three countries. A petition supporting the new code received overwhelming support from the federations at the 1999 world championships. But when the executive committee finally voted on whether to proceed with the proposed code, the United States, Romania, and Japan voted against it.[108] The first two were among the top-ranked teams in women's artistic gymnastics, and Japan was the top-ranked team in men's artistic gymnastics. China, also one of the top nations in women's gymnastics, shortly joined the group opposing the code. Soon enough more of the world's top teams had joined the chorus of opposition to block the executive committee's plans. Grandi conceded defeat and bided his time until multiple judging scandals at the Athens Olympics in 2004 allowed him to force the change.

The new, post-10 code was introduced in 2006. It was missing some elements of Titov, Grandi, and Fink's vision. It was not universal, and it still required updating every four years. It also removed the formula the technical committees had earlier insisted on that held the top score at 10. This has fueled tension between the value assigned to execution and that assigned to difficulty. Many gymnastics fans were scandalized when Vanessa Ferrari of Italy won the 2006 world championships despite having fallen on one event. But the post-10 code separated difficulty and execution scores, and it allowed for the creation of records. With the upper limit of 10 removed, the sport could once again pursue quantifiable records, as scores reached

FIGURE 4.8. Vanessa Ferrari of Italy won the first world championships that used the post-10 code of points in 2006. She is pictured here competing at the 2016 Olympic Games. © 2016 IOC / Jason Evans—All rights reserved.

well into the teens. And ultimately, it has fulfilled one of the core aims of its creation: dividing the judging panels so that scores can be more objective, in theory.

Doping and Age Falsification

The scoring system was but one of the problems with gymnastics' rules. Gymnastics programs in a several countries were also devising other ways of gaining competitive advantage, disregarding age and doping rules. In doing so, they refused to abide with the international agreement on the rules of the sport, failing to cooperate with both the organizations and countries involved in international gymnastics.

Age falsification was the most prolific form of cheating in women's artistic gymnastics. In the early 1970s, the FIG instituted a minimum age of fourteen for the discipline, which it updated to fifteen in 1980 (effective from 1982). In 1996, it raised the age to sixteen. North Korea was one of the first countries found guilty of breaking this rule, with repeated false declarations of Kim Gwang-Suk's age. Uneven bars champion at the 1991 world championships Gwang-Suk had also participated in the world championships in 1989 and the Asian games in 1990. But at each of these competitions, over three years, her age had been listed as fifteen—the minimum age required. Then when she competed at the 1992 Olympic Games, her age was listed as seventeen. When the FIG finally noted the discrepancy and asked for an explanation, the Democratic People's Republic of Korea provided a birth year of 1975 and "regretted the oversight" in birthdates listed as 1974 and 1976. But the FIG was not satisfied, believing that it was not simply the mistake of only one official. "The executive committee finds it very hard to believe that Mrs Li Jong-Ae is the only person in the PRK federation who knew about the real age of Kim Gwang Suk," the secretary general reported in 1993.[109] The FIG considered that it was not Gwang-Suk but the officials who falsified records that should be held accountable. Once again, officials had put their country's interests ahead of the gymnast. On this basis, the FIG allowed Gwang-Suk to keep her medals. But as punishment for the administrative error, which the FIG suspected was intentional, the North Korean women's team was banned from competing in the 1993 world championships. Yet, North Korea made the same false declarations two decades later. Hong Su Jong competed at the 2004 Olympics, but at various international competitions before and after, her birth year had been listed as 1985, 1986, and 1989. Again, the FIG chose not to strip the gymnast of her medals—a silver on vault from the 2007 world championships—but it did ban both the men's and women's programs from participating in the 2010 world championships.[110] In both incidents, the FIG caught North Korean officials falsifying ages close to or at the time they were doing it.

Although the FIG dealt with North Korea's age falsification relatively consistently over two decades, it employed completely different disciplinary measures when a Chinese athlete was found to have falsified her age. In 2008, Dong Fangxiao registered to serve as a line judge for the Beijing Olympic Games, with a birth year of 1986—the same year given on her résumé. But when she had competed at the 1999 world championships and 2000 Olympic Games, her birth year had been listed as 1983. If her correct birth year was really 1986, it meant that she would have been thirteen at the world championships and fourteen at the Olympics. After a sixteen-month investigation, for which the FIG billed the Chinese Gymnastics Association for costs, it determined that Fangxiao's age had been falsified and her results from the 1999 world championships were nullified.[111] China was stripped of the bronze medal it had won in the team event. It made this announcement in February 2010 and recommended to the IOC that it nullify her scores from the 2000 Olympic Games too. Usually, the IOC has employed an eight-year statute of limitations for modifying any results.[112]

FIGURE 4.9. Dong Fangxiao competes on the uneven bars at the 2000 Olympic Games in Sydney. In 2008, the IOC found that her age had been falsified and she was likely only fourteen at these games instead of the minimum sixteen. © 2000 IOC / Stephen Munday—All rights reserved.

FIGURE 4.10. The Chinese team was stripped of its bronze medal from the 2000 Olympic Games and the 1999 World Championships after Fangxiao's scores were nullified. Pictured here, the Chinese team celebrates their bronze medal at the 2000 games. © 2000 IOC / Stephen Munday—All rights reserved.

But this statute appears to exist for doping-related offences only. The IOC announced that the executive board agreed with the FIG and stripped the Chinese team of its bronze medal from the 2000 Olympic Games.[113]

Although both age falsifications took place under similar circumstances, several differences in the revelation of cheating may explain the FIG's different responses. First, the FIG had more evidence about Fangxiao's age than it had about Gwang-Suk, whose age is still unknown. Moreover, as Fangxiao's age discrepancies did not come to light until eight years later, it would not have made sense to ban the Chinese team from the next world championships, as this would have punished athletes (and possibly coaches and officials) who had not been involved at the time of the infraction. Whereas Gwang-Suk was seen as a victim of officials who had forged her documents, Chinese officials claimed that Fangxiao herself had faked her age.[114] However, as journalists have noted, it seems unlikely that a thirteen-year-old could have forged government-issued documentation like the passport used to prove her age.[115]

The fact that Chinese officials blamed Fangxiao, and that the evidence appeared eight years after the incident, go some way to explaining the

FIG's exaggerated response in comparison to how it deal with North Korean cheating. Moreover, Fangxiao's case happened at a time of intense scrutiny of the Chinese team in 2008, with many media outlets claiming that the 2008 team was also underage.[116] However, those allegations were based on journalists' assessment of the Chinese gymnasts' physical appearance, without hard evidence or documentation to support their claims of cheating. The FIG was assured that the 2008 team were not cheating, but it had an interest in appearing strict and decisive when presented with evidence of Fangxiao being underage. It is also possible there was a racialized element to how FIG and IOC leaders dealt with Fangxiao, as Chinese people have long been characterized as sneaky and untrustworthy in many Western cultures.[117] Indeed, the gap in time between Fangxiao's competitive career and her reckoning cannot fully account for the actions taken against her when these measures were not also applied to Romanian gymnasts found to have competed underage after their careers had ended.

In 2002, Romanian star Daniela Silivaş revealed that officials had misrepresented her age by two years so she could compete as a senior at the 1985 world championships when she was only thirteen.[118] She claimed that the Romanian Gymnastics Federation had changed the date on her passport without asking her, and had done the same for at least three other gymnasts. Lavinia Agache claimed the Romanian Gymnastics Federation did the same to her when she competed at the 1981 world championships also at age thirteen.[119] Alexandra Marinescu agreed. She said officials had changed her age by a year to make her eligible for the 1995 and 1996 world championships and Olympics.[120] Marinescu's claim in particular fell well within the informal eight-year statute of limitations. Moreover, when longtime leader of the Romanian Gymnastics Federation, Nicolae Vieru, was asked to comment on these allegations, he admitted to the cheating. "Changing the ages was a worldwide practice . . . we copied this from others." Ion Ţiriac, head of the Romanian Olympic Committee, agreed: "this was a practice employed by everybody."[121] Despite these admissions, however, all of these gymnasts kept their medals, none of the officials received sanctions, and the Romanian Gymnastics Federations remained active in the international gymnastics community. Perhaps the FIG did not have the evidence to revoke their titles, yet there is no indication that it undertook the same kind of strenuous investigation it did for Fangxiao. Moreover, unlike the Chinese case, the accounts of various Romanian gymnasts over several generations, alongside the comments made by officials, suggest

FIGURE 4.11. Romanian Daniela Silivaș competes on the beam during the 1988 Olympic Games. It was revealed in 2002 that Romanian officials had falsified her age for the 1985 world championships.

that Romanian age-falsification was systematic and remained an ongoing policy.

The admissions of Romanian age falsification arose in the wake of gymnastics' biggest doping scandals. At the Sydney 2000 Olympics, Romanian gymnast Andreea Răducan tested positive for a banned substance, pseudoephedrine. As a result, she was stripped of her gold medal for the all-around competition. It was only the second positive doping test gymnastics had seen.[122] William Sands, a sports scientist who specializes in gymnastics, theorizes that the relative absence of doping in the sport is because of its nature. Certainly, strength and speed are necessary components, but ultimately it is a sport of skill and precision that relies on superior coordination and air sense. "When a drug interferes with control (as most do), their benefit to gymnasts is highly questionable."[123]

Prescribed cold medicine by the team doctor, Răducan had unwittingly taken pseudoephedrine—a substance banned because of its energy-enhancing effects. Although at the time the FIG did not ban the drug, the IOC did. The IOC rules prevailed, and Răducan's medal was awarded to her teammate Simona Amânar. The FIG clearly sympathized with Răducan, its executive committee voting unanimously not to impose any further sanctions on her or the Romanians, the loss of her medal being "punishment enough for an athlete who was innocent in this situation."[124] Across these three countries and decades, it is clear that officials, coaches, and even medical staff put the medals before welfare, making child athletes compete internationally, even though the rules prohibited it, and leaving the athletes to take the blame if caught.

Both the IOC and FIG supported sanctions against the team doctor. But was the FIG turning a blind eye to systematic and state-sponsored doping? There is evidence that it was not uncommon for Romanian team doctors to prescribe pills to gymnasts before competition. But, as Sands outlined, it is unlikely that these offered any chemical enhancements to the gymnasts. More likely, pills were prescribed for the psychological effect of a confidence boost. One FIG executive committee member who was present at the emergency meetings in Sydney said that the Romanian team leader pleaded for leniency with Răducan, arguing that everyone on the team had taken pseudoephedrine, she just got caught because she was the smallest and it had not passed through her body yet.[125] Romanian Olympic head Țiriac later made these claims in public.[126] Such public admissions of doping should have disqualified the entire team on the basis of the drug being banned at the time. But the narrative never became one of systematic doping, it simply focused on the personal tragedy for Răducan, a sixteen-year-old who had wrongly put her faith in the team doctor.

There have been several positive doping tests since then, spread throughout the globe.[127] Almost every case of doping in women's gymnastics has been related to the use of furosemide. The drug is banned because it can mask other drugs. But it is also a diuretic, used to lose weight quickly. When female gymnasts use it, seeking to keep their body weight low, they often abuse the drug for months.[128] The gymnasts who have tested positive have invariably been banned for at least a year, but as none of these tests derived from Olympic or world championship medal-winning performances, no medals have been withdrawn.

Conclusion

The making and breaking of the rules in gymnastics demonstrate the varying levels of international cooperation and collaboration in the sport. At the outset, FIG leaders from around the world collaborated to develop the rules laid out in the Code of Points. This offered a form of standardization that would transcend national boundaries. Through the code the FIG could quantify performances, awarding points based on efficiency of movement.

It also allowed the FIG to meet the IOC's criteria for sports it included in its program—it provided a measurable system of judgment that rationalized the sport. But the FIG had to continue negotiating and compromising with the IOC, as the latter questioned gymnastics' validity as a team sport, along with the number of medals available. Changes to the sport's structure, including team size, competition format, and a limit on the number of athletes per country in the finals, allowed the FIG to satisfy the IOC's concerns. Soviet leaders played a great role in this last initiative, which is consistent with the idea that the Soviet Union tried to democratize international sports to promote its own agenda.[129]

While the FIG cooperated with the IOC's demands for a fair and measurable sport, judges were collaborating to break the rules that underpinned this. At best, judging was inherently subjective, judges had biases and sometimes judged a gymnast's reputation as much as her performance on the day. But at worst, judges made agreements to elevate the scores of certain gymnasts preordained for a medal. Gymnasts were deprived of influence, even after their best performances, as judges and officials conspired to fix the scores. Most of the allegations concur that it was Eastern-bloc judges responsible for this, but other judges may have gone along with it in order to keep their scores in line with their peers'. Moreover, some of those allegedly responsible were part of the FIG leadership. The number of ties awarded began to draw suspicion from the IOC, which suspected a problem with the judging. While the FIG continued awarding *ex aequo* results throughout the 1980s, by the 1990s the IOC demanded that the FIG stop. The FIG cooperated, introducing a tie-break rule, but this was only ever applied at the Olympic Games, and was not required of all Olympic sports.

Meanwhile, as president of the FIG, Titov worked tirelessly to improve judges' objectivity. Under his leadership, the FIG implemented a number of computerized technologies to monitor judges' work. But as problems continued, he asked the men's and women's technical committees to collaborate on devising a new scoring system. The new system removed the cap on scores of 10 points and aimed to provide a universal and permanent Code of Points. Although the two groups worked on the new code together, they could not agree. The women's technical committee and several member nations opposed it so strongly that they stopped the new code from coming into force for the year 2000. While the FIG had worked tirelessly with the IOC, and judges collaborated to fix scores, FIG members refused to cooperate on the new code. Only after yet another judging scandal in 2006 could the FIG leadership could finally push through the post-10 code.

Yet, for all its focus on subjective judging and devising a new scoring system to prevent it, the FIG did relatively little about the most brazen cheating of all: age falsification. Despite some officials' claims, it is inconceivable that children forged their own government-issued documentation to falsify their age. Clearly, the gymnasts were entirely victims of the actions of officials determined to win at any cost. Neither the North Korean nor the Romanian gymnasts had their medals removed when their age falsifications were retrospectively revealed. The North Korean federation received minor sanctions, excluded from the world championships for a year, while the Romanian federation was never punished. Yet, when it emerged that the Chinese federation had falsified the records of one of its gymnasts at the 2000 Olympics, the FIG stripped the team of its medal a decade after the fact. Although each situation of age falsification differed, it is also clear there has been a racialized element to the way the FIG has responded. By its nature, age falsification involves officials cheating on behalf of children. It is evidence of collaboration to break the rules within a national regime and of a refusal to play by the rules internationally. And despite this being true of age falsification in North Korea, China, and Romania, the Chinese gymnasts were the only ones for whom the FIG and IOC revoked medals. Doping, on the other hand, appears to be an example of isolated cheating. A small number of gymnasts, from a variety of different countries, have tested positive for doping with furosemide, and each has been banned for at least one year for that transgression. Comment from Romanian officials and FIG insiders, however, suggests that doping in Romania was more systematic, at least until the year 2000, when Răducan was stripped of her gold medal in the all-around after the team doctor gave her, and allegedly the entire team, pseudoephedrine. This evidence shows that over the last four decades, at least, coaches, officials, and even medical staff have conspired to break the rules in order to win medals, thereby jeopardizing gymnasts' careers and health.

Through the making and breaking of rules, it is clear that cooperation and collaboration occurred internationally between sports organizations, administrators, judges, and gymnasts. While the FIG inconsistently disciplined those who broke the rules, it focused on creating new, stricter rules designed to improve the objectivity of the sport and retain its place in the Olympic movement. This was a balancing act, as FIG had to appeal to both the IOC's sense of fairness and neutrality in sports, but also to the values of those within the sport. As the central body responsible for the sport's governance, the FIG cooperated with its constituent gymnasts, coaches, and officials, and had to hope they in turn cooperated with the federation. Most did so. Some collaborated with other international actors to break those rules and avoid any disciplinary action. Others limited their cooperation to within their national programs, where officials worked together to evade international rules and attain an advantage.

5
FEMININE AND FEMINIST?

Women's artistic gymnastics was designed to be inherently feminine and uniquely appropriate for women. But over the decades following its 1952 debut, the style of the sport changed from balletic to acrobatic, from art to spectacle.[1] Alongside these changes, the gymnast's body also transformed. Through these stylistic and bodily changes, gymnasts demonstrated different interpretations of femininity—which remained the fundamental principle underscoring the sport. Gymnasts adopted different ways of masking their efforts and apologizing for their transgressions of gender. But these remained largely applicable to White women only. Racialized women faced an entirely different set of circumstances in entering the sport.

This chapter explores the different forms of femininity expressed in gymnastics as the sport changed over the twentieth century, showing how collaboration across borders can be subtle. It argues that officials, technologies, gymnasts, and coaches from around the world worked together to inscribe social ideals of race and gender on gymnastics. Together, and successively, these actors shaped gymnastics to align with contemporary ideals of womanhood. It is therefore not only an analysis of physical movement, but equally a study of what the gymnasts themselves were trying to communicate about the space for women within the sport. As such, it also analyzes gender performativity. The stylistic developments of the sport are inherently linked with the fluctuations in social constructions of femininity.

That is, iterations of femininity are situational, evolving based on time, style of gymnastics, bodily ideals, and race. In traversing this history, ultimately, a new question arises: can a sport that was designed and constrained as feminine offer some kind of feminist experience for the gymnasts involved?

The chapter begins with a study of the basis on which women's gymnastics was distinguished from the men's, then chronologically examines the evolution of the sport over the twentieth and early twenty-first centuries, including the FIG's role in shaping various developments. The FIG created rules governing style that gymnasts and coaches had to uphold, although gymnasts and coaches consistently innovated, presenting styles the FIG had never anticipated. The international cooperation that is revealed in this chapter, unlike others, is not always cooperation in unison. It is a push and pull between those practicing gymnastics and those governing it over successive generations. Each of the styles appears to build on those that went before it, hence implying a kind of evolution. But that is by no means to say that the transformations to the sport can always be considered progress. The question of race was rarely considered in the sport, until the first Black gymnasts in the 1980s challenged the Euro-centrism of gymnastics' values. Finally, the chapter considers the experience of bodily autonomy and control that the evolution of the sport has created and situates this within a feminist understanding of movement.

Distinguishing Masculine and Feminine Gymnastics

Women's gymnastics was designed to be inherently different to the men's sport so that it posed no threat to masculinity. This difference prevented any direct comparison between the performances of male and female athletes. Sports scholar Mary Louise Adams explains that this was by no means unique to gymnastics, but a principle that sports leaders widely employed. "The link between masculinity and sport could be stronger if women were not encouraged to engage in sport on the same terms as men."[2] For women in gymnastics, the apparatuses were modified versions of the men's apparatuses (e.g., the vaulting horse turned sideway), or completely new in competition (e.g., the balance beam). The requirements of the ideal performance were totally different too. Where the men's discipline emphasized masculinity and strength, the women's emphasized femininity and fluidity. Women performed the floor exercise to music, which drew attention to timing, rhythm, dance, and grace, in contrast with the men's slower-paced and silent show of strength on the floor.

The FIG took great pains to ensure that the definition of artistry in the women's Code of Points was rooted in conceptions of appropriate bodily movement for women, described as "harmonious flexibility and feminine grace."[3] Creating these differences in expectations between genders ensured both that women gymnasts posed no threat to masculinity in the sport and that gender ideals remained firmly separated. On this basis, the FIG was able to get women's artistic gymnastics accepted into the Olympic program, promoting the discipline as "appropriate" for women and "in harmony with their constitutions."[4]

Women competed in bare legs. Even as early as the 1928 games, gymnasts wore leotards with loose shorts over the top for some exercises, while for others they wore looser fitting tunics. In both cases, their outfits were cropped above the knee to allow the gymnasts to perform the leg balances and jumps during their routines. By 1948, the shorts were even shorter and tighter. In 1952, the shorts were gone, but the leotard remained, conservatively cut and somewhat loose. By 1960, the standard uniform was settled, with women wearing tight, long-sleeved leotards cut at the hip to lengthen and exhibit the legs, while the wide necklines emphasized the décolletage and elongated the neck. Elastic cinched in the waist, showcasing the hourglass figures women were expected to have. The uniform was required by the FIG, but it also evolved as new elastic materials became available and as gymnasts needed to demonstrate larger movements. The tightness and cut of the women's leotard from 1960 onward were designed to reveal women's body shapes and reaffirm the idea that women's participation in gymnastics posed no challenge to the sport as a temple of masculinity. Men, meanwhile, have worn a sleeveless leotard with shorts or trousers over the top with little change over the last half century.

While the men's leotard remains constructed of a plain fabric (although occasionally men wear velour leotards), women's leotards have become spectacles in themselves. They are now often adorned with metallic, reflective fabrics, usually in bright colors (representing fun and cuteness) or white (representing purity and innocence), and they are often covered in diamantés. These glittering outfits are designed to catch the eye and direct it to the women's bodies. Whereas women in other sports like track and field or swimming also wear high-cut briefs or cropped tops to allow freedom of movement and minimal drag, the materials used in those sports are plain (although there are elements of the sexualization and commodification of women's bodies in such attire, too). Women's gymnastics also has aerodynamic justifications for the tight-fitting attire, but there is no mechanical

FIGURE 5.1. By 1936, women were competing in shorts and leotards. Vlasta Děkanová of Czechoslovakia competes on the uneven bars, which had been modified for women's competition.

FIGURE 5.2. By 1960, the standard uniform was set, being a long-sleeved leotard cinched in at the waist, often with a wide neckline and low cut hipline. Eva Bosáková-Hlaváčková of Czechoslovakia performs on the bars.

reason for gymnasts to be so decoratively adorned. Indeed, men's leotards abstain from these glitzy decorative elements, maintaining a plain and serious look that appropriately directs focus to their athletic feats instead of their visual appeal. The dazzling leotards that women gymnasts wear, then, speak to the construction of femininity in gymnastics and its centrality to the sport. They affirm the historical understanding that women should be visually appealing to the spectator. Hence, the leotard shows how women engage in the sport in very mediated, acceptable, and separate gender terms.

These rules about apparatuses and leotards casts the very first institutional instructions as to how femininity would be performed in gymnastics, differentiated from masculinity.[5] Scholars have shown that gender is performed, displayed, and "done" (through choice of hairstyles, clothing, behaviors, language, demeanor, tone, and so forth).[6] Women's artistic gymnastics embodied all of this, and additionally, inscribed gender through movement styles. But as the sport developed, so too did its constructions of femininity.

Balletic Beauty Queens

Women gymnasts had competed on varied apparatuses in the first half of the twentieth century. When women's artistic gymnastics became a permanent part of the Olympic program in 1952, the apparatuses were set as vault, uneven bars, balance beam, and floor exercise. But at those games and in 1956, gymnasts also contested an additional event: the portable apparatuses. The portable apparatuses will be familiar to viewers of what is now rhythmic gymnastics. A group event, teams had to perform to music on the floor using ball, ribbon, rope, clubs, or hoop. The official Olympic report from the Melbourne games described it as "a spectacle of controlled rhythm and concerted movement that has never been seen in Australia before."[7] The discourse surrounding appropriate gymnastics performance for women echoed that promoting dance as a feminine activity. Women's physical activity should promote grace, health, beauty, rhythm, and discipline.[8] These passive ideals posed no threat to women's perceived fragility and drew on decades of social expectations (in the Western world) that women look appealing and act compliantly.

These ideas were reflected in the gymnastics of the first few Olympics. The report from the 1956 games declared "The increasing artistic trend in all gymnastics was in evidence in the Games at Melbourne. This was most marked in the women's work, by the including of more ballet-like

movements, along with agility, control and speed."[9] Champions for the
following decade were often former ballerinas with training in classical
dance. But ballet shares the same existential question as artistic gymnastics:
is expression and artistry the core of the sport, or is technical virtuosity
more important? This question has underscored the differences between
the men's and women's disciplines of gymnastics.

In ballet, women were assumed to be naturally more expressive than
men. The men of King Louis XIV's ballet used the dance to exhibit masculine
power.[10] The concept of expressiveness opened the practice to female dancers, in the same way that the concept of artistry created a space for women
in gymnastics.[11] Because women were stereotyped as more emotional than
men, they were supposedly more expressive too. By the mid-twentieth century, the developing ideals of women's artistic gymnastics mirrored trends
in ballet. Under Russian George Balanchine's influence, ballet demonstrated
modernity through the optical illusion of grace and weightlessness. Performances were formal, minimalist, and prioritized technique to accentuate
human movement above all. This also meant that a ballerina would reduce
her expression of emotion in order to appear controlled and precise. These
observations are all equally applicable to mid-twentieth-century women's
artistic gymnastics and share their origins in the Ballets Russes—the Paris-
based Russian ballet company of the early twentieth century.[12]

Women gymnasts performed a kind of outward passivity, appearing to
float through the air with ease, their limbs appearing weightless, their movement light, soft, effortless. But this was obviously an act—great physical
effort is needed to perform even the simplest skills. Take, for example, the
split leap. The gymnast hops from one foot to the other while moving forward.
It is the same as a hurdle in track and field. But a hurdle is not graceful. The
gymnast must appear to pause in midair. The greater her height at the apex
of her leap, the greater the illusion of ease. She must fully extend her body,
reaching her torso upright, gliding her arms beside her, and stretching her
legs to a 180-degree split. Keeping all of these parts in place requires effort,
but in adhering to this style, the gymnast appears to move passively and effortlessly, like a doll swept up by a light wind. But this femininity only appears
to be passive. Internally, gymnasts were "voluptuously active."[13] When they
swung down from the high bar to beat their hips against the low bar, they
were even violently active. In Melbourne, at least nine sets of the women's
uneven bars were broken in practice before the games, and one during the
competition, so intense were the forces going through them.[14]

The FIG and the gymnasts themselves cooperated with social expectations. Gymnasts appeared passive and weak to appeal to social norms of femininity, underpinned in the FIG's Code of Points. While the adherence to traditional gender roles might have limited the sport's feminism, it was in fact crucial to allowing women to practice gymnastics at all. Performing gymnastics gave women new power. They could experiment with energy, control, and strength rippling through their bodies, even if it had to be masked. However, this power could only be concealed for so long before it became apparent in the new skills women gymnasts performed.

Former ballerina Larisa Latynina of the Soviet Union was the reigning champion throughout the 1950s and 1960s, winning eighteen Olympic medals—a record she held until US swimmer Michael Phelps broke it in 2012. Commentators likened her body to a sylph, the spirit of the air.[15] Latynina was nineteen when she made her international debut two years before the 1956 games, and thirty-two when she ended her illustrious career. For all of her international competitions and victories, she was a fully

FIGURE 5.3. Nelli Kim beats her hips against the low bar as she descends from a swing on the high bar at the 1980 games. The bars bend under the pressure. © 1980 IOC—All rights reserved.

grown adult. This was the norm. In many ways, she was the ideal of the "new Soviet woman." Historian Pat Simpson explains that "everything heroic, triumphant, and hopeful in the USSR was to be perceived as invested in the Soviet athletic girl."[16] Latynina demonstrated will, training, national purity, and good hygiene, which were all associated with Soviet woman as mother. At the 1958 world championships she won every gold medal but one (the silver for floor exercise) when she was four months pregnant. Neither this nor a second child stopped her Olympic career. She went on to compete at two more Olympic Games. Latynina embodied the feminine ideals of the time and performed them through her gymnastics. But far from limiting what was appropriate for women athletes, she legitimized the sport as appropriate for women. Her balletic grace, her motherhood, and her victories all served to quash any concern about the dangers of physical activity and competition for women. Working within the confines of her time, she was able to expand the boundaries for women gymnasts performing ease and femininity while internally exploring her own limits.

Latynina's dominance was not usurped until Czechoslovakian Věra Čáslavská won the Olympic all-around in 1964 and again at the 1968 games. Čáslavská modeled a similar kind of balletic gymnastics—although she

FIGURE 5.4. A former ballerina, Larisa Latynina dominated the sport in the 1950s and 1960s, performing in a typically classical style. After her competing career, she went on to coach the national team. She is pictured here performing her floor routine at the 1964 games. © 1964 IOC—All rights reserved.

no longer had to compete with the portable apparatuses. Čáslavská also represented a superficial shift in the performance of female gymnasts. At the 1968 games in Mexico City, she presented a floor routine to the tune of "Jarabe Tapatío," also known as the Mexican hat dance—a nod to the hosts and the home audience. This kind of performance was designed to appeal to spectators as much as its technical aspects were designed to appeal to the judges. Čáslavská thus added to gymnastics the idea of spectacle: performance, not just technical mastery, or art, but actively as entertainment. She showed how the most popular of gymnasts cooperated with both audiences and judges. This notion was only enhanced by her purposefully curated look. She often gathered her long blonde hair into a bouffant for her competitions—a popular style of the day. Apparently, a former coach described her as "someone you'd take to high school prom," while various media touted her beauty.[17] When she died in 2016, obituaries around the world reminded readers how popular she was for her appearance. She performed not only gymnastics, but equally, beauty, and therefore, the femininity expected of women at the time.

At twenty-six years old during the 1968 games, as an adult woman Čáslavská was also fully engaged in society and astute to political issues. During the Prague Spring of that year, she signed the "Two Thousand Words" petition calling for greater openness in the Czechoslovakian government. When the Soviet Union's Red Army invaded the country two months later (and only two months before the Olympics), Čáslavská went into hiding to avoid being imprisoned. She fled to a small town in the Jeseniky Mountains, where she continued her Olympic preparations in the forest, using a fallen tree as a balance beam and branches as bars.[18] It worked. She won the gold for every apparatus except beam, where she won silver. Many suggested score fixing was at play when she had to share the gold medal for the floor exercise with Soviet Larisa Petrik, whose preliminary scores were mysteriously upgraded.[19]

The medal ceremonies for balance beam and then floor both played the Soviet national anthem as the flag ascended. Standing on the second-place podium, then again when she shared the top podium for gold, Čáslavská bowed her head and turned her face away from the flag, in silent protest of the Soviet occupation of her country. "It is understandable that every Czechoslovak citizen is deeply disturbed. I am a Czechoslovak citizen," she told media a few months later. "We all tried harder to win in Mexico because it would turn the eyes of the world on our unfortunate country."[20] Čáslavská

FIGURE 5.5. Czechoslovakian gymnast Věra Čáslavská was renowned for being a beauty queen, but she was also two-time Olympic champion in the all-around and a medalist across several apparatuses in the 1960s. Here she competes on the beam at the 1964 games. © 1964 IOC—All rights reserved.

is an example of how gymnasts' visibility can work against regimes as well as for them. But her protest had severe personal consequences. Her government barred her from international travel, and she was no longer allowed to compete, coach, or judge in gymnastics. Čáslavská's impact then was not only in the spectacular nature of her gymnastics but in her political engagement and civic-mindedness. She thought about politics and she used her platform to protest and draw the world's attention to her people's cause. She represented not only the mature bodies of 1960s' gymnastics but also the mature minds behind them.

Acrobatic Adolescents

As Čáslavská was winning her final Olympic medals in Mexico, women's gymnastics was gradually shifting toward a more dynamic style practiced by much younger athletes. The United States had always used younger gymnasts in women's artistic gymnastics both because of the amateur rule as well as the way sports were embedded in the education system—it was simply harder for adult women to engage in extracurricular activities like gymnastics when they were under social pressures to contribute to domestic life. But in the 1960s, the average age of women gymnasts started dropping in Europe too. At the 1968 games, Čáslavská shared her floor gold medal with Russian gymnast Larisa Petrik. Nineteen at the time, Petrik had debuted at the world championships just after turning seventeen. Before that, she had won the Soviet national championships in 1964 at the age of fifteen. She was not alone in her youthful success. Her compatriot, Natalia Kuchinskaya, won a gold medal at the 1966 world championships at age sixteen.[21] Ludmilla Tourischeva also joined the Soviet team at the 1968 games at age sixteen. If physiologically immature teenagers could demonstrate the feminine ideal, then it points to underlying changes in what that ideal was. From the mid-1960s onward it became youth and dynamicity.

This downward trend in age concerned the FIG. Prepubescent girls could not perform the femininity that the FIG envisioned. In 1971 it issued a caution: "Medical reports have given a warning and pointed out the dangers of abusive training without necessary control . . . how much surer it is to obtain high-class gymnastic champions whose fullness is manifested in their psychic and physiological 'flowering'."[22] On the one hand, the FIG foresaw the abusive territory that elite sports like women's artistic gymnastics could stray into when working with children: overtraining, undereating, and pressures to stay thin or prepubescent. The FIG wanted to avoid the very things that the sport would become known for. But on the other hand, medical discourse has long been used to limit women's involvement in sports.[23] Nonetheless, few heeded the FIG's advice. At the same time, a number of male coaches were moving from men's gymnastics to women's artistic gymnastics. Rules restricting men from accessing training halls and competition floors in women's artistic gymnastics were dismantled. Coaching roles that had gone exclusively to women were now open to men.

The entry of male coaches into women's artistic gymnastics had a remarkable impact on the sport. Men brought with them a wealth of assumptions about the bodies in the sport and the gymnastics they should be performing. They expected that because of their experience in men's gymnastics, they could excel as coaches in what they assumed was an easier discipline, women's gymnastics. Despite the deliberate measures taken to make women's gymnastics distinct from men's, these coaches assumed that women should aspire to the acrobatic, strength-based style of gymnastics that characterized the men's sport. They further assumed that this was only possible if women retained a more androgynous body type, devoid of the breasts and hips that typically indicate femininity. While male gymnasts were rarely competitive before they had reached peak strength at full maturity in their early twenties, women reached their peak strength when they went through puberty. Puberty could even reduce women's strength-to-weight ratio as their bodies began to hold more fat, so male coaches preferred working with prepubescent athletes. Sports scholar Natalie Barker-Ruchti notes that undeveloped girls resemble the boys that male coaches were accustomed to working with.[24] Ironically, these coaches failed to appreciate that women's gymnastics was designed to showcase femininity through movement. Why would a man be better placed to teach that than a woman who has lived it all of her life? Male coaches thus started teaching young female gymnasts the acrobatics that had previously been limited to the men.[25] But muscularity and risk were sanctioned masculine traits. For women, this was not the feminine ideal that the FIG had envisioned.

A US gymnast during the 1950s and 1960s who turned coach in the 1970s, Muriel Grossfeld recalls that international scoring swung like a pendulum: "One time the more artistic gymnast won, but maybe the next time the more athletic gymnast won."[26] In her view, Čáslavská succeeded because she had both. Even when she was acrobatic, Čáslavská remained a mature adult. So despite the FIG's opposition to acrobatization, it was still rewarded by judges. And when the best won using the acrobatic style, it became socially expected within the international gymnastic community. Gymnasts and coaches then began to adapt their own routines to achieve the same rewards. They moved away from simple poses and backbends, replacing them with tumbling on floor and beam. On bars, where gymnasts had once stood and held positions, there was a shift toward swing-based routines.

Soviet gymnast Ludmilla Tourischeva represents the turning point between the old and new styles of gymnastics. She joined the national team as a teenager but achieved her most stunning results at her second Olympic Games in 1972, when she was twenty years old. At Munich, Tourischeva won the prestigious all-around competition, in addition to a silver on floor and a bronze medal on vault. Her body was mature, but the growing link between femininity and youth was demonstrated in the pigtails and ribbons that held up her hair. In her comportment, she was reminiscent of the civic-minded Čáslavská. Tourischeva was seen in the Soviet Union as self-controlled and composed, reliable and trustworthy, which contributed to her status as a sporting hero.[27] After serving as captain of the team, she was elected to the Central Committee of the All-Union Lenin Young Communist

FIGURE 5.6. Ludmilla
Tourischeva prepares for
her beam routine at the
1976 Olympics. She was
the last of the "older"
classical gymnasts, with
a long career and civically
engaged. © 1976 IOC—All
rights reserved.

League—Komsomol. Like Čáslavská, Tourischeva used the platform of her gymnastic success to promote a political agenda. However, it is unclear to what extent that was her own decision. As a popular role model, she would have been a desirable figure for party propaganda. Further, cooperation with sports leaders was an important tactic for Eastern-bloc athletes to advance their interests: medals, successful careers, and material interests.[28]

Tourischeva's gymnastics style was also a hybrid of old and new. Like her peers, she was trained in ballet and performed the graceful, flowing movements of her predecessors. But she also performed the new acrobatic style that had been necessary to achieve national victories within the Soviet Union, characterized by greater complexity and height. At the 1969 European championships, Tourischeva lost points for the acrobatic nature of her performances.[29] The judges advised her coach to change her routines to the more classical style of women's artistic gymnastics. But her coach refused, seeing acrobatic gymnastics as the future of the sport. His assessment was correct. At the world championships a year later, Tourischeva was awarded first place.[30] This about-face might be explained by considering the influence that Eastern-bloc judges had internationally, and the growing influence of their collaborative judging. It also suggests that acrobatics were more palatable when they were performed by (even slightly) older bodies. Gymnasts like Tourischeva, performing the new acrobatic style yet not departing too far from expectations of mature womanly bodies, played an important role in popularizing acrobatics. On the other hand, a change in how judges perceived acrobatics was already underway. In 1970, the FIG released a new Code of Points requiring gymnasts to show "difficulty and connections" and even specifically required acrobatics on the floor.[31] Audiences also pressured judges to reward more acrobatic routines.[32] The FIG still demanded femininity, but the sport had also reached a point where difficulty was a major consideration.

Tourischeva's male coach, Vladislav Rastorotsky, drew on the Russian circus tradition to inform his work, and became renowned for inventing new, dynamic, acrobatic gymnastics elements.[33] Indeed, soon the Russian Gymnastics Federation invited circus experts to work with their coaches and gymnasts on acrobatics.[34] The circus was a symbol of patriotism in the Soviet Union, celebrated for its unique acrobatics and contortion.[35] It was as highly regarded and culturally important as Russian ballet. Hence, as a medium of performance and spectacle, gymnastics shared similarities with these two national treasures. If the Soviet Union was going to use sports to communicate the Soviet way of life, it makes sense that it would appropriate aspects of these two institutions to promote Soviet cultural values in gymnastics. As the Soviets dominated the sport, other nations tried to emulate them to win.

But of course, the acrobatic turn is far from entirely attributable to the Soviet Union. In some ways, it was inevitable. Sports historians Kevin Wamsley and Gordon Macdonald argue that the changes to women's gymnastics were "the direct result of a general trend to demonstrate measurable progress," that underpinned twentieth-century sports.[36] Women's artistic gymnastics had already reached the boundaries of the classical style by the 1960s. Yet, the fundamental tenets of Olympic sports—faster, higher, stronger—held, and demanded, limitless potential. Women's gymnastics found this in the creation of increasingly difficult acrobatic elements in which "bodies leave the earth, master gravity and centrifugal force, and seemingly defy natural laws," according to historian Ann Chisholm.[37] Mastery over one's body in time and space is essential to the sport. Navigating the body through increasingly complex spaces is required to be the best. With its much longer history (and different gender ideals), men's gymnastics was acrobatic because the ground-based limits of the sport had been reached decades ago. In a globalized sport, women approached those limits faster, with the added advantage of observing the men's sport to see what more might be possible. Forward rolls were replaced with front somersaults in the air, and tumbling on the floor was transferred to the beam.

Olga Korbut of the Soviet republic Belarus (then known as Byelorussia) brought the world's attention to the new style of acrobatic gymnastics when she presented routines at the 1972 Olympic Games that were at the forefront of the sport's new direction. She was not the first to perform youthful, acrobatic gymnastics, but she was responsible for raising popular awareness of it. Like Tourischeva, Korbut's coach, Renald Knysh, advocated for the acrobatic turn, considering gymnastics to be "acrobatics on the apparatus."[38] At the 1972 games, Korbut debuted a backward-tucked somersault on the four-inch-wide balance beam, as well as a now eponymous back handspring that finished with her swinging her legs down to straddle the beam. These skills stunned audiences. But she was equally breathtaking on the uneven bars, where she not only displayed the photogenic hyper-arched positions she used on the beam and floor, but also some of her most daring acrobatics. She stood atop the high bar, jumped backward, her arched body rotating so that her hands could clasp the bar where her feet stood only moments earlier. This was the first high-bar release move for women.

Unlike Tourischeva, Korbut also represented the sport's trend toward youth. It was awe-inspiring to see such risk and spectacle being performed so effortlessly by someone who appeared to be a child. She was seventeen at the Munich Games, but she appeared younger. Her body was prepubescent and she too wore her hair in pigtails. She appeared to act like a child too, with wild emotions on display throughout the competition. Korbut smiled during her performances, which Knysh designed to mimic child's play. She laughed with her peers in front of the cameras. She flirted with audiences. And when she fell from the uneven bars, she cried. Live broadcasting collided with soap-opera storytelling to grip audiences. Closeups captured her tears, and slow-motion replays theatricalized and eroticized her body.[39] The media cast Korbut as the heroic rebel fighting against the establishment—represented by the likes of Tourischeva.

Audiences had never seen such emotional range from a Soviet athlete before, who had a reputation for being extremely stoic. The injection of personality into her performances was a strategy intentionally developed by Korbut and Knysh. She was told to smile to mask the difficulty, risk, and fear of her performances.[40] Doing so upheld the tenets of women's sports: effort must be hidden, and women must appear to move with ease. But she also removed the barrier between the performer and the audience, actively engaging with them and inviting them to share in her emotions. Audiences related to her and rooted for her. Perhaps they also felt some kind of protection for her, in the childishness and vulnerability she displayed. She could not have been more different from the composed, poised, and controlled women who had previously represented the sport. While those gymnasts had been publicly adored, the celebrity status that Korbut reached was unprecedented.

Awestruck audiences could not anticipate the FIG's reaction to this new brand of gymnastics. The women's technical committee was especially concerned about several of the new skills Korbut presented in Munich: the

FIGURE 5.7. Olga Korbut popularized an acrobatic style of gymnastics while performing to the crowd, coached to smile. Here she performs her namesake element on the beam at the 1972 games. © 1972 IOC / United Archives—All rights reserved.

Korbut loop on the bars, the Korbut flip to straddle the beam, and the backward somersault on the beam. They had additional concerns about her use of hyper-arched positions—on the beam she lay on her chest, body stretched over her, legs extended along the beam in front of her, while on the floor she performed a backward somersault to her chest.

The group asked the medical commission to provide some justification for eliminating "movements with too pronounced or over exaggerated back bends."[41] Meanwhile, it determined that pauses in routines would incur penalties. This precluded the Korbut loop on bars, as it required the gymnast to cease swinging while she stood on top of the bars.[42] Her dismount from the bars also required that she stand on the bar before somersaulting off it. The women's technical committee decided that a dismount without grip was not in keeping with regulations and would be subject to deductions.[43]

The women's technical committee also disliked Korbut's innovations on the beam because the risky nature of her tumbling encouraged gymnasts to pause. It reported on the Munich Games that the beam exercises "remained static in spite of tremendous efforts and they risk becoming even more so if the floor exercises continue to be exploited on this apparatus." Moreover, the women's technical committee was concerned that such elements raised "the risk of causing serious accidents."[44] Six months later it explained that at Munich there had been "too many acrobatics" on the beam, and that "the technicians should understand that acrobatics should be reserved for the floor exercise." The problem was not simply in the tumbling on the beam, but also the "jerky" routines with "frequent pauses" it caused. The women's technical committee preferred routines based on "balance positions, turns, [and] rhythmic steps"—the classical style of women's artistic gymnastics.[45]

The committee clarified that the backward somersault was especially dangerous and undesirable, and attempted to outlaw it because it was not an element "peculiar to the beam."[46] In response to this proposal, Korbut threatened to retire from international competition. "If the decision is put into effect then I simply do not see any place for myself in gymnastics," she told the Associated Press.[47] Although Eastern-bloc athletes' interactions with the press were strictly controlled, Korbut was notoriously unpredictable, and authorities struggled to restrain her, which goes some way to explaining why she would make such a bold, public statement.[48] In any case, the women's technical committee continued to seek proposals on how to eliminate the somersault from the beam.[49] Adriena Gotta of Italy and Ellen Berger suggested that the backward somersault "should not be considered as a specific beam exercise," recommending that the question be put to the medical commission to produce further justification for its prohibition. But the skill was not banned. Indeed, acrobatic elements became ubiquitous on the beam, with gymnasts performing walkovers and cartwheels with no hands over the following years. The FIG was already too late.

In fact, the FIG had promoted acrobatization in many ways. As it continued trying to rationalize a sport that was supposed to be artistic, it claimed that only acrobatic skills had a rigid technique that could be objectively judged. The angles, lines, heights, and distances of acrobatics could be impartially evaluated in a way that broader, subjective concepts like artistry could not. This pursuit of objectivity was particularly important, as the IOC was pressuring international federations to be fair and transparent in their contests at this time. The FIG specified that a minimum of two of the six elements in every routine should be of "superior difficulty," the highest level of difficulty. Although these did not need to be acrobatic skills, in 1973 it proposed requiring three to six specifically acrobatic difficulties in each routine.[50] The FIG reserved 1.5 points to be awarded for the gymnast's creative choreography, diversity, and originality.[51] But it did not anticipate that gymnasts would seek those points from acrobatics rather than from the leaps and turns that had previously characterized the sport. This freedom also allowed for the emergence of national styles of gymnastics. For example, where the Soviet Union presented ballet-based choreography, the entire Romanian team demonstrated a contemporary style that caricatured child's play.

Moreover, the FIG endorsed modifications to the equipment that only facilitated acrobatization. In 1971, the women's technical committee allowed the uneven bars to be set at the gymnast's preferred width, between 54 and 78 centimeters.[52] Tension cables also secured the apparatus to the ground, so it could withstand greater torque as gymnastics swung farther from the bar. The bars themselves were changed from oval-shaped wood used in the men's parallel bars, to round fiberglass coated in wood.[53] This allowed gymnasts to grip them better for swinging. These modifications made it possible for Korbut to perform her famous Korbut loop. The FIG also introduced springs to the floor in 1971, which not only softened the impact of gymnasts' landings, but also aided them in getting higher off the floor. This would be necessary when women completed the first double somersaults five years later at the 1976 Olympic Games. The once sharp, wooden beam was upholstered with leather, which provided better grip and minimized injury if the gymnast slipped.[54] After Korbut's innovations in 1972, the FIG made padding regulation for balance beams to allow for softer landings after aerial skills.[55] The FIG reaffirmed this direction, declaring that balance beams must be both padded and covered in artificial leather from 1975 onward.[56] On vault, the springboard was covered in carpet after 1971, and only three years later its height was raised to 15 centimeters. A corresponding elevation of the vaulting horse to 120 centimeters allowed gymnasts to gain greater propulsion and height in the air. Hence, two years after these adjustments, Nelli Kim became the first women to complete the first full twisting Tsukahara (a double somersaulting) vault, previously only performed by men.

Thus, there appears a contradiction in the FIG's stance on acrobatic gymnastics. It reacted strongly and swiftly to Korbut's gymnastics after the 1972 games, attempting to prevent acrobatics on any apparatus but the floor. On the one hand, it opposed what gymnasts like Korbut were doing. But at the same time, it enacted a number of rules to specifically demand greater difficulty and more acrobatics. Its modifications to apparatuses made the equipment safer but also enabled greater risk to be performed on them. So, on the other hand, it cooperated with gymnasts to provide the means for them to perform the acrobatic style. The FIG's conflicting stance can be explained by considering these issues in terms of femininity.

In 1964, the women's technical committee had defined artistry as "harmonious flexibility and feminine grace." As acrobatics became more prevalent, the FIG complained that gymnasts lacked musicality, rhythm, and artistic grace—the ideals that it considered feminine and thus central to the sport when performed by women. By 1971, criticisms from the women's technical committee echoed refrains about the sport today.[57] "For every good and intelligent composition there were so many dreary background dronings . . . so many catch-tunes tagged together, waltzes which allow the gymnast to arrive at the end more or less in time with the music, not to mention all the massacred classical music."[58] This raised an existential problem for the FIG. What exactly, was "feminine"? Was it about dance and music? Did it exclude acrobatics? Did artistry mean something different depending on whether women or men were performing?

In these complaints, along with its efforts to prevent acrobatics, it is evident that the FIG was mourning the loss of its previous constructions of "feminine grace." Barker-Ruchti suggests that "feminine qualities require gymnasts to perform gracefully and effortlessly; the acrobatics on the other hand, demand muscle power, fitness and courage, which are perceived masculine characteristics."[59] The question of (masculine) risk versus (feminine) artistry was finally brought before the FIG General Assembly in 1975. President Arthur Gander told delegates: "We should perhaps now ask ourselves if the moment has not now arrived when we should mitigate the trend towards 'risk' and 'difficulty' which are rapidly becoming more important than deportment and execution. We should take care that artistic gymnastics do not degenerate into pure acrobatics with risk to life and limb."[60]

The FIG did not want gymnasts to injure themselves, but neither did it approve of the shift in focus that acrobatics required: from aesthetic execution to mere attainment of the skills. When Gander mentioned gymnasts' deportment, he identified the FIG's concern. The gymnasts should adhere to the gendered expectations of bodily movement that the FIG had set out.[61] Gender performance was fundamental to the FIG's interpretations of artistry. Women's artistic gymnastics had been created to fulfil the need for women's participation in sports without comprising their femininity. Its existence was premised on the idea that women could compete without "masculine" qualities (strength, power, risk) compromising their feminine qualities (beauty, grace, and ease of movement) or endangering their reproductive capabilities.[62] Acrobatization thus threatened the unique position that the FIG had carved within the international sporting landscape for gymnastics. Rather than acrobatization itself, it was the associated masculine qualities, so far removed from the original purpose of women's artistic gymnastics and its interpretation of artistry, that drew resistance from the FIG.

The muscled, young bodies that characterized acrobatic gymnastics further problematized acrobatics. They were far removed from the mature, healthy women's bodies that had demonstrated femininity in gymnastics until the 1960s. They undermined gymnastics' claim of being a feminine-appropriate sport. The FIG moved to put a stop to it. "Let us hope that we shall see less of these children . . . incapable of mature and harmonious work," the women's technical committee declared when it implemented its first minimum age rule (fourteen years old) in 1971.[63] But enforcing a minimum age rule proved difficult (see chapter 4). National federations assumed responsibility for ensuring that gymnasts were fourteen before competing internationally.[64] Effectively, the officials responsible for enforcing a minimum age rules were the same ones who could falsify ages. In 1976, the FIG complained of gymnasts as young as twelve and thirteen competing internationally, and determined to reexamine minimum age requirements after the Olympic Games.[65] But the most famous child-gymnast appeared at the 1976 games, securing the marriage between gymnastics and youth in the public imagination.

Performing at the age of fourteen at the Montreal Olympic Games, Nadia Comăneci's gymnastics were perfect. When she competed in 1976, there was no question that she was the best gymnast in the arena. Delivering her routines with assuredness, confidence, and composure, she made skills that were considered almost death-defying four years earlier look easy. Her concentration was such that she appeared to be in a world of her own, unflappable, stable, perfect. Achieving a perfect 10 on the bars and the beam an astounding seven times throughout the competition, Comăneci showed that acrobatic gymnastics could be executed flawlessly. A *Sports Illustrated* reporter explains the awesomeness of her performance: in only twenty-three seconds she exuded a "spectacular burst of energy" on the bars, while on the beam "her pace magnifies her balance. Her command and distance hush the crowd." But equally, the same observer noted that it was her 10s that brought her

FIGURE 5.8. Comăneci was only fourteen when she won the all-around at the 1976 games. © 1976 IOC / United Archives—All rights reserved.

attention more than her skill. Her talent was unquestionable, but her record-breaking performances attracted publicity for the sport.[66]

Comăneci introduced a precision of movement, demonstrated in photographs that show every muscle tensing in even the simplest of positions. When Korbut had performed acrobatics, she was still able to display soft, passive body movements, seen in the way she held her arms below her shoulders and slightly bent, like a ballerina. Comăneci held every limb as straight as possible, right down to her hyperextended fingers. This kind of stiff, precise movement sparked a postural shift among gymnasts. The soft, fluid bodily movements were replaced with rigid extension of every limb. Instead of a bodily movement, malleability or docility became a desirable personality trait.

Where Korbut had given the impression of a child playing in her performances four years earlier, Comăneci was actually a child. But she did not act like one. Although her choreography mimicked child's play, she was never able to appear carefree and childish. She assumed a serious, reclusive demeanor throughout the competitions and in press interviews. Her coach, Béla Károlyi, purportedly had to teach her to smile and wave to the audience and cameras that followed her after her performances. Some were concerned about her lack of expression. Reporters asked if she missed her childhood but followed up with questions about her favorite dolls. Since it was not apparent in her performances, Comăneci had to explain that she enjoyed gymnastics. The media invited audiences to assume a protective, parental role in relation to Comăneci by describing her as "frail-looking," "grim-faced," with "dark circles above her cheeks," a "solemn wisp of a girl," "a fragile-looking child."[67] This language echoed that describing the weakness and frailty of women in the nineteenth and early twentieth centuries. Sports scholar Margaret Carlisle Duncan argues that these characterizations trivialized Comăneci's successes.[68] Incongruously, however, it made acrobatic gymnastics for women more palatable to some people. Rather than the empowered, adult gymnasts who had gone before, gymnasts like Comăneci appealed to audiences uncomfortable with the power women were gaining elsewhere in society as a result of third-wave feminism, higher education, employment, and birth control. Her gymnastics demonstrated a type of reversion to the subordination of women through physical belittlement, childlike innocence and docility, and her dependence on her overbearing and physically large male coach as the indisputable authority.

It was not only display of fragility that offset the gender transgressions of acrobatics. Comăneci also deployed "cuteness" to apologize for her masculinity. Chisholm explains that this too invited viewers to assume a parental role, but it also had pedophilic connotations that appealed to a sense of domesticated femininity.[69] Korbut had used the same "cute" appeal four years earlier. She had won fame for doing so, even though she was not champion of the 1972 games: her compatriot Tourischeva was. But Tourischeva was cool, calm, and adult, and did not perform the cute style of gymnastics. As a twenty-three-year-old, Tourischeva placed third in the all-around at the 1976 games, but otherwise she drew little attention. Korbut, meanwhile, found that by 1976, she no longer had the currency of youth to effectively perform cuteness. The media cast her as a rival to Comăneci, the "aging, disappointed woman yielding reluctantly to the flower of youth."[70] Korbut was then twenty-one.

While young gymnasts attracted audiences and received high scores from the judges, the FIG continued to resist youthful, cute, acrobatic gymnastics.

FIGURE 5.10. Korbut watches a gymnast perform while she waits for her turn at the 1976 Olympics. The archival caption alleges: "Korbut tenses up as she watches the tally mount for Nadia Comăneci." © 1976 IOC / United Archives—All rights reserved.

It commissioned a sports physiologist to investigate the problem of children in elite gymnastics. But the specialist concluded that the decreasing age was no more marked in gymnastics than it was in any other Olympic sport. Most Olympic sports had seen a decrease in average age between the first modern Olympics in 1896 and the 1976 Games, largely due to a decline in participants over the age of thirty. He found that the trend was more visible in gymnastics because of the large number of medalists in the youngest demographic. But he also noted that a trend toward youth was inevitable in a sport designed for women, as their relative strength decreases after puberty. Thus, he said, "top performances at around fifteen are normal for women and are a result of the typical development of their physique."[71] However, if this logic held, then all women's sports would see a proliferation of teenage champions, yet only gymnastics has become notorious for youth. Nonetheless, instead of finding the medical rationale for the exclusion of youths from gymnastics, the women's technical committee was instead told that there was no physiological or medical reason to prohibit gymnasts as young as thirteen or fourteen.

Without gaining the medical rationale it was looking for, the FIG resolved nonetheless in 1980 to increase the minimum age to fifteen. A year later, the IOC intervened. Arpad Csanádi, the IOC sports director, insisted that the FIG reconsider its age limits, and do so under the guidance of the FIG's medical commission.[72] The IOC appeared unaware that the FIG had long been thinking about the age problem in the sport and had already appealed to medical science to support any changes. The minimum age remained at fifteen for the following decade.

The FIG was thus grappling with conflicting directions for the sport. With acrobatics and risk attracting spectators, gymnasts and coaches were eager to take gymnastics in that direction. But it could be dangerous for athletes, and young gymnasts and their acrobatics did not align with the FIG's conceptions of femininity. The relationship between decreasing age and acrobatization was central to the FIG's concerns. The acrobatics invoked masculine qualities like risk, and the bodies performing them tended to be leaner and younger. Both of these were far removed from the FIG's original conception of femininity that had justified the creation of the sport decades earlier.

But the FIG was so concerned with what it meant to appear feminine that there was no evident discussion of what it meant to be physically female. Sex verification was essential to Cold War Olympic sports, and between 1968 and 2000 the IOC demanded that every female athlete undergo a sex test.[73] Yet, this is not mentioned once in FIG documents or correspondence with the IOC. Instead, through its quadrennial rule book, the FIG determined gender by performance ideals. This explains its preoccupation with the questions of acrobatization, risk, and femininity.

Powerful Pixies

At the 1980 Olympic Games in Moscow, Comăneci competed again. She nearly won again, but Soviet gymnast Elena Davydova was just 0.075 points higher in the all-around. It was Davydova's first Olympic Games, after having narrowly missed out on selection to the Soviet Olympic team four years earlier. At eighteen, she was the same age as Comăneci. Her teammates were older. Natalia Shaposhnikova made her Olympic debut at nineteen, while it was Nelli Kim's second Olympic Games at twenty-two. Despite acrobatics and cuteness, the value of experience and age remained important to teams vying for gold. These women all placed in the top five in the all-around in Moscow, interrupted only by the presence of fifteen-year-old East German Maxi Gnauck in second equal. Outside the Soviet team, the rest of the Eastern bloc saw a sharp drop in the average age of their gymnasts, with many fifteen- and sixteen-year-olds from Czechoslovakia, Bulgaria, Hungary, and East Germany. Even on the Romanian team, Comăneci was the only Olympic alumna, with the rest of the team aged between fourteen and sixteen.

The gymnasts of the 1980s often had cropped hair. Comăneci, Davydova, and Mary Lou Retton all sported practical hairstyles that required no ponytails, ribbons, or other hair fasteners. They exhibited an austere femininity that demanded a focus on the forms of their bodies and the expression of their movement. For Comăneci, at least, this was a way of distancing herself from the child gymnast that the world met in 1976. The women did

FIGURE 5.11. Nadia Comăneci competed again at the 1980 Olympic Games, sporting a cropped hairstyle that was popular among female gymnasts in the 1980s.
© 1980 IOC—All rights reserved.

not want to be seen as children but rather taken seriously as adults. They wanted the world to pay attention to their gymnastics, not their cuteness.

On the vault, gymnasts used a new style created by Natalia Yurchenko. She debuted her eponymous skill at the 1982 world cup, where, instead of traversing the vaulting horse forward as gymnasts always had, she performed a back handspring over the horse. In doing so she created an entire new family of vaults.[74] She and her coach, Vladislav Rastorotsky, devised the vault as a solution to the problem of getting increasingly small gymnasts over a vaulting horse as tall as them.[75] Like the Fosbury flop in high jump, the backward style movement of the Yurchenko was a solution to the challenge of height. But equally, the FIG had pushed the gymnasts to innovate on vault when it created a rule limiting the number of identical vaults that a team could use.[76]

The Yurchenko vault was extremely dangerous, as the entry to the springboard and vaulting horse were both done blindly. In reward for this danger, it garnered a lot of points, according to US coach Beverly Mackes.[77] So much so, that by the Seoul Olympic Games in 1988, it was the most common vault.[78] But that year, fifteen-year-old US gymnast Julissa Gomez broke her neck attempting the vault.[79] US coaches reported feeling pressure that doing the Yurchenko was necessary to keep pace with the Soviets.[80] The FIG never commented on the Yurchenko vault specifically, but it did note that the world championships the year prior had been "murderous," with seventeen gymnasts requiring emergency hospital visits.[81] Thereafter, the FIG recommended using a safety collar around the springboard to avoid more injuries like Gomez's. But it did not make the equipment mandatory until 1997.[82] Around the same time, the FIG also began developing a new apparatus to replace the vaulting horse: a padded table with a larger surface area that both men and women would use.[83] The vaulting table is now in use, and as a result, the Yurchenko has been popularized for men, while women's vaults have become faster and higher. This is a rare example of a trend in women's gymnastics transferring to the men's discipline.

While Yurchenko was developing a way to get smaller gymnasts over the horse, Mary Lou Retton was developing a new US style of gymnastics. The ebullient sixteen-year-old introduced it at the 1984 Games. The energy and raw power that Retton brought to her gymnastics had never been seen before. It was so popular that it became the typical style of US gymnastics. "Retton's natural elfin exultation would absolutely explode if anyone else

FIGURE 5.12. Xijing Tang of China performs a Yurchenko using the padded vaulting table at the 2018 Youth Olympic Games. © 2018 IOC / Lukas Schulze—All rights reserved.

touched a spark to it," wrote *Sports Illustrated*. Months earlier, the magazine had described her energy as bubbling, like a volcano.[84] Like Korbut before her, she had the personality that Americans adored and made into stars. But her gymnastics were equally explosive. She scored perfect 10s on the vault and the floor—the two most leg-dominated, fast-moving events. Only a muscular, powerful body could excel in these events, and indeed, rather than "fragile" like her predecessors, Retton was "sturdy."[85] Her style on the floor was aided by a recent FIG rule change that allowed gymnasts to perform to music on a cassette tape rather than a live piano. This opened up the genres of music that gymnasts could perform too, and in turn, allowed for different types of expression through dance. Retton used a fast-paced music that matched her energy and got the crowd to clap along.

Eighteen months before the games, she had moved from her home in West Virginia to work with the recently defected Károlyis in Texas. Until then, Retton had been unknown in the international gymnastic community. In winning her Olympic gold, Retton broke the barrier to international success for US gymnasts. While a handful of US gymnasts had won apparatus medals at the world championships before this, clinching an Olympic all-around medal proved that past US successes were no fluke. In a radio address, President Reagan told the nation that Retton's hard work and spirit

FIGURE 5.13. The ebullient Mary Lou Retton won the United States' first Olympic gold medal in 1984, exhibiting a fast, dynamic, energetic style of gymnastics. © 1984 IOC / United Archives—All rights reserved.

were the keys to her success, utilizing her story to inspire Americans to rise to new challenges and underpin the neoliberalist agenda for his reelection campaign.[86]

When Retton won the Olympic gold for the all-around, she provided the international reputation necessary for US gymnastics to be taken seriously. While the artistic style defined and driven by Soviet gymnasts continued to dominate, Retton's success exemplified the powerful, albeit marginalized, style of gymnastics beginning to emerge internationally. Though competitors like Elena Shushunova (USSR) had also demonstrated this powerful style of gymnastics too, it was not typical of Eastern-bloc gymnastics, nor was it as noticeable in the presence of strong dance training that offset displays of strength and power. It was a style that came to define US gymnastics, perpetuated in the 1990s by the likes of Kim Zmeskal (another Károlyi student) and Vanessa Atler, and in the 2000s, Carly Patterson and Shawn Johnson. By 2014, Simone Biles's raw strength, dynamicity, and ability to perform extremely complex twists and turns at great heights on all apparatuses secured the US style of powerful gymnastics as the future of the sport. By 2020, Biles had become widely regarded as the greatest of all time.

When Retton made history for US gymnastics in 1984, nearly all of the
Eastern bloc was absent.[87] Those games were also the first at which the
People's Republic of China competed, since the IOC had not previously
recognized the country.[88] The Chinese gymnasts impressed spectators with
their artistry, leaps, and turns, and famously, their innovations on the bars.
On bars, they adopted the style emerging around the world, which was
shifting toward greater use of giant circles (swinging 360 degrees around
the high bar), and release moves that required the gymnast to let go of the
bar, perform a somersault or fly over top of the bar, then re-catch it. This
style of bar work became so predominant that the FIG widened the bars
further to allow for bigger swings.[89]

Like the Soviet Union had decades earlier, the People's Republic of China
drew on its cultural traditions to create its own style of gymnastics. In the
1970s, the government had sent acrobatic troupes to tour the United States,
showcasing through their performances the state agenda of a modern,
national culture.[90] Acrobatics was culturally important in China, but the
Chinese government also used the sport to project onto the world stage
the image of a modern China. The US media interpreted Chinese women's
acrobatics through an Orientalist lens, that racialized Asian peoples as
small, sneaky, and submissive.[91] Thus, in parallel with how Western media portrayed gymnasts as cute, it referred to Chinese female acrobats as
pigtailed, mystical, and juvenile. These portrayals not only facilitated a
hierarchy of difference between men and women, but also a hierarchy of
cultures in which feminized China was of little threat to the strong, free
West.[92]

The Orientalist lens allowed for East Asian women to perform acrobatic gymnastics without calling into question their femininity. Rather,
Western assumptions about the submissiveness of East Asian cultures
aligned with historical Western ideals about femininity and enhanced the
acceptance of Chinese gymnasts. To some extent, the entry of the Chinese
to Olympic gymnastics was eased by the long-time participation and high
rankings of Japanese gymnasts since the 1952 games. Asian bodies had
already been accepted in gymnastics. But the United States and many
other Western countries have a long history of considering China and
its people as effeminate and slight, a perception that has shaped China's
place in the sport.[93] Although it facilitated their acceptance in gymnastics
in the 1980s, three decades later, Western media leveraged these racialized ideas to suggest that Chinese gymnasts were underage and the state

dishonest and corrupt for such alleged cheating. But as scholar Michelle Murray Yang points out, the only evidence for it in 2008 was media assessments of gymnasts' physicality.[94]

Racialized Gymnasts

Gymnastics' early history reveals its European origins. As international sports codified and internationalized in the early twentieth century, it remained the employ of the elite, who were still predominantly White Europeans. As gymnastics was rationalized, it internalized this context. Performance studies scholar Shani Shakur-Bruno observes that the illustrations in the Code of Points portray a White body.[95] Although it is intended to be a neutral illustration without facial features, the gymnast's hair is straight and pulled back into a ponytail, which precludes many non-White hair types and styles. The illustrations outlay expectations of performance based on ideals of performance White womanhood. At the same time though, there has been room within understandings of White womanhood in gymnastics beyond its Western European origins. This is seen in the performances of a range of light-skinned women who could be considered to be on the margins of White femininity. For instance, 1984 Olympian Tracee Talavera is a Latina who, in her gymnastics, conformed to preexisting ideas about White femininity. She was small and young. She wore her hair in both the popular crop of the 1980s as well as the classic gymnast's ponytail secured with ribbons, and her gymnastics fit within normal performances of the time. Nelli Kim of the Soviet state of Tajik in Central Asia is part Sakhalin Korean and part Tartar. Her presence pointed to the history of Soviet imperialism in the region and the Soviet Union's push for a cohesive national identity.[96] Her gymnastics was therefore consistent with that of her teammates, and she had the support of Soviet officials. Although anti-Slavic sentiment could have been a problem for Soviet gymnasts displaying White femininity, through their judging and their winning, their style of gymnastics was quickly accepted and adopted within the sport. Kim was also able to draw on the history of Asian women's relatively consistent representation in the sport. The Japanese women, for instance, won the bronze medal at the 1964 games. But orientalist assumptions about Asian states at large being fragile and effeminate meant that the presence of Asian gymnasts did not really challenge existing understandings of femininity. It simply expanded Whiteness to include a broader range of light-skinned nationalities.

Moreover, such an expansion in conceptions of race in gymnastics was advanced with the support of the nations behind them. The Soviet Union had its judges and officials promoting its style of gymnastics. Chinese and Japanese gymnasts worked with judges, coaches, and teammates in a shared national and ethnic context that could contribute to developing a cohesive gymnastics culture, showcasing it on the world stage, and carving out a space for themselves within international gymnastics ideals.

But Black women were not afforded this opportunity. The African Gymnastics Union was only founded in 1990, and no African gymnast had ever competed in women's artistic gymnastics at the games. There is little evidence of Black women competing for diverse nations throughout much of the Cold War either. Black gymnasts thus operated within the confines of a White world, surrounded by White coaches and judges. Black women were hyper-visible in women's artistic gymnastics because they were such an anomaly. They were not only national representatives but racial representatives too.[97] But this hyper-visibility meant that they were often over-scrutinized.[98]

In Cold War sports more broadly, when the United States realized that it had to employ women athletes to meet the challenge presented by the large number of Soviet women athletes at the Olympic Games, it sent Black woman athletes as ambassadors. This attempted to quash Soviet claims of racial inequality in the United States and counter the Soviet Union's strong team of women athletes. Black women were already characterized as "aggressive, coarse and passionate, and physical—the same qualities assigned to manliness and sport."[99] The use of Black women athletes enabled the United States to project an image of equality and athleticism abroad while still protecting notions of femininity for White women at home. The success of Black athletes in track and field, however, undermined the reconciliation of their athleticism with femininity. "Even though these athletes helped dismantle certain racial prejudices, their triumphs simultaneously reinforced stereotypes of Black women as being less feminine than white women," explains historian Lindsay Parks Pieper.[100] Their athletic successes implied that they were strong, competitive, and aggressive women. They were seen to excel because of their masculinity. This did not align with the ideal of femininity in women's gymnastics as passive and fragile. Therefore, Black women gymnasts were already faced with a perception of them being less feminine than their White counterparts before they even began to perform.

Young, cute, acrobatic (and predominantly White) gymnasts became part of the curious "freakshow" spectacle of human performance—often pictured alongside taller athletes to suggest a giant-dwarf configuration, their bodies carrying injuries and disfigurements from gymnastics like the sideshow "freak." Being cast as less than human allowed the gymnasts to display exceptional, superhuman abilities.[101] White gymnasts compensated for their transgressions of gender by portraying femininity through cuteness.[102] This also offset the near-nakedness of their performances and any suggestions of gymnasts' sexuality.[103] If viewers were sexually aroused by cute White gymnasts, it was (perversely) through the innocence the gymnasts portrayed.[104] But for Black women, performing cuteness was not enough to apologize for their gender transgressions. Black femininity has long been sexualized and Black women long accused of inviting sexual engagement. As enslaved people, they were sexually exploited, and their suffering was masked by portrayals of Africans as "savage, immoral and hypersexual."[105] Thus, even if the Black female gymnast performed cuteness, audiences could not as easily see innocence in her performance.

The FIG wanted feminine performances, in the sense of womanly, demure, and graceful. Audiences wanted spectacular performances, with femininity mediated through cuteness. Neither wanted femininity to be sexy. Even White gymnasts like the Soviet Belarussian Svetlana Boguinskaya, 1989 world champion in the all-around, were booed for this reason.[106] Her mature body and soulful routines were considered too sexy for the sport. Black gymnasts thus had to navigate their own paths to find an acceptable form of femininity within the women's artistic gymnastics community. Arguably, they did this by initially embodying White ideals and styles of balletic gymnastics, beginning with biracial (Whiter) representation.

In addition, Black people have had less access to gymnastics clubs. The sport requires a large training space and specialized, expensive equipment. In the United States, clubs are mostly situated outside the densely populated urban areas where the majority of the Black community resides.[107] The number of hours required for training at the elite level equally means that families must pay for thirty to forty hours of tuition per week.[108] Hence, economic access is an issue that (for the most part) constrains participation in capitalist countries to those in the middle class or higher. But the design of the sport and those who have predominantly practiced it has historically created barriers to diverse participation.

When Retton was winning her Olympic gold medal, her former teammate Dianne Durham was watching from home. Durham, an African American gymnast, had been the national champion in 1983, after having moved to work with Károlyi a year earlier.[109] She too exhibited the power-packed, fastmoving, big-air gymnastics that Retton became famous for. Her talent was unquestionable, and she was rewarded by judges and fans. However, like most US gymnasts of the time, she received little media coverage. The coverage she did receive described her as muscular and powerful. In a 2016 interview, Durham accepted that she was a powerful gymnast, but she also commented that she wanted to be seen as a beautiful gymnast.[110] This points to the struggle she faced in finding her own form of femininity that would be accepted in the sport. Media emphasized the promise that she showed as an athlete, evidenced in the agreement between US judges and coaches that she could be the nation's great gymnastics hope for the 1984 games. But an injury precluded her from Olympic trials, and Durham missed her opportunity. Shakur-Bruno suggests that Károlyi withheld bureaucratic procedures that could have allowed her to be eligible for Olympic selection after an injury.[111] That was the end of Durham's career.

Another Károlyi protégé, Betty Okino, a Ugandan Romanian gymnast, graced the US team in 1992. Her gymnastics was the lithe, long-lined style. She was accompanied by another Black athlete, Dominque Dawes—the first African American Olympic gymnast, who went on to compete in two more Olympics. Biracial Tasha Schwikert joined Dawes on the Olympic team in 2000. Then, in 2004, Annia Hatch was selected to the US Olympic team. Hatch was a naturalized US citizen who had immigrated from Cuba seven years earlier. The "community of color" within US Olympic gymnasts was disproportionally represented by biracial and international Black athletes. Shakur-Bruno reasons that this demonstrated that "reward is conferred upon the black female gymnast who most closely approximates whiteness and/or most exotically exceptionalizes (African American) blackness."[112] But the representation these gymnasts gave to Blackness within the gymnastics community made it easier for their successors.[113]

Daiane dos Santos of Brazil found her success by appealing to both exotic and exceptional narratives. She became world champion on floor exercise in 2003, becoming the first gymnast of African descent to win a gold medal at the world championships. Dos Santos's gymnastics pushed the acrobatic boundaries of the sport on her strongest event, floor exercise. She competed some of the most difficult tumbling possible at the time and was the first in the world to compete two new skills on the floor. In the first, known as the Dos Santos 1, the gymnast does a half twist into a double somersault forward in the pike position (a piked double arabian). In the Dos Santos 2, the gymnast completes the somersaults in a straight position.[114] An extreme amount of power, strength, and explosive energy is needed to complete these skills. To some extent, racist ideas in Brazil helped propel her career. "Many Brazilians believe that blacks are inherently swifter and have better muscular coordination than whites," explained a *New York Times* article. But in the same vein, this stereotype meant that she faced pressure from Brazilian sports administrators to pursue sprinting rather than gymnastics.[115] Her coach further identified the racialized and age-based obstacles she faced as a Black woman in a mature body: "Daiane has the body not only of a woman, but of a Brazilian woman."[116] The media focused on her body type as the key to her gymnastics success, as "unusually muscular," and "not a waif," which invited direct comparisons (and contrasts) with the White, lithe young women who had dominated the sport. Dos Santos also did not begin training in gymnastics until she was twelve, so her success challenged the idea in gymnastics that early specialization was necessary to achieve success. Her older age may also have played a part in finding an acceptable form of femininity, as it adhered to the FIG's earlier aspirations of mature women athletes. But both racially and in terms of her age, dos Santos was accepted as an exception to what coaches, judges, and fans knew of gymnastics.

Dos Santos performed with a big smile on her face as she danced and tumbled to fast-paced, high energy music. The music she used in 2004–5 and again in 2008, "Brasileirinho," was a version of a famous Brazilian composition. In appealing to nationalism in these performances, she appeared exotic in a sport that had been predominantly White and European. Exoticism is not possible without recalling colonialism, imperialism, and, in the context of gender, subjugation. In this sense, it presents no challenge to masculinity. Historian Patty O'Brien describes exotic femininity in the Pacific as "unselfconsciously naked . . . physically perfect, passive, and pleasing."[117] Although dos Santos is not from the Pacific, with her dark skin, petite body, and formfitting leotard, she used music, movement, and facial expressions to invoke a similar kind of femininity. Exoticism was the interpretation of femininity that dos Santos used to create a place for herself in the sport.

Over the nine years following her 2003 world championship medal, she won several more medals for her floor exercise at various international events. She also competed at the 2004, 2008, and 2012 Olympic Games, in spite of a series of injuries that slowed her career. Dos Santos demonstrated unusual longevity despite the FIG banning her for five months in 2009 after she tested positive for furosemide, a drug used to lose weight. The use of this drug in particular suggests that despite finding her own form of femininity in the sport, she still felt pressured to manipulate her physical maturity and muscular body type in order to comply with the sport's feminine ideals.

In 2012, US Gabby Douglas became the first gymnast of African descent to win the Olympic all-around gold in 2012. Her style of gymnastics was similar to Okino's in that she excelled in the "finesse" apparatuses of bars and beam, demonstrating a graceful style that emphasized long limbs, elegance of movement, and bodily lines.[118] Nevertheless, Douglas still faced criticism for her racialized femininity. In 2012, the media focused on the widespread criticism of her hair on social media. Like her teammates, Douglas wore her hair in a slick, high ponytail. Her hair appeared chemically straightened to achieve the same look as her White peers, which could be seen as an appeal to the White standards of femininity so prevalent in gymnastics. But viewers criticized her for having "kinks" at her hairline that did not match the straightness of her ponytail. They disparaged her for looking "unkempt" and said she should have had her hair done professionally because she was representing Black communities on the world stage.[119] Although other public commentators spoke out in her defense, the majority of the narrative surrounding Douglas was not about her gymnastic success, but over the importance of hairstyles and their appropriateness. Her public reception tarred her Olympic experience and certainly dampened her victories, but Douglas nonetheless made a bid for a second Olympic team in 2016.

Her second Olympic experience was equally difficult. Douglas again excelled in the competition, helping to bring the team to another gold medal. But again, she was the subject of further public criticism. When the US national anthem played during the medal ceremony for the team competition, Douglas was the only US gymnast not to place hand over her heart. Then, as her teammates competed in the all-around final, she was accused of not

FIGURE 5.15. American Gabby Douglas became the first black Olympic all-around champion in 2012. © 2012 IOC / John Huet—All rights reserved.

FIGURE 5.16. Douglas's victory received less attention online than did her hair, which was heavily criticized. © 2012 IOC / John Huet—All rights reserved.

cheering enough for them, instead looking "salty" as she watched from the stands, failing to stand up and clap.[120] Twitter users started the hashtag "CrabbyGabby," and in the midst of hurtful media coverage at her second Olympics, Douglas was criticized for not smiling enough. But only four years earlier, McKayla Maroney had famously pulled an unhappy face when she was receiving her second-place medal on vault. Numerous memes were borne from Maroney's experience, but she did not face much criticism. Yet Maroney's actions were very similar to Douglas's. This suggests that Douglas was subject to racialized scrutiny, demanding she meet impossible standards of comportment. While she was not the first Black gymnast, she was the first to achieve the highest level of success—Olympic all-around gold—and the first to do so in the age of social media. Despite the struggles she faced, Douglas's all-around victory in 2012 became one of the most important milestones in creating a space for racialized gymnasts in the sport. Her success required audiences to adjust their conceptions of femininity in gymnastics in order to make sense of her success, while the criticisms she faced equipped those younger than her with lessons about what pressures they too might face.

At the 2016 games, Douglas competed alongside another African American gymnast, Simone Biles. Their proximity, competing at the same time

and in contrast with one another, meant Biles had quite a different public reception than Douglas. Biles won the Olympic all-around in 2016. In
fact, Biles won every international competition she entered after 2014, her
first year as a senior international gymnast. In doing so, she accumulated
more world championship medals than any other gymnasts in the world,
male or female. She performed excellent gymnastics, exhibiting a powerful
style enabled by her compact, muscular body that allowed her to perform
elements others could not dream of. She mastered skills that few male
gymnasts could do and had some of the hardest possible elements named
after her on three apparatuses. Her sheer dominance inspired awe instead
of criticism. Media coverage has been all but hagiographic. But she also
appealed to audiences in a way that Douglas never did, adhering to the
little-girl traits that have prevailed in the sport. Although she never wore
pigtails, she was reminiscent of Korbut in the enormous grin she wore during her performances and the pure fun she appeared to be having. Adding
to the idea of this youthful femininity, media coverage often showed her
laughing alongside her teammates. No one could criticize her for not being
supportive, patriotic, or happy enough.

Biles combined the traits of the most celebrated gymnasts in gymnastics' history. Like Latynina, her dominance in the sport was both astounding and lasting. Like Čáslavská, she used her athletic success to speak out
on civic issues. Biles was publicly critical of US Gymnastics Federation's
care of its gymnasts and organizational mismanagement in the wake of
team doctor, Larry Nassar, being accused of sexually assaulting hundreds
of gymnasts.[121] Like Retton, her gymnastics were explosive and energetic.
She appeared invincible, with no limits to her gymnastic abilities. Like
Comăneci, she appeared calm and at ease on all of the apparatuses, consistent and stable. Moreover, she too broke records. Her routines included
original skills that were previously considered too difficult to be possible.
Both Biles and Comăneci showed awe-inspiring gymnastics. Like Korbut,
Biles expressed unreserved, total delight on the competition floor. This
utter joy offset the explosive power that underscored Biles's gymnastics.
Her smiling, giggling, fun persona counteracted any suggestion that her
gymnastics were not feminine. Through Biles, racialized women were
finally accepted in gymnastics. But her acceptance came after racialized
athletes before her had paved the way, in a kind of intergenerational
cooperation.

FIGURE 5.17. Simone Biles became Olympic champion in 2016 exhibiting a powerful style of gymnastics like Retton's. Her dominance was akin to Comăneci's, her visible joy was reminiscent of Korbut, and the way she used her success as a platform for social change was like Čáslavská. © 2016 IOC / Ian Jones—All rights reserved.

Gymnastics as a Bodily Experience

Dance scholars Markula and Clark argue that "the perfect feminine ballet physique becomes a disembodied body whose movements (extensions, weightlessness), roles (fairies and swans), and size (petite) are defined by patriarchal structures."[122] They highlight how the ballet body maintains traditional gender roles and power arrangements, the dancers induced to do what it takes (diet, extreme training) to achieve and sustain this ideal. The same could be said of gymnastics. While many call the 1970s to the 1980s the golden era for gymnastics, it can better be understood as a dark age. Even into the 1990s, gymnasts were dying for their sport.[123] Beyond traumatic injuries, the effect is abundantly clear by observation. The bodies of the sport during that time were young and prepubescent. If the gymnasts themselves were not young, they had stalled the onset of puberty to appear so. Such an understanding of femininity as androgynous came to permeate popular culture more broadly in the mid-1990s. Fashion and women's magazines promoted "heroin chic" à la Kate Moss, which celebrated a pale, emaciated appearance. Scholar Alphonso McClendon argues that heroin chic reflected the pessimism and despair that pervaded culture at the time.[124] For that matter, the mature femininity of the 1950s gymnast was rooted in postwar desires for domesticity and population regrowth. At the height of the Cold War in the 1970s, the child gymnasts reflected a call to think of the children and moreover, invest in them as a source of hope for the world.[125] This investment continued throughout the 1980s and 1990.

Some have explained that the child athlete was a necessary precondition for the acrobatic style of gymnastics. For instance, Wamsley and Gordon note the correlation between acrobatization and child athletes: "The direct results of this shifting emphasis in performance have been decreased ages, heights, and weights of participants."[126] But we now know this is more correlation than causation. While the use of child gymnasts found justification in physiology and biomechanics, the predominance of child gymnasts really existed to apologize for gender transgressions within the sport.[127] Gymnastics was only cast as a child's sport for this reason. Since about 2010, a growing number of gymnasts have reminded the world that the sport is, in fact, perfectly suitable for fully grown women.

Since 2014 the average age of female elite gymnasts at the world championships has been over twenty. The most famous of "older gymnasts," Oksana Chusovitina, has competed at seven Olympic Games. She is competing into her forties, demonstrating that older gymnasts can compete—and win. Her presence has influenced a generation of gymnasts to prolong their careers. Adult gymnasts in the sport further diversify what the gymnastics body looks like. It remains lean and generally small in stature, but it now allows for postpubescent athletes and muscular gymnasts. Recent editions of the Code of Points have aided in this regard, rewarding aerial difficulty that requires great strength. From Alicia Sacramone to Simon Biles, the United States in particular has shown that there can be a new postmodern, feminist gymnastics body.

Studies reveal that older gymnasts are sustained by an immense love of women's artistic gymnastics.[128] The shift toward acrobatics allowed gymnasts to access power previously attributed only to men.[129] Dynamic gymnastics required hypersensitive proprioception—awareness of one's body in space and how to manipulate it. Alone on the apparatus, the gymnast has complete control of herself and her body. Comăneci explains this feeling in her autobiography: "Gymnasts develop an 'air sense' on all of the apparatus pieces, especially the beam. . . . An imaginary beam is created in the gymnast's mind, so even when she can't see it, she knows it's there.

I always knew when I was crooked going into an aerial on the beam. Just like all elite gymnasts, I'd make tiny corrections while in the air. Those split-second judgements made the difference between falling off the beam and hurting myself or completing a successful skill that allowed me to win competitions."[130] Thus, although many coaches have used disciplinary methods that demanded docility, at the same time gymnasts learned to think about themselves, their bodies, and make midair decisions to control their situations.

Feminist historians of sports conclude that "the rules, practice, consumption and governance of sport have produced a sporting culture hierarchy, which imposes power and control on women, while also providing opportunities for women to push the challenge and go beyond these constraints." In gymnastics, women are given the opportunity to go beyond their usual social constraints through the bodily experience and authority it gives them.[131] Dance studies scholar Eluned Summers-Bremner wrote that "dancing can feel like unlimited freedom."[132] Add to dance the flight of gymnastics and one has (temporarily) removed the bounds of gravity from the human experience. The gymnast masters fear, controverting the myth of feminine fragility and angst.[133] She experiences unfettered, unlimited, boundless movement through dance and flight. Such freedom allows the gymnast to escape the limits of patriarchal inscription and has allowed women of different heritages to expand inclusion in the sport.

In itself, the acts of gymnastics allow the woman to experience and know her body and herself, in space and time, without limits. Gymnastics gives athletes power usually not afforded to women, and the gymnast knows exactly how much she is capable of. So, to this extent, gymnastics must be feminist. But when we consider the narrow view of femininity the gymnast is expected to adhere to, the way she is (subordinately) compared to the male body and its gymnastics, and the way her own body and psyche are shaped by the pressures of coaches, officials, and administrators, this feminist potential becomes limited. Yet, women have shown time and again that they will overcome these barriers to access previously male spaces, like acrobatics, and even lead them, as with the Yurchenko vault. Despite the narrow, White-centric construction of femininity in gymnastics, racialized women have fought for and won space within the sport. In 2020, gymnasts around the world are leading the push for athlete rights in sport. They are not afraid. They are self-reliant and confident, using the skills they have learned in the sport and about themselves to push for women athletes'

FIGURE 5.18. Biles demonstrates the gymnast's experience of freedom, unbound from the limits of gravity as she flies through the air, completely and totally in control of her own body and where it goes. © 2016 IOC / Ian Jones—All rights reserved.

liberation. So despite the feminist problems that gymnastics poses, the gymnasts show that the sport indeed can be feminist both in the gymnastics itself and in the social liberation that its participants demand.

Conclusion

When women's artistic gymnastics entered the Olympic program in 1952, it merged the men's gymnastics competition that had gone before it, with softer, more passive bodily movements that were considered appropriate for women. But the limits of this style were quickly reached. By the late 1960s, gymnasts looked to men's gymnastics for inspiration about how to push the boundaries further, how to do something never accomplished by a woman before, and how to stand out as a performer beyond the poise and grace that nearly all female gymnasts shared at the time. Soviet coaches drew on the Russian traditions of ballet and circus, as the sport transitioned from balletic passivity to dynamic acrobatics. They worked with judges to ensure this new style was rewarded, and the FIG too contributed to acrobatization. It added difficulty and acrobatic requirements in the Code of Points, as well as modifying the equipment, which allowed gymnasts to take greater risks. So, the FIG cooperated with gymnasts and coaches to drive the sport in an acrobatic direction, although it was displeased when young bodies performed those acrobatics. Concurrently, more male coaches worked with female gymnasts, teaching them the gymnastic skills that had hitherto been confined to the men's discipline. Gymnasts around the world then emulated the style of the most dominant of nations. Although the fundamental masking of effort still remained, the newly muscled, petite bodies revealed the extreme strength and hardiness necessary to perform acrobatics.

From the 1960s onward, female gymnasts intentionally designed their performances for audiences, selecting music and facial expressions to appeal to spectators. This showed gymnasts cooperating not only with audiences, but with broader social expectations about femininity. As the gymnast became more acrobatic, her performance of femininity changed from mature, classical ballerina to cute, fun child. By the late 1970s, gymnasts not only performed this youthful brand of femininity, they were actually children, with Olympic medalists being as young as fourteen. This was a significant divergence from the FIG's conceptions of femininity, which had shaped the sport at the outset. Despite claims that young bodies were necessary to perform acrobatics, the success of adult gymnasts in the early twenty-first century—performing even more acrobatics—debunks such an assumption. Rather, the young bodies were part of a broader redefinition of femininity, that focused on youth and cuteness.

These styles of gymnastics were united by a femininity conceived by Europeans. It derived from cooperation across Europe when FIG leaders outlined the rules for the sport, and it excluded non-White ideas about feminine performance. African countries had both negligible representation in the FIG and within international gymnastics competitions. The Code of Points illustrated a White gymnast that drew on movements like ballet, a dance style important to European cultures. Black gymnasts had to overcome geographic and class barriers to sustaining the full-time training that was necessary by the 1970s, and if they overcame this, they were still faced with operating within a definitively White context in terms of peers, coaches, and judges. A steady stream of Black gymnasts since the

1980s have helped to overcome these problems, demonstrating a kind of intergenerational cooperation to find an acceptable form of femininity for Black gymnasts. This started with biracial athletes and culminated two decades later in the first African American Olympic all-around champion, Gabby Douglas, who was succeeded by Simone Biles, who is widely regarded as the greatest gymnast of all time.

Social ideals about race and gender from around the world were inscribed on the sport and the bodies that practice it. As officials, technologies, gymnasts, and coaches collaborated over time, each left their mark on gymnastics, continuing to shape and expand the sport to align with contemporary ideals of womanhood. The very acceptance of women into gymnastics, governed uniquely and exclusively by women, cemented its potential as a feminist space in sport in the early twentieth century. A century later, the increased diversity of gymnasts' race, increased age, and longer careers points to the sustained feminist potential of the sport. However, this potential has not always been met—from the difficulties racialized gymnasts have had finding a place in the sport, through to the abusive coaching methods and other negative impacts women's gymnastics has had on many lives (see chapter 6).[134] Yet, the development of gymnastics through the cooperative and responsive efforts of the FIG, gymnasts, and coaches, has enabled varied interpretations of bodily movement and expression. These are united by a demand that gymnasts have intense awareness and control over their bodies in space and time. Such agency over one's own trajectory is imperative to feminism. The act of gymnastics, is therefore, feminist. But the demand to conform to a limited ideal of femininity, and some of the disciplinary measures used to enforce this, can curtail the extent to which the sport offers a completely feminist experience for the gymnasts.

6

COACHING AND CULTURE

Women's artistic gymnastics was created as a space for women in sports, and the bodily movements that it allowed became a source of emancipation for women. But soon after its inclusion in the Olympic Games, coaching became gendered as women coaches were displaced by men. When the Soviet Union collapsed, coaches from the Eastern bloc moved westward in search of work. Until recently, scholarship on sports migration has focused on players rather than on coaches.[1] In a sport like gymnastics, this gap is a major oversight. Many immigrants attained head-coach positions around the world and elevated the quality of gymnastics in a number of countries. But their outsider status made them easy scapegoats when allegations of abuse scandalized the sport and how the public perceived it in the 1990s. Claims of abuse thus prompted little change inside the sport. The issues were dismissed as isolated incidents that involved other people, rather than a pervasive part of the sport's culture. That is how, two decades later, the US Gymnastics Federation could be rocked by one of the largest sexual assault scandals in history when its team doctor was accused of molesting hundreds of gymnasts. Then, when even that did not result in sweeping changes to the sport, in 2020 gymnasts around the world began sharing their own stories of abuse in the sport under the banner "gymnast alliance." In doing so, they showed that not only has abuse in the sport not gone away, it is everywhere. This chapter argues that women's artistic gymnastics has a problematic culture based on fear that stems from the imbalance of power between child gymnasts and the adults employed to achieve sporting victory. But it also offers hope that this culture can be repaired when gymnasts, coaches, and officials cooperate to create more positive training environments. This collaboration is essential to ensuring that the sport fulfills it feminist potential.

First, this chapter looks to the past to understand the coach-athlete relationship in gymnastics, its gendering and power dynamics. Then, it asks how that changed when a diaspora of former Eastern-bloc coaches took their expertise to the West, and what the impacts of immigration were. Moreover, it looks beyond the coach-athlete relationship to examine the other actors, like federations and officials, who contribute to the culture of fear that leaves gymnasts vulnerable to predators, using the Károlyis' ranch as an example. It then contextualizes the US situation and the global abuse allegations of 2020 with the long history of abuse in gymnastics around the world. Finally, it shows that a number of coaches have proven that a more protective approach can yield successful careers both in terms of athletic excellence and longevity, and they do so using collaborative methods. Ultimately this chapter demonstrates that, although gymnastics may be theoretically feminist, coaches, officials, and the elite sport cultures they create have been the gatekeepers allowing or preventing it from being a feminist experience in practice.

Gendering Coaching

In the 1970s, a demographic shift happened not only in the gymnasts performing women's artistic gymnastics, but also in the coaches behind them. Until then, it was one of few sports providing professional opportunities for women to work as coaches. Educative gymnastics and physical education had been made available to women through female physical educators. The educators were trained not only in bodily movements, but also in upholding femininity for women who engaged in sports.[2] Female teachers mediated women's involvement in physical activity in order to protect their womanliness. This assumption was carried over into sports, particularly sports like gymnastics that demanded gendered performance.

Hence, female coaches were the foundation of women's artistic gymnastics in its first decades, consistent with social expectations about who should teach physical activity to women, and how they would manage femininity and prevent manliness. Women-led coaching was supported by rules that barred men from training halls and competitions floors. Sports perceived as feminine have historically provided more coaching opportunities for women, and for its first decades, women's artistic gymnastics continued this trend.[3] This gendering extended to the sport's governance too, where only women served on the women's technical committee.[4] Governed by women, performed by women, judged by women, and coached by women, women's gymnastics had been molded in every way as a place for and by women.

Many women gymnasts thus went on to pursue coaching after their competitive careers ended. Larisa Latynina, Olympic champion from 1956 to 1964, became the Soviet Union's head coach for women's artistic gymnastics after she retired from competition.[5] Latynina used her exceptional athletic career to reach the top coaching position in the Soviet Union. When she was competing, her main coach had been a man.[6] However, due to the international rules at the time barring men from the competition floor, he could never have been appointed to the top position of national head coach. Because of this rule, the top coaching roles were reserved for women. Latynina's post-competitive career transition into coaching was by no means unusual. Her former teammate Polina Astakhova also pursued a coaching career in Soviet Ukraine, serving as a national team coach at the

FIGURE 6.1. Polina Astakhova of the Soviet Union was one of many women who pursued a coaching career after a successful time as a gymnast. Here she competes on the bars at the 1964 games. © 1964 IOC—All rights reserved.

1972 and 1980 games. Their contemporaries in the West did the same. In the United States, Muriel Davis Grossfeld also enjoyed a long career as a national coach after competing at the 1956, 1960, and 1964 games. She was the head national coach from 1974 to 1976 and went on to coach the United States' first world championships gold medalist in 1978, Marcia Frederick.[7]

But by the 1970s, a shift was underway. More male coaches worked in women's gymnastics as the sport became more acrobatic. By 1979, male coaches were allowed on the competition floor, but they were to serve as assistant coaches only. Women coaches were the only ones allowed to "chaperone" the gymnasts and accompany them onto the podium on which the apparatuses sat. While the head coach roles remained open only to women, permitting men on the competition floor, even in an assistant capacity, made new space for male coaches' expertise in the sport.[8] This shift was consistent with what was happening in sports more broadly. Expert coaches using scientific methods were necessary to meet the standards of elite sports in the Cold War, which led to a professionalization of coaching.[9] This had already happened in the Soviet Union, where sports were practiced professionally and coaches were educated at tertiary institutions. Wherever coaching became more professional, men began working with women's sports. According to sports historian Susan Cahn, in the United States "as the status of women's sports rose and the salary levels moved closer to parity with men's, more and more men grew interested in coaching women's sports."[10]

In gymnastics, when Korbut and Comăneci attracted so much media and spectator attention, it raised the profile of the sport. They had also both worked with male coaches, proving that there was a place for men in women's gymnastics. Cahn also links the growth of male coaches to the 1972 passage of Title 9 in the United States, which prevented sex discrimination in education.[11] Schools had to offer sports programs to both men and women. Many schools merged their men's and women's athletic departments, which resulted in men being appointed to the top positions. But this explanation does not account for the shift in the gendering of gymnastics coaching around the world. Rather, while coaching was becoming more professional and men began to be permitted on the competition floor, the nature of women's gymnastics was also changing.

As women's gymnastics became based less on ballet and more on gymnastic techniques, body angles, and periodized training, it was seen as more skillful and scientific. Masculinity has long been associated with skill and reason, while femininity has been associated with emotion. So, as the sport became acrobatic, with greater technical demands, men were perceived as being better equipped to coach it in both East and West. At the same time, acrobatization challenged the patriarchal assumption that women's gymnastics was a lesser, easier version of the men's sport. So in order to reestablish the superiority of men in gymnastics, men assumed a new role within the women's sport.

Hegemonic masculinity demands that men dominate in society, which requires that women be subordinate.[12] It positions men in power and requires them to assume masculine gender roles to promote their dominance.[13] In gymnastics, hegemonic masculinity explains why male coaches assumed responsibility for the "masculine" acrobatics and shared apparatuses of the vault, bars, and floor (tumbling only). The ideology encourages men to avoid displays of (perceived) femininity. Hence, many male coaches refuse to work on the beam and dance because they are considered too feminine.[14] So while previous studies have found that women coaches are advantaged in feminine sports because they do not suffer the still-prevalent lesbian stigma, women gymnastics coaches have been limited by their gender, as it is perceived that their contribution is more limited than the male coaches'.[15] Therefore, through coaching structures as well as the recruitment and sensationalizing of young, docile gymnasts, the understanding of femininity in gymnastics also appears to encompass an idea of female subordination.[16] Despite the feminist potential of gymnastics as an empowering activity for women, coaching structures that uphold hegemonic masculinity can undermine the potential of women's emancipation through the sport.

The ideological expectation that men conform to masculine behaviors may also explain some of the social conditions that have been normalized in the sport. One might posit that empathetic behaviors like care and compassion could be seen as feminine, and thus, they were removed from the coach's arsenal. Male coaches might avoid such behaviors because they do not demonstrate masculinity, while women coaches may also eschew them in an attempt to be seen as more masculine and taken more seriously.[17]

Although some female gymnasts had male coaches before, women were still predominantly the main coaches until the 1970s. But by 1972, at least half the Soviet Olympic gymnastics team were coached by men.[18] This shift toward male coaches was justified in the need for larger, stronger coaches to lift and catch gymnasts learning acrobatic skills.[19] The inverse is also true. Gymnasts became lighter and smaller (which often meant younger), making them easier to lift and catch. Victor Khomutov, coach to 1972

Olympic gymnast Antonina Koshel, explained the value of male coaches in women's gymnastics to the Australian gymnastics community in 1978: "Spotting is physically difficult, and requires the strength of a man. Girls in the teen years, relate better to a man and work harder." It seems unlikely that teenage girls relate better to adult men than the female coaches they previously worked with. An alternative explanation for why these girls might work harder for a male coach may be that the power imbalance between gymnast and coach is amplified. Gymnasts were already subject to a subordinate status in the coach athlete relationship, defined by the binaries of adult/child, expert/novice. Male coaches added a gendered dynamic of man/woman to that hierarchy. In most Western societies, men hold more social capital, which gives them power over women. In addition, their larger body size can also add physical intimidation to their arsenal of power, even if they do not consciously use it this way. Thus, the entry of male coaches into women's gymnastics consolidated these binary power differentials, solidifying the authority of the coach and the subordination of the gymnast. Gymnasts may have been motivated by fear or a desire to please the coach.

Khomutov also related the role of men in women's gymnastics to the technical developments in the sport becoming more dynamic and acrobatic, implying that it was beyond the expertise of women coaches. "Women's work is now very complicated, and requires the technique understanding of men's work."[20] As in other spheres, male coaches were seen as more competent in the complex and scientific expertise required for acrobatics. Acrobatics, then, were not only seen as masculine in terms of performance of risk, musculature, and dynamics, but also in the masculine logic and intelligence necessary to coach them.

Commissioned by both the FIG and the Australian Gymnastics Federation to undertake a coach education program in Australia, Khomutov advised that in "all top countries, the top coaches are men." By publishing his views in the Australian Gymnastics Federation's official magazine, the Australians tacitly endorsed this gendered view of coaching. Indeed, Khomutov's advice was presented alongside his evaluation of women's gymnastics in Australia and his recommendations on how to improve it based on the best practices in the USSR. At the same time, the advice that Khomutov shared would have been approved by Soviet government officials (and likely limited to prevent Australia becoming a real threat to Soviet dominance). His expertise was also broadly endorsed by the FIG who, with

Soviet officials (it is unclear if these were gymnastic or broader government officials), selected Khomutov as the coach to send on this educative tour.[21] It is therefore unlikely that the views Khomutov shared were purely his own; rather, they seemed to reflect common coaching practice in the Soviet Union.

In the Soviet Union, head coaches in most clubs were men, while women worked as assistant coaches. A contemporary observer, PhD student Catherine O'Brien, confirmed that women seemed to specialize in the dance elements of beam and floor, while men did most of the other coaching.[22] The Soviet Union's unbeatable results seemed to legitimize this gendered division of labor and justify the place of men in women's gymnastics. This division could have occurred organically in the West due to professionalization of coaching and acrobatization of women's gymnastics, but it was certainly cemented when the most dominant gymnastics nation promoted it on the world stage, with the support of the FIG. Global networks of cooperation and education therefore facilitated this shift. The gendered division of labor became so ubiquitous that when Western gymnastics organizations began recruiting Soviet coaches after the fall of the Soviet Union, they actively sought male coaches for head coach roles.[23]

Soviet Coach Migration

Known as a brawn drain, a trickle of coaches and players across a number of sports had moved from East to West since the beginning of the Cold War, almost en masse at one point in the late 1950s.[24] These migrations had been seen in the West as defections. But, as historian Johanna Mellis argues, from 1956 onward, communist states incentivized top coaches and athletes to stay, which stopped the westward flow of expertise.[25] Not only did coaches and athletes receive material benefits in the Eastern bloc—top housing, cars, and salaries—they were also unencumbered to reach their sporting goals. They had state support to pursue their careers, they had a large supply of athletes to work with, and they did not have to attract and maintain paying customers as coaches had to in the West.

Despite these incentives, there were still occasional defections across a range of sports from the 1960s to the 1980s. During the Cold War, Western countries accepted Eastern-bloc coaches as political refugees—proof of the ills of communism and Western nations' "unbending commitment to anticommunism."[26] They were also highly prized for their expertise. But there remained a cultural gulf between these migrants and their new communities. They did not receive the living assistance they were accustomed to at home, and yet, often without language skills and social networks, were expected to forge their own way forward in new, unfamiliar countries. Because of these limitations, and a perceived harshness of Eastern-bloc methods, many émigrés found it difficult to find suitable coaching jobs in their new nations. So, it is fair to say that Western countries received Eastern-bloc sports migrants with some ambivalence. This ambivalent reception continued after the Cold War ended. Although the struggles these migrants faced did not disappear, changing economic circumstances in the East propelled a new wave of migrants to seek their fortunes in the West.

After the Soviet Union's costly involvement in the war in Afghanistan and Soviet leader Mikhail Gorbachev's policies of glasnost and perestroika in the 1980s, the ideology behind the Soviet Union began losing its appeal.[27] The public started to withdraw its support for the Communist Party, and on Christmas Day 1991, the Soviet Union dissolved.[28] In the months before then, communist regimes throughout the Eastern bloc had fallen. Coaches previously employed by the state were suddenly unemployed. Until then, gymnastics coaches in the Eastern bloc had been among the privileged of society—with one or more gymnasts on the national team, coaches had good salaries, plus perks including cars, housing, and international travel.[29] After 1991, coaching was less lucrative. "They all moved out of Russia because there was no way to make a living for them," asserts Liz Chetkovich, who employed the first former-Soviet coach in the West, Andrei Rodionenko. "They were driving taxis, doing all sorts of things."[30] So they started accepting coaching offers in other countries. This loss of status, employment, and social security were the push factors that spurred on a diaspora of Soviet coaches. Additionally, lucrative opportunities for coaches abroad, both financially and in terms of improved chances of making the national team in Western countries, acted as pull factors to attract coaches westward.

Rodionenko pioneered the post–Cold War migration. As former head coach of the Soviet national team, he had fallen out of favor after their loss to Romania at the 1987 world championships. When the Soviet Union collapsed, he placed an advertisement in *International Gymnast* magazine seeking work. Chetkovich saw it and asked him to move to Perth, Australia. "And so, he came here, and his wife followed him about a month later I suppose, and then all the programs around Australia wanted a Russian coach."[31] Having settled in Australia, Rodionenko secured positions for his close friends from the national team. The Shorinovs and the Koudinovs moved to New Zealand; and the Beloussovs and Lapchines moved to Australia. Andrei Popov moved to Great Britain in 1991. National team gymnasts Valeri Liukin and Yevgeny Marchenko moved to the United States in 1992.[32] Less data is available about US recruitment of Soviet coaches, but it is clear that many former coaches established their own gymnastics clubs there.[33] This first wave of migrants were settlers, accepting permanent jobs in their new home countries.[34] Emigrating coaches tended to move as couples. The men often became head coaches, while women worked as assistant coaches, usually responsible for the beam and floor dance, as Khomutov had advocated in 1978.[35]

In Australia and New Zealand, gymnastics clubs facilitated recruiting male coaches. They relied on Rodionenko's old boys' network to find suitable coaches for roles in the West. Scholars have shown that, in women's gymnastics, "male coaches in positions of power recruit other males of similar status, thereby ensuring that only males received high level roles."[36] Women only became involved in coach migrations through their husbands. "Most of the Soviet coaches we brought out were men. We didn't bring out any women on their own to coach. They came with their husbands. We never recruited any females," a gym administrator explained. "But most of the Russian female coaches were married to male coaches. It was like a husband-wife thing. They all had wives. . . . Most of them. Maybe 80 percent of them had wives that coach."[37] This administrator explained that recruitment was gendered because Western countries already had women coaches. Men were recruited to teach acrobatics, which were culturally valued as more technical (and thus scientific, rational, and therefore considered appropriate for men). Women's work on the beam and dance—which as any ballet school would assert is arguably just as technical—was, by contrast, seen as not as important. The devaluing of coaching skills regarded as feminine buttressed the structures of hegemonic masculinity that underpin the sport.

Notwithstanding the Soviet relationships and networks that facilitated the migration of the 1990s, many coaches nonetheless suffered from culture shock in their new countries. They eventually adapted to the new culture, softening their coaching style (in some cases), vacationing around the country, and adopting local leisure activities. But, unsurprisingly, many former Soviet coaches still have pride in the accomplishments of Russians and former Russians. International competitions are a reunion of sorts where they meet and socialize with their former colleagues. A Western coach explains: "When they're at international competitions, the Russian coaches from all around the world form a tiny little private club. I see still in them a great deal of pride any time a Russian does well. So, when Nastia Liukin won that Olympic gold medal [in the all-around in 2008, for the United States] . . . they considered her to be Russian. And that result also reflected on Russia."[38]

The Soviet diaspora increased the quality of gymnastics around the world, while the former Soviet Union struggled to maintain its past dominance. "While they were giving their expertise to everyone else, they were losing it at the same time," mused one coach.[39] The once formidable juggernaut was broken into fifteen smaller, weaker teams representing fifteen new nations. But it also meant that judging problems in the sport escalated. Coaches, judges, and administrators continued collaborating on scores in their new affiliations, meaning many more nations were now in on the game.[40]

Beyond score fixing, Soviet coaches shared a significant amount of technical knowledge with the countries they emigrated to. One former Soviet gymnast and FIG official recalled that in the past climate of Cold War suspicion, gymnastics knowledge was a secret.[41] Nobody shared their experience or expertise. After 1991, these barriers were broken. In their new countries, former Soviet coaches shared technique, conditioning, programming, as well as broader ideas about nationally structuring the sport. "There was an immediate increase in quality everywhere in the world where they were," remarked another FIG official.[42] Another coach commented that "Soviet emigration allowed other countries to learn the technical things that they didn't actually know."[43] Contrary to popular caricatures of Soviet coaches, the Soviet position (according to Khomutov) was actually that a coach must work quietly and patiently, and never shout.[44] But while this knowledge and these methods were highly effective in improving Western gymnastics, they were less useful in educating other coaches. Former Soviet coaches may have worked alongside coaches in their new homelands, but there was seldom any collaboration.

In the 1970s, Soviet gymnastics had progressed from a sports machine with various moving parts—scientists, doctors, nutritionists, psychologists—into an insular, self-sufficient system. To facilitate this self-reliance, national head coach for men's gymnastics Leonid Arkaev promoted a highly specialized system where coaches were expected to fulfill these specialist roles instead. Coaches had to be graduates of an Institute of Physical Culture, which only accepted candidates who had achieved a master of sport in gymnastics (attained by meeting a benchmark score at the highest level of national competition). Coaches had years of gymnastics-specific practical training in these institutes, relying on biomechanics, physiology, history, sociology, and psychology, giving them the most relevant knowledge available and no need for outsiders.[45] Why seek a sports scientist who has no experience of gymnastics, when coaches were themselves trained in sports science and experts in gymnastics? The production of knowledge in Soviet gymnastics became insular. Moreover, gymnastics coaches specialized even further, becoming experts in different aspects of the sport. But rather than becoming expert in nutrition, or pedagogy, their specializations were instead centered on the specific skills or apparatuses. One observer explained that one would be a handstand coach, one would be a bars coach, and so on, so no one but the head coach saw the whole process.[46] Hence, when these coaches moved into Western systems, they were both reluctant to lean on medical, nutrition, psychological, or other support for their athletes, and also unable to make broad contributions to coach education.

Some point to the Soviet influence in gymnastics being the negative coaching styles that plague the sport. "They just knew one thing: this is how you coach; this is how you produce an athlete. We all know but we wouldn't do it," said one official. This person claimed that Western coaches emulated the psychological abuse and overtraining that they saw Soviet coaches doing.[47] But abusive coaching was evident before Soviet immigration. Moreover, it was shaped by broader environmental factors that allowed abuse to take place. A closer examination of the US system demonstrates how this can reach an extreme.

The Károlyis, the Ranch, and the Culture of Gymnastics

Even before the fall of communism catalyzed a diaspora of Eastern-bloc coaches immigrating to the West, two of gymnastics' most famous coaches had defected. After Nadia Comăneci's victory in Montreal in 1976, she and her coaches, Márta and Béla Károlyi, were closely watched by the Romanian government, who wanted to use them as political tools to enhance the image of the communist regime. "All of a sudden they forget everything I do," recalled Károlyi. "I am 'controversial'."[48] So at the end of a government-controlled tour of the United States in 1981, the Károlyis and their colleague, choreographer Geza Pozsar, checked the team in for their flight home, then slipped out of the airport. After the flight departed, they sought political asylum. A few months later, Paul Ziert, a gymnastics coach at the University of Oklahoma, offered them work at his gym, and off they went.

A year later, the Károlyis moved to Houston and started their own club. Advertising on lampposts around the community, they initially attracted only twenty-four students. Word spread, however, and in eighteen months their gym had five hundred girls enrolled, including the next Olympic champion, Mary Lou Retton.[49] Having coached Retton for fewer than eighteen months, the Károlyis were responsible only for a small portion of her gymnastics education. But Retton was not the only gymnast to transfer to the Károlyis' club after her formative training in anticipation of upcoming Olympic Games. The Károlyis became renowned as a kind of finishing school for female gymnasts. One gymnastics official commented: "[Béla] didn't do all that preparation for Mary Lou Retton, or [Kim] Zmeskal or anyone. But suddenly he arrives in town, they all go to him and they're champions. They would have been champions without him, but he did do that final bit of psychological touch-up, whatever you want to call it. I'm not sure what it was, but it put them over the top—that last little bit that they needed."[50]

In the lead-up to the games, the Károlyis had purchased a large plot of land in the Sam Houston National Forest. Within a year, they had built gymnastics facilities and dormitories on the site, which would become known as

FIGURE 6.2. US gymnast Phoebe Mills smiles after her performance at the 1988 Olympic Games, while coach Márta Károlyi has her arm around her. © 1988 IOC / Richard Avery Lyon—All rights reserved.

the Károlyi Ranch. After Retton's 1984 victory, enrollments ballooned. By the early 1990s, the Károlyis were celebrated coaches in the United States. Mike Jacki, executive director of the US Gymnastics Federation, commented that "the one thing over the past 10 years that's had the most effect on U.S. gymnastics, overwhelmingly, is the presence of Béla Károlyi."[51]

But the Károlyis' methods quickly came under scrutiny. *Sports Illustrated* reported that US coaches saw Béla as Coach Dracula. Though possibly referring to his Transylvanian roots, this term also connected Károlyi and his coaching methods with the superhuman character known for his inhumane, torturous treatment of others. Károlyi was accused of "menacing the red-blooded American system" and violating child labor laws.[52] On the one hand, this type of media coverage exposes a type of territorialism from rival coaches attempting to undermine the Károlyis. It is also consistent with the anti-Eastern European sentiment that many immigrants encountered during the Cold War. For instance, US media described Hungarian track coach Mihály Iglói in 1962 as "autocratic," making athletes live a "Spartan life of punishing severity" under "backbreaking training methods."[53] They contrasted this with the laissez-faire, unregimented, do-it-yourself spirit of US sports. Similar criticisms followed Eastern-bloc gymnastics coaches around the world after the Cold War. This framing cast Eastern-bloc coaches as Others, regardless of how long they had been in their new homes. On the other hand, numerous gymnasts have since accused the Károlyis of employing inappropriate, if not abusive, coaching practices. Their former pupils in Romania, Emilia Eberle and Ekaterina Szabo, accused the coaches of beating and starving them, which team choreographer Geza Pozsar corroborated.[54] Their US protégée Dominique Moceanu echoed these claims a decade later, adding emotional abuse to the accusations.[55]

The Károlyis always denied these allegations, and a number of gymnasts came to their defense. For example, Betty Okino explained that their methods were nothing more than was necessary for any elite athlete: "[Béla] Károlyi structured his training in a way that built your physical and mental strength to such a remarkable level, that even *he* couldn't tear you down. Béla wanted to know that when push came to shove, his athletes could handle any situation thrown at them. If you are not an individual who thrives under intense pressure, and high physical demands, then you are foolish to believe you can handle being an elite athlete."[56]

Earlier champions Retton and Comăneci echoed this sentiment.[57] Comăneci explained: "Béla Károlyi is a great coach; he is a masterful motivator and a powerful man who is as complex as any human being. I do not know the details of his coaching relationship with other gymnasts, but I do know that he is a good person."[58] Comăneci and Okino may not have experienced maltreatment at the hands of their coaches, but it is possible that they also do not consider their treatment to have been unacceptable or unusual. Scholars have shown that many gymnasts who have witnessed or experienced maltreatment from their coaches do not always recognize it, for such behaviors are normalized within the sport's culture. A gymnast's position as the coach's favorite might spare her from the abuse that her teammates allege. This manipulation of relationships and the use of favoritism and neglect allows the coach to create a hierarchical system within the group, in which multiple and contradicting realities exist. The line between appropriate and abusive behavior becomes blurred. Gymnasts' "admiration and fear for the coach prevented them from questioning the coaches' behaviors or admitting to themselves that the abusive coaching behaviors may be wrong," explain psychologists Ashley Stirling and Gretchen Kerr.[59] As seen in Okino's explanation, the success of the gymnasts they coached is seen to legitimize their methods. Gymnasts see such coaching as necessary for gymnastic victory—and many coaches agree.

Béla was the personal coach to at least nine Olympic gymnasts between 1984 and 1996, and he served as head coach of the 1992 Olympic team. Only three years after his retirement in 1996, the US Gymnastics Federation asked him to be the national team coordinator, a position he held until 2001. In the lead-up to the Sydney 2000 Olympics, Károlyi instituted the national team camp system, requiring athletes to attend closed training sessions at his ranch in Texas every few weeks. This was based on the semi-centralized model that Eastern-bloc countries employed. US champion Vanessa Atler recalled the pressures on the athletes at the camps: it was not only competitions scores that determined their selection to the Olympic team, but their every move in training, what they ate, and their ability to ignore injuries.[60]

Béla was the face of the Károlyi operation, but his wife, Márta, was widely renowned as the real gymnastics technician. When Béla retired in 2001, Márta replaced him as national team coordinator—a role she held until 2016. During that time, the US came to dominate the sport.

But when US team doctor Larry Nassar was publicly accused in 2016 of sexually assaulting hundreds of gymnasts over this period and the decade before it, the Károlyi regime came under scrutiny. Much of the abuse had taken place during national team training camps at the Károlyi Ranch—the official national team training center since 2001. [61]

Although gymnasts' personal coaches accompanied their charges to the ranch for monthly training camps, while there the athletes were subjugated by the Károlyis' hierarchy. Coaches too were under pressure to prove how good their gymnasts were, how much they could handle, and ensure they impressed decision makers at the top of the hierarchy. A former athletic trainer at the ranch, Melanie Seaman, described how personal coaches would not let her give ice to their gymnasts when they were injured.[62] Like the gymnasts, coaches too were teammates and rivals, both working together and trying to outdo each other. And they might have seen this as acting in the athletes' interests, helping them achieve favor with the fickle decision makers at the top of the women's program. This goal could also have made them hesitate about raising any concerns, out of fear of rocking the boat and harming their gymnast's standing.

Madison Kocian, a 2016 Olympian, describes the ranch as fostering a "culture of fear, a culture of silence."[63] Various gymnasts reported being afraid to show, let alone report, pain. The ranch culture demanded that Olympic hopefuls avoid being seen as difficult.[64] After 2012 and 2016 Olympian Aly Raisman retired from the sport, she described how the gymnasts were afraid to ask for things as basic as soap.[65] Such testimony also points to the lack of amenities provided to the athletes. By several accounts, the food was awful and gymnasts felt watched when eating.[66] Coaches were housed separately and were not present in the gymnasts' dormitories, where Nassar treated the youngsters, rather than in an infirmary. There was no Wi-Fi and no cell-phone reception. The only contact with the outside world was via one of two pay phones at the ranch.

Although the Károlyis established the camp system and venue, many more people were responsible for creating and sustaining the environment over the seventeen years the ranch operated as the national team training center. The behaviors and culture there were shaped and upheld by successive personal coaches, support staff, and by US Gymnastics Federation (and later USA Gymnastics) officials. At best, all of these adults conspired to create and sustain an insular environment cut off from the rest of the world. But at worst, everyone knew that if the behaviors were made public, the system would have to change and they would be held accountable for the abuse.

FIGURE 6.3. Aly Raisman, an 2012 and 2016 Olympian, has been vocal about conditions at the Károlyis' ranch, the culture of fear, and the failures of the US Gymnastics Federation. © 2016 IOC / Jason Evans—All rights reserved.

Former elite gymnast Mattie Larson described her experience at the ranch:

> There is an eerie feeling as soon as you step foot onto the Károlyi Ranch. It is completely removed from all civilization. In the case of an emergency, the closest hospital is so far away, you'd need to be helicoptered there. To get to the ranch, you must drive up a dirt road for what seems like an eternity, . . . On top of that, there is no cell service. It's completely isolated, and that's no mistake. That is how the Károlyis wanted it. The complete detachment from the outside world, on top of careless and neglectful adults, made the ranch the perfect environment for abusers and molesters to thrive.[67]

Over the years, the Károlyis increased and solidified their power as coaches in the United States to the extent that they had full control over the national team: where they trained, how often they trained, what they ate, if they were in pain, when they could speak, and who had access to them. This setup was supported by the gymnasts' personal coaches and by federation officials, who, although not necessarily leaders, were part of the culture. The power imbalance between (often child) gymnasts and (adult) coaches created an opportune environment for predators. Even if they were older, gymnasts were afraid to challenge authority for fear of repercussions on their careers, and if they did so, few in authority were willing to listen.[68] There are few known examples of personal coaches withdrawing their athletes from the ranch because of the abuse they identified there, except for Simone Biles's coach, Aimee Boorman.[69] The gymnasts at the ranch were vulnerable and isolated. Their careers were dependent on the adults around them, and those adults were prioritizing gymnastics over the well-being of their charges. This dependence enabled the adults to create a culture of fear in which the gymnasts became susceptible to abuse. And Nassar leveraged this situation to prey on the gymnasts.

In testimony after testimony, the athletes speak of Nassar as a friend and confidant; someone who brought the gymnasts candy when their coaches pressured them not to eat much in front of everyone at camps; someone who cooperated in hiding injuries so decision makers would not exclude athletes from the team; someone whom coaches made the gymnasts see regularly in an attempt to mitigate the symptoms of overtraining; and someone whose abuse continued unreported for decades because of a carefully cultivated atmosphere of silence and fear. In an environment of fear and a culture of abusive coaching, Nassar deliberately and painstakingly built up trust with the impressionable and susceptible gymnasts in order to prey on them.

While Nassar was cast as a lone actor, an exception, media coverage of the crimes at the ranch and the women's elite program more broadly focused on the role of the Károlyis. Despite some disparaging articles, by and large the Károlyis were celebrated for their successful gymnasts in the 1990s and 2000s. The media had touted their pursuit of the American dream, immigrants who came to the United States with nothing, built a gymnastic empire, and adopted the Texan rancher lifestyle. When the Nassar scandal broke, they were recast (again) as foreigners, introducing a foreign, regimented, depersonalized system into the United States. This explained that Others were responsible for the abuse that happened, rather than something Americans were also responsible for. It absolved US anxieties about the system Americans had created, sustained, and supported. It also drew on anticommunist rhetoric that had pervaded the way Eastern-bloc sport was presented in the West during the Cold War. For instance, the podcast *Heavy Medals* perpetuated Red Scare discourse, contrasting the Károlyis' harsh methods with the US narrative of sporting freedom.[70] This rationalized the abuse that has taken place in gymnastics as the result of a foreign system, rather than as something that became integral to US gymnastics and involved dozens of citizens. Not only did it limit examination of US involvement in the problems, it hampered any interrogation of the culture of women's gymnastics itself, around the world.

Abusive Gymnastics

The abundant, visceral accounts of the experience at the ranch make for a compelling case study of abuse in gymnastics. But in 2020, complaints around the world about gymnastics culture, raised under the hashtag "gymnast alliance," showed that it was by no means the only time or place that gymnasts have been trapped in a culture of abuse, fear, and silence. It is a problem that permeates how women's gymnastics is practiced around the globe. Indeed, historical evidence reveals a long history of abuse in gymnastics.

The Nassar case was shocking in scale, but sexual misconduct by gymnastics coaches was not new. Before the arrival of Eastern-bloc coaches, 1978 world champion on bars Marcia Frederick was allegedly sexually assaulted by one of her coaches after her record-breaking competition.[71] Only six years earlier, on the other side of the world, Korbut's coach allegedly raped her.[72] Head coach of the 1984 US Olympic team Don Peters was accused of sexually assaulting gymnasts in the 1980s and is now permanently banned from the sport.[73] There appear to be no national or temporal limits to allegations of sexual abuse in gymnastics.[74] But abuse in the sport goes beyond sexual. At its root, young gymnasts have been vulnerable when they have been entrusted to adults who should have cared for them. All too often, the national sports agenda and gymnastics officials' objectives have superseded gymnasts' welfare. This has led to serious injuries and even death.

After world champion Elena Mukhina broke her neck in 1980, she claimed that everyone around her had prioritized the interests of the nation, and its sporting supremacy, over her own safety. The Soviet gymnast had been practicing a Thomas salto—$1\frac{1}{2}$ twists with $1\frac{1}{2}$ vertical rotations, landing headfirst and forward-rolling out of the somersault. She under-rotated her somersault, crashing her head into the ground while her body flipped over her, instantly breaking her neck.[75] Mukhina saw her paralysis as an "inevitable" symptom of the broken gymnastics system in which she trained: "There are such concepts as the honor of the club, the honor of the team, the honor of the national squad, the honor of the flag. They are words behind which the person isn't perceived. I was injured because everyone around me was observing neutrality and keeping silent. After all, they saw that I wasn't ready to perform that element. But they kept quiet."[76]

Mukhina's paralysis, however, was downplayed for most of the 1980s as a minor injury.[77] In an interview, Mukhina explained that fans wrote her asking when she would be returning to competition. The usual narrative for athletes was that they would return to the competition despite fractures and concussions, proving their heroism and devotion to their country. "Why?," she asked. "For what purpose? In order to report that 'the task of the Homeland' has been completed?"[78] An expert on the Soviet sports system, Dufraisse argues that Mukhina's paralysis illuminated "the dysfunction of the elite sports training process: training in defiance of physical limitations, the exploitation of young children and adolescents, the race for acrobatization, excessive medicalization." Mukhina's injury seemed to support critics' arguments that Soviet sports were the "product of a mechanized and dehumanized system."[79] Yet, these same arguments could be made for what happened in the United States thirty years later. Young girls' physical, mental, and emotional health were exploited for sports success and the athletes were overly medicalized to disguise excessive training, all to achieve a larger goal—the success of the nation. When the flaws of the system were exposed—through Mukhina's paralysis and in the Nassar trial—governing bodies sought to reframe coverage of the incidents rather than address the problems that had caused them, as we see below.[80]

Sadly, Mukhina's was not the only catastrophic injury of that decade. In 1988, when performing her vault at the World Sports Fair, fifteen-year-old US gymnast Julissa Gomez missed her foot on the springboard after her round-off, slamming headfirst into the vaulting horse behind her.[81] She was instantly paralyzed, dying three years later from complications. The danger in gymnastics was not only in the risky skills that gymnasts were performing in less than ideal conditions, it was also in the culture itself. In 1994, another American, Christy Heinrich, died of anorexia, having been told by a judge that she would never be internationally competitive unless she were smaller. Her story was one of many abusive practices in gymnastics publicized in Joan Ryan's 1995 exposé, *Little Girls in Pretty Boxes*.

Allegations of abusive coaching surfaced in Australia too. In 1995, Head Coach Ju Ping Tian was accused of running a gymnastics program that caused anorexia nervosa in its gymnasts and subjected them to hitting, smacking, kicking, denial of access to medical care, abusive language, and intimidation.[82] An inquiry cleared Tian of the allegations, but sports scholar Varney argues that the inquiry itself legitimized practices that were part of the culture of gymnastics worldwide.[83]

But even before Ryan's best-selling book and the various investigations into gymnastics culture around the world, problems in the sport were becoming public. As it became more popular with each Olympics, women's gymnastics attracted more attention as well as more scrutiny. Commentary changed from emphasizing the exceptional nature of child prodigies to noting that child athletes had become the worrying norm in women's gymnastics. The sport was losing credibility. Between serious injuries and "social and psychological problems caused by inordinate, single-minded devotion to this isolating sport," according to the *New York Times*, gymnastics' reputation was falling fast. Such was its decline that Dave Anderson, a regular gymnastics' reporter to the *New York Times* suggested the IOC should drop women's artistic gymnastics entirely. "More than any other sport, gymnastics steals a kid's life. . . . Women's gymnastics isn't a sport so much as it is a show and sometimes a sham the Olympics could do without."[84]

Rather than responding to these criticisms by interrogating the sport or trying to tackle the issues raised, the FIG instead launched a public relations program to improve viewers' opinion of the sport. It considered such negative commentary unfair representations of the sport. For example, in his 1993 report, Michel Leglise, president of the FIG Medical Commission wrote: "This year once again, our sport has not been spared press criticism in the field of health and safety. In the vast majority of cases, however, the articles in question have been provocative and tendentious, providing no evidence, no concrete element and no objective truth. The intention has been not so much to cause damage as to merely write something sensational. These criticisms may hurt us, but they should not discourage us. We should continue to provide explanations, to bring forward concrete elements and to add to public comprehension on the basis of our experience and scientific work."[85]

Leading the defense against negative media coverage, the FIG Medical Commission introduced "Operation Universal Bibliography," a collation of every piece of research on gymnastics that could be deployed to rebut any criticism. The commission explained: "Scientific, objective, factual and rational explanation are certainly the only reasonable response to sensational reporting. Scandal-seeking newspapers all too often base their stories on subjective arguments without scientific foundation."[86]

The FIG's defensive response arose in the context of its threatened position in the Olympic movement. As ESPN's X Games became popular in the mid-1990s, they rivaled gymnastics' monopoly as a dynamic, risky, and aerial sport. With a half million spectators in attendance at those first Summer X Games, it was hard for the IOC not to see the rise of extreme sports as a challenge to its own games, which focused on more traditional sports. Moreover, after suffering a decline in youth spectatorship during the 1990s, the IOC was looking to contemporary sports as a way to reclaim this market.[87] The FIG worried that the IOC might annex extreme sports, and if gymnastics was perceived as problematic, extreme sports might even replace gymnastics. Changing the public discourse surrounding the sport was faster than changing gymnastics' culture.

Even decades later, the culture appears not to have changed much. After the June 2020 release of the documentary *Athlete A*—in which US gymnasts from the 1990s to 2020 detailed their abuse from coaches, officials, and the team doctor—others have found the courage to speak out. In direct response to that documentary, a number of gymnasts throughout Europe and Oceania have alleged that over three decades, they too trained in an abusive environment in which bullying, gaslighting, and hitting were part of their everyday experience. They were taught to fear their coach above anything else.[88] Moreover, this abuse took place in a broader elite sports culture in which athletes and coaches from a range of sports were discouraged from speaking up for fear of reprisal.[89]

Gymnastics' culture of abuse goes beyond Britain and the United States. In addition to the Australian abuse detailed in 1995, gymnasts in the Netherlands made similar allegations of emotional, psychological, and physical abuse in 2013. In 2012 the Swedes investigated the culture of elite gymnastics in Sweden and ongoing reports of abuse in 2013. In Switzerland, the head of high-performance gymnastics and two rhythmic gymnastics coaches were suspended after allegations of bullying in 2020.[90]

At the end of 2020, more stories continue to emerge as gymnasts are inspired by their peers speaking out, and it remains to be seen what the ramifications will be. At least three countries have ordered independent investigations. But gymnasts are wary of their national governing bodies' ability to implement any change.[91] This echoes Aly Raisman's and Simone Biles's criticisms of how USA Gymnastics has handled, or failed to handle, complaints. In each of these countries, allegations of abuse in women's artistic gymnastics have vastly outnumbered allegations of abuse in the other disciplines. This shows that gymnastics is facing a problem not only of child abuse but also of gender discrimination. The similarities between these experiences also suggest that not only is abuse part of the global culture of women's gymnastics, but so too perhaps is a failure to listen to the gymnasts at the heart of this sport. Gymnastics officials who prized the docile, compliant, child gymnasts, who are seen and not heard, continued to restrict women to that role long after they have grown up.

These problems run deep in the global culture of gymnastics. Some commentators have called for gymnasts to unionize in order to protect themselves.[92] Organizations responsible for educating coaches about acceptable behaviors and indeed, advocating for gymnasts, already exist—these are the national governing bodies. President Watanabe observed: "without gymnasts, Gymnastics federations in the world have no place to exist."[93] Yet, many of these organizations have clearly not been operating with this ethos. An international body, comprised of national unions, may make gymnasts' voices harder to ignore at every level. Drawing on gymnasts' expertise would help address the fundamental issue of what is considered acceptable behavior in the sport and has long gone unchecked.

Emotional manipulation, bullying, ignoring injury, and body shaming have been normalized in the culture of gymnastics around the world. When US gymnast Kerri Strug landed her vault on one foot at the 1996 Olympics, she collapsed to the ground in agony. In the media, this was widely lauded as heroic. She was injured before starting the vault, and video footage shows Coach Béla Károlyi telling her that she needed to do the vault anyway. It was not only Americans who learned from this. Coaches and gymnasts from around the world observed this kind of attitude and determination as what was necessary to win; health consequences were secondary. This win-at-all-costs mentality is not only tied to the ambitions of the state. Everyone involved has a vested interest in prioritizing medals over athlete welfare. Gymnastics programs lose funding if they do not produce winning results, governing bodies are forced to downsize, and coaches get fired.[94] Their replacements are brought in to do whatever it takes to get results. These adults are all paid to win medals, not produce healthy athletes. It is the athletes who pay the price of that approach. That is why a number of scholars have likened youth sports to child labor.[95]

Canadian Olympian and sports scholar Bruce Kidd explains elite sports in general: "As underpaid professionals, athletes are 'sweat-suited philanthropists,' subsidizing the careers of hundreds of fully paid coaches, sports scientists, and bureaucrats, not to mention the ambitions of the federal state and the products and ideology of the corporations which sponsor teams and competitions."[96] This power imbalance between athletes and staff affects a number of elite sports. However, in gymnastics the athletes are even more vulnerable because of their youth.

These issues occur at both a sports system level (of camps, selection criteria, domestic programs, and competitions) and at the level of the coach-athlete relationship. The coach-athlete relationship is predicated on trust. When the coach catches the gymnast before she hits the ground in a mistimed skill, they have her life in their hands. But the trust seldom goes both ways. Comăneci explained her relationship with her coaches: "the Károlyis understood that, as children, we young gymnasts were incapable of disciplining ourselves, so they had to do it for us."[97] Many coaches assume that their female, child gymnasts are not able to regulate themselves, so the coach becomes all-controlling. Symptoms of this can be seen in the way coaches deny gymnasts food and refuse to believe or act on their complaints of pain and injury. This strict control is also described in academic studies on gymnastics coaching.[98] The control described here suggests that cooperation and collaboration have rarely been the norm in women's artistic gymnastics around the world.

Stirling and Kerr find that positive qualities in a coach-athlete relationship—closeness and being parental or familial—can be also used negatively when "a culture of sport idealizes and prioritizes athletic performance above the interests of well-being of the athlete."[99] They recommended that the absolute authority of the coach could be reduced by diluting it with contributions from parents, nutritionists, psychologists and other sports experts—that is, collaboration across different roles in the sports system. But as Kidd explains, these people too can have a vested interest in prioritizing athletic outcomes over athlete well-being. Moreover, if those services are provided as part of an elite athlete assistance program by the national sports organization, then they become another element of control. Athletes can be threatened with losing this support, have no alternative support organization they can turn to, and may have little option but to quit.[100] Either way, there is a clear need for independent actors to advocate for athletes.

Protective Coaching

Gymnastics can in fact be practiced in a supportive, empowering environment. Moreover, various coaches have shown that positive, athlete-centered
coaching does not come at the expense of international success: some of the
world's best gymnasts in the late 2000s and 2010s have attributed their success to their coaches' protective style. Studies on older elite gymnasts found
that all sustainable coach-athlete relationships shifted toward partnership
and collaboration. Some gymnasts even started coaching themselves.[101]
Leveling the coach-athlete hierarchy allowed gymnasts to have more say
in their training regimen and speak up to both coaches and administrators. Gymnasts needed to negotiate training hours and workloads in order
to manage their bodies, preventing fatigue and injury. Coaches had to be
willing to relinquish their previously unquestioned authority in order to
facilitate these changes.[102] The swelling number of older gymnasts enjoying
international success points to the efficacy of such coaching.

Some have been able to employ these kinds of methods even when
working with younger gymnasts. For example, Vladislav Rastorotksy was
widely regarded as a patient and calm coach, whose gymnasts had different
body shapes and performed unique styles of gymnastics.[103] Liang Chow
and Liwen Zhuang, coaches to 2008 Olympic champion Shawn Johnson,
were famous for their caring approach to coaching, laughing and smiling
in the gym and asking their gymnasts to train "only" twenty-five hours per
week rather than the standard thirty-plus.[104] This approach not only kept
their athletes happy and motivated to continue training, but it has also
protected their bodies from injury. Both Chow and Zhuang had competed
on the Chinese national team and purposefully created a different experience for their own gymnasts in the United States. More recently, coach
Aimee Boorman used a similar approach with Simone Biles. Boorman
worried that, if she pushed Biles, she would simply quit. Other gymnasts
noticed: "Simone's coach Aimee lets her smile, which I'm super jealous
of," 2012 Olympian McKayla Maroney remarked on a 2016 podcast.[105] Like
Chow, Boorman also limited training hours in order to keep Biles in the
sport and prevent injury. She emphasized fun in training and competing. She even declined an invitation to a national team camp in order to
protect Biles from Márta's criticism.[106] But by and large, such coaching
is still considered exceptional or unusual, and this is highlighted in the
media coverage it attracts. A culture shift may be underway in gymnastics

as people see the successes achieved with the style of coaching, but it is certainly far from universally accepted. Indeed, despite these coaches' efforts, both Biles and Johnson have described various types of abuse or treatment in their gymnastics experience due to the broader structure of the sport.

In the wake of the Larry Nassar case, the US Gymnastics Federation and the FIG have both instituted a range of safeguarding policies to protect athletes. In December 2018 the FIG established an independent Gymnastics Ethics Foundation with an investment of 2 million Swiss francs.[107] This new foundation is organized into three sections. First, a safeguarding unit receives reports of abuse, harassment, or intentional harm, determines if any FIG rules have been broken, and if an investigation is necessary, who should be involved in it (including external experts). Second, a disciplinary section may conduct investigations and impose disciplinary sanctions. This section also includes an appeal tribunal. The FIG emphasized that an important role of the tribunal is to clear the name of those wrongly accused, which though an important principle of justice, casts some doubt over the FIG's will to create an athlete-centered reporting mechanism.[108] Third, a compliance unit seeks to monitor good governance and the application of the FIG's ethical principles.[109] The FIG's role is to create policies, deliver education, and support to member federations. This appears to mirror a similar establishment at the IOC level.[110] A gymnastics code of ethics had been established in 2001, but no one was responsible for enforcing it. The FIG created a new code of ethics in 2019, which is one of the core documents that the Gymnastics Ethics Foundation uses in its assessment of complaints and monitoring of compliance. An FIG athletes' network ensures athletes are involved in finding solutions to these problems. President Watanabe explained in 2019: "The athletes are the best people to know what is happening on site and I believe that young athletes themselves must create their own future. . . . The FIG will entrust our bright future to the young generation."[111] The spirit of this initiative is athlete empowerment, but it remains to be seen if this is working. There is little information about how athletes for the working group are selected into this space for building a new gymnastics culture, nor what gender or national quotas will be used to ensure a balanced and diverse group, nor how, or if, each gymnastics discipline will be represented.

The link to the Larry Nassar case is clear. When setting up the new safeguarding structures, the FIG explained that "if we had taken action earlier, the cases in the USA might not have occurred."[112]

Conclusion

Women's artistic gymnastics was created as a space for women in sports: a place where they could practice athleticism without comprising their femininity. This space for women existed not only for athletes but also in the sport's governance, wherein only women could judge the sport and serve on the women's technical committee for the first few decades. Gymnastics was also a space for women coaches. Through their lived experience, women were best placed to teach gymnasts how to participate and compete in sports while protecting, and even promoting, femininity. But by the 1970s, the acrobatic turn was used to legitimize the superiority of male coaches in women's gymnastics. Supposedly, men's larger builds better suited them to spotting female gymnasts through acrobatics elements on each of the apparatuses. Moreover, men were also seen as more scientific and rational, thereby making it more appropriate for them to supervise the periodization of training and coach the precise techniques of acrobatics. Meanwhile, women, being stereotyped as more emotional, were relegated to coaching the expressive "feminine" skills. Women coaches thus became relegated to the "women's work" of dance elements on floor and the beam, while men served as the main coaches. The gendering of coaching reflected conceptions of femininity in gymnastics, defined in terms of hegemonic masculinity that positioned women as subordinate to men. This division, combined with an old boys' network of coach recruitment, led to a dominance of male head coaches in the sport. International cooperation and exchange on coaching methods popularized and perpetuated this dynamic, which was further entrenched during the emigration of former Eastern-bloc coaches.

After the fall of the Soviet Union, Eastern-bloc coaches emigrated to the West. Many clubs actively recruited male head coaches, while women coaches—often the wives—were usually seen as a "bonus." Eastern-bloc coaches brought with them a vast understanding of gymnastics techniques that enabled many countries to improve their gymnastics. But many also worked in an insular manner. They had a highly specialized understanding of gymnastics, but they eschewed support from sports scientists and other support services. They did not see the value in cooperating with other experts, nor were they known for collaborating with their new colleagues. Although their education for gymnasts was excellent, due to this insularity they made far less of an impact on the education of coaches in their new countries. As allegations of abusive coaching arose around the world in the 1990s, many pointed to foreign coaches as the source of the problem. But there is little evidence that problematic coaching is a uniquely Eastern-bloc phenomenon. Such accusations enabled Western coaches and administrators to remove themselves from culpability and to scapegoat foreign coaches.

Although the ranch was set up by two immigrants, Béla and Márta Károlyi, the culture at the national team training center was created and supported by US coaches and officials. They reinforced an isolated training regime that demanded the utmost docility and compliance. Far from being supported, gymnasts were not furnished with sanitary living conditions or adequate nutrition. Many feared speaking up, believing (perhaps correctly) that doing so would put their Olympic ambitions in jeopardy. Their every move was watched, both in the gym and outside, creating a culture of fear in which gymnasts were vulnerable to being preyed upon. The Larry Nassar case was an example of the potential consequences of such an environment.

When the interests of coaching staff, national federations, and the nation itself are prioritized over athlete welfare, it can be very dangerous for the gymnasts. In this environment, the interests of gymnasts have been neglected with alarming frequency. Around the world, and for decades, gymnasts have been telling stories of being abused. There appears to be a globally shared understanding that emotional manipulation, bullying, ignoring injury, and body shaming are requirements for victory in gymnastics. The continued employment of coaches, officials, bureaucrats, and medical staff relies on winning results, so staff in these professional roles are incentivized to do whatever it takes. And if they fail, they are replaced by someone else willing to do it. This model fails to recognize that at the heart of this labor are the gymnasts: real people, often children who do not know any better and who pay for this win-at-all-costs mentality at great cost to their health and well-being.

But several coaches have demonstrated that employing a more protective approach with their athletes can lead to better outcomes. This protective approach has been marked by a willingness to listen to and collaborate with athletes about what their training looks like. It often results in reduced training hours, smaller training loads that reduce injury, and lengthened careers that last into the gymnasts' twenties, if not longer. An emphasis on athlete enjoyment and long-term well-being underpins the decisions made in these relationships. But even when coach-athlete relationships operate at their best, gymnasts have not been shielded from abuse when working within a national team system in which other officials can and do abuse their power, knowing athletes have no recourse available. They cannot simply take their athletic talents elsewhere and compete for another country.

The practice of gymnastics may not be inherently abusive, but it becomes disempowering when gymnasts are consistently relegated to subordinate positions. Gymnasts are seen as children, females, and novices, in relation to coaches and officials who are adults, often men, and cast as experts. In each of these binaries, coaches and officials are positioned as authority figures who have control not only over the gymnasts' day-to-day experiences, but the trajectory of their careers. This is a feature of the hegemonic masculinity that underpins the sport and has resulted in a lack of care for and empowerment of the athletes themselves.

The solution must be in restoring the balance of power between gymnasts and the coaches and officials involved in the sport. This will enable meaningful collaboration with the gymnasts themselves. While there is certainly a place for men in the sport, women could be favored for head coach roles, in which they could model compassionate leadership rather than being pressured to demonstrate so-called masculine leadership styles. This would contribute to shifting the imbalance between male/female values in the sport. To rebalance the novice/expert dynamic, gymnasts' experience could be valued not only in their athletic careers but in their involvement in the sport thereafter, particularly with reference to governing bodies or alternative unions. Governance roles could be made available by requiring athlete representatives on technical, disciplinary, and other committees and commissions so that athletes are embedded in decision-making processes rather than limited to the separate, consultative role of Athletes Commissions. And to address the child/adult dynamic, higher minimum age limits could be put in place to make adult gymnasts a key part of the sport. Higher ages would also rebalance the dynamic of novice and expert, as the gymnast is more experienced, confident, and assertive in their own feeling of their own body and thus able to challenge decisions that will harm their long-term health. These changes would empower gymnasts, facilitate their ability to collaborate with coaches and officials, and create a new athlete-centered culture for the sport.

CONCLUSION

In his 2016 speech to the International Sports Press Association, FIG president Bruno Grandi reflected on the effect of the Cold War on gymnastics. "The geopolitical battles between East and West, which were also played out in sports arenas, now fortunately belong to the last century. But we have taken drastic measures to prevent those little arrangements between friends, as we also did in the past."[1] Beyond the score fixing that Grandi alluded to, the quest to prove national superiority through sports spurred growth and innovation in gymnastics. It changed how women participated in sports more broadly, paradoxically requiring gymnasts to adhere to feminine ideals while also reshaping those ideals as the sport acrobatized and diversified. Despite some resorting to cheating and abuse to achieve victory at any cost, economic shifts reoriented who could triumph. The global conflict shaped gymnastics throughout the second half of the twentieth century. But this book shows that Cold War gymnastics was also punctuated by collaboration and cooperation: between nations, between the FIG and the IOC, and between judges, officials, coaches, and gymnasts. Those interactions all shaped the sport's development and continue to influence gymnastics today.

In the drive to prove ideological supremacy, sports became a key Cold War battleground. Through sports, nations could prove their physical prowess, which represented the health of the people. Athletic victories suggested a strong and fit population, ready to go into battle if necessary. They were also put forward as evidence of a flourishing society, demonstrating the state's cultural values and support for talented citizens. For the United States, sporting victory demonstrated the ascendency of the laissez-faire system providing for individual freedom. For the Soviet Union, its triumphs proved the efficacy of a systematic approach to sports, sponsored and supported by the state. The Cold War lent new meaning to the Olympic Games, elevating their importance to a quadrennial contest of culture between East and West. But from the Soviet Union's first entry in the games in 1952, its large contingent of women athletes won a significant proportion of its medals. The only way for the West to compete with this was to reevaluate its assumptions about the appropriateness of sports for women.

Women in the West had largely been discouraged from sports participation in the early twentieth century, for fears that rigorous exercise would harm women's reproductive health and encourage masculine traits like competitiveness or hard, muscular bodies. Light gymnastics were one of the few forms of exercise widely available to women. The FIG had been formed in the late nineteenth century to organize sportive gymnastics for men. Further, as a European organization, rather than a truly international one, it advocated for gymnastics competitions derived from various European gymnastic traditions. These were nationalist, focused on drill, and aimed to develop healthy bodies. Although the organization became more international in the early twentieth century, it continued its adherence to these European values, and gymnastics competition remained exclusive to men.

In response to Alice Milliat pressuring the IOC to allow women's sports in the 1920s, international federations sought to establish women's divisions through which they could control women's sports. The FIG began developing an international women's gymnastics program. International gymnastics leaders collaborated to develop a standardized international competition program, guiding women's gymnastics through the process of sportification. But many remained cautious of, if not opposed to, women's participation in sports by the middle of twentieth century. Nonetheless, women's gymnastics secured a permanent place on the Olympic roster in 1952 as women's *artistic* gymnastics, a sport in which femininity was the object of competition. Gymnastics gained Olympic and social acceptance as athletes performed in appropriately feminine ways, guided by the FIG's promise that the sport promoted feminine charm and grace. To achieve this, the international members of the women's technical committee negotiated a definition of femininity that would govern the sport. They distinguished the women's apparatuses from the men's, which prevented any kind of comparison between male and female performance, and defined performance expectations based on perceived traits of femininity. Gymnasts performed movements that appeared passive, their bodies limber but delicate. Of course, this was an act designed to fit within understandings of feminine subordination. In fact, appearing to move with such ease masked the huge effort required of gymnasts.

The Cold War imperative to increase women's participation in sports in order to win medals was essential to the development of gymnastics. Women's artistic gymnastics provided a way for women to practice sports without threatening their femininity. Athletes were fully grown women, many of whom had come to gymnastics after earlier training in dance. Soviet gymnasts intentionally performed in a balletic style that reflected the nation's cultural ballet heritage. But the limits of this style were reached within the first two decades of the sport, and by the late 1960s, gymnasts were looking to men's gymnastics for greater complexity and acrobatic innovation. Maintaining the link to their heritage, Soviet gymnasts and coaches also drew on the Russian circus to create new acrobatics. When they continued their dominance using this more dynamic, risky version of women's gymnastics, other nations followed suit and adopted this style. Gymnasts still appeared to perform with ease, but their petite, muscled bodies were evidence of the intense training and effort required for this style of gymnastics.

The acrobatic turn hastened a trend toward youth that was already underway. Women apologized for their acrobatics that transgressed gender by reframing femininity and linking it with youth. The world's best gymnasts today have shown that youth is not physiologically necessary for acrobatics, although it was an important way for acrobatics to be accepted into the women's sport. Young, cute gymnasts could be seen as innocent, docile, and submissive. These traits replaced the passive, mature style of femininity that had characterized the first two decades of the sport. But this interpretation of femininity remained the domain of White women. For Black women, who have long been sexualized, it was perverse for them to be accepted as cute. Moreover, the athletic achievements of Black women in other sports also contributed to an idea that they were less feminine than White women. For Chinese women, performing cuteness invited allegations of age-falsification that drew on Western stereotypes of them as sneaky and untrustworthy. Although these allegations proved true in 2000, media have disproportionately made accusations of Chinese cheating both before and since. Meanwhile, Romanian gymnasts have not been subject to the same allegations, despite substantial evidence of systematic age falsification. This difference highlights the racialized femininities of gymnastics.

Although the early acrobatic gymnasts were not necessarily young in age, they curated an image of youth and cuteness by styling their hair in pigtails and performing routines choreographed to mimic child's play. But on the other hand, US gymnasts were actually children and teenagers before the acrobatic turn in the late 1960s. Since the first women's gymnastics competitions at the games, the United States had been using younger gymnasts than the rest of the world. Over the next twenty years, the age of US gymnasts continued to decline to as low as thirteen. Due to the amateur rules at the time, children were the most readily available demographic who were not required to work for income and could thus afford to train without pay. In the Eastern bloc, state support meant that adult athletes were released from work commitments and could practice gymnastics for a living. However, by the late 1960s the Soviet Union began using younger gymnasts too, although not quite as young as the Americans. Many coaches preferred younger gymnasts for the ease of spotting them through difficult maneuvers, their lack of fear, and their compliance. The success of wunderkinds like fourteen-year-old Nadia Comăneci in the 1970s reinforced an idea around the world that the sport was best suited to girls rather than women.

The FIG supported neither the acrobatic turn nor the trend toward youth. While gymnastics fans today look to the 1970s as a golden era for the sport, FIG commentary at the time complained about the lack of dance skills and connection to music—problems they attributed to acrobatization. The FIG responded in a way typical of sporting leaders: by turning to medical expertise in an attempt to police women's participation in sports. It claimed that the acrobatics on the apparatuses were too dangerous and that young gymnasts could not possibly perform the classical femininity it championed. But medical and scientific experts did not provide the justifications the FIG sought to ban acrobatics. Moreover, the FIG had created the conditions for acrobatization to occur. It modified the equipment to make falls safer, while also making technical upgrades to propel gymnasts higher, like spring floors. In addition, it codified this style through its demands that gymnasts perform acrobatic elements of high difficulty. The popularity of gymnasts fronting this style in the 1970s cemented acrobatics' place in the sport. Olga Korbut was renowned for her acrobatics and her childish nature, becoming a celebrity in Western nations around the world. When Comăneci became the first gymnast to achieve a perfect 10 four years later, she secured the popularity of youthful, acrobatic women's gymnastics in the public imagination.

The celebrity of these gymnasts provided the basis for their states to use them in international diplomacy. For the Eastern bloc, the gymnasts' successes not only proved their sporting superiority and gender equality over the West, they also demonstrated the freedom of movement, liberation, and joy enjoyed by their citizens. Their popular appeal provided for connection across cultures—between the gymnasts, their fans, and even politicians. Both the Soviet Union and Romania sent their star gymnasts on tours of the United States, the United Kingdom, and Australia after their Olympic success, in an effort to gather support and raise funds for their regimes. The gymnasts used bodily discourses to communicate with Western audiences. Through the gymnasts' acrobatics, unbound by the laws of gravity, Western audiences could understand, despite the language barrier, how "free" life in the Eastern bloc was. Meanwhile, Western audiences were more interested in hearing about how their favorite Eastern-bloc athletes loved the West. The gymnasts' exposure to American ideas, experiences, and values were a form of cultural infiltration that sought to undermine the Soviet Union. This discourse enabled the gymnasts to be welcome visitors in the United States, and their popularity catalyzed immense growth in the sport. Despite the disconnect between the Eastern bloc's intended representation of the gymnasts and how the West interpreted their presence, the gymnasts' use in diplomacy ultimately suited both Eastern-bloc and Western leaders. Gymnasts became sporting ambassadors in political negotiations. They represented cooperation between East and West.

But just as sports were used to aid in achieving détente, they were also used as a weapon in the following decade, when two Olympic Games were boycotted. The political reasons different countries gave for their boycotts exemplified the suspicion that pervaded this period, denying opponents a chance to host a propaganda-filled Olympics as Adolf Hitler had in Berlin in 1936. The problems surrounding the 1980s games highlight the importance of viewing the IOC and FIG as international nongovernmental organizations that are nonetheless actors in international diplomacy. Both organizations facilitated relations between the superpowers and globalized the sport. Until the 1980s, the Olympic Games were one of the few sites where the powers engaged directly with one another. After the boycotts, the IOC increased its political presence, overseeing negotiations for cooperation and even collaboration between East and West through sports. In this way the IOC acted not only as a political entity but also as the leader of world sports, including gymnastics.

Much of the way women's gymnastics is practiced comes from IOC directives and pressures. The FIG consistently cooperated, comprised, and negotiated with the IOC in order to keep gymnastics in the Olympic family. The Olympic Games have always been the pinnacle event in gymnastics, and it is only relatively recently that the FIG developed an international program with annual events like world championships and world cups. The FIG's commitment to amateur sports while the rest of international sports movement was professionalizing further intensified its reliance on the IOC and its attendant funding.[2] Gymnastics needed to be included in the Olympic Games, but the IOC constantly threatened the FIG with reducing or eliminating the gymnastics program. When extreme sports intruded on gymnastics' monopoly over aerial contests in the 1990s, the FIG moved to make gymnastics more entertaining. It shortened competition times and removed compulsory routines, and it abolished cumulative scoring so that only scores in the final competition round counted toward the end result.

The biggest change to gymnastics came when the FIG abandoned the perfect 10. "Everyone loved the 10 because it was the symbol of perfection," recalls Grandi, the FIG president responsible for pushing through the open-ended Code of Points in 2006. "But the 10 was in fact restrictive, because it did not permit the judges to separate the difficulty level of exercises and the quality of their execution."[3] The 10 put a cap on scores, limiting the distance that could be achieved between good and exceptional performers. The open-ended, post-10 Code was the result of Olympic pressure, after sustained scrutiny over gymnastics' subjective judging. There had been too much collaboration where there should have been none. Judges, coaches, and officials conspired to arrange the final results by fixing the scores. The United States had been largely excluded from the arrangements between judges and officials due to its status as Cold War adversary of the most notorious of cheaters, but also because its officials failed to engage in the political networking that happened off the competition floor. The dissolution of the USSR created more countries attempting to fix scores. To reduce such cheating, the FIG introduced computer-aided refereeing, but this could not prevent subjective judging. Suspicious about the number of ties being awarded in gymnastics judging, the IOC made the FIG enact a tie-breaking rule after 1996—a rule that has undergone numerous changes since then and has only ever been applied in Olympic competition.

As judging problems and IOC pressure only increased, the FIG undertook developing a more objective scoring system. Men's and women's technical committee members from around the world collaborated on the new system, but strong opposition from some of gymnastics' top countries was enough to stop it from being implemented at the turn of the twenty-first century. However, another judging scandal at the 2004 Olympics provided the opportunity for FIG leaders to push through the open-ended code. With the post-10 code, gymnastics was reframed as a sport in which athletes could break numerical records and spectators could witness history in the making. It was designed to appeal to the modern audience. The changes to gymnastics scoring system restored gymnastics' position as a top-tier sport in the Olympic movement, paralleled only by swimming and track and field.[4] The open-ended code was part of a wider program designed to improve public perceptions of gymnastics and thus attract spectators and money for the FIG. But the new code came at the cost of the perfect 10 that had been fundamental to gymnastics' identity, the ideal score around which the sport had been built.

The United States' rise came as Olympic sports were shifting away from amateurism. In the 1980s, it became possible for athletes in the United States to pursue sponsorships and other commercial benefits from their athletic success. Until then, Eastern-bloc athletes had a great advantage due to the system of incentives and rewards bestowed on successful athletes and coaches. State support meant that they also did not need to find resources to support their training costs in the same way Western athletes did. Western commentators criticized the IOC's economic policy that allowed this, claiming it broke the amateur rule. By the 1980s, the IOC relaxed its position to allow athletes to profit from their sport. But the FIG remained opposed to any kind of professionalization, showing economic policy to be a place of challenge, rather than cooperation, between both sports organizations as well as athletes and fans. When the West professionalized, economic opportunities grew, and simultaneously, so did their gymnastic success. Mary Lou Retton was the first to capitalize on her Olympic fame, and scores of US gymnasts followed in her footsteps. Meanwhile, economic opportunities for Eastern-bloc gymnasts were in decline as sports funding was cut under glasnost and perestroika. By the 1990s, economic downturn after the collapse of the Soviet Union pushed many coaches to migrate to the West in search of work.

Western gymnastics clubs recruited mostly male coaches, with their wives seen as bonuses to employ in subordinate positions. As in the practice of gymnastics, its coaching was gendered too. Although women's gymnastics' demand for performance of femininity meant that women coaches were not stigmatized as lesbians, as they were in other sports, women's gymnastics still employed a hegemonic masculinity that often placed female coaches below male head coaches. As coaching professionalized in the 1970s, more men began working in women's sports. In women's gymnastics, the ascension of male coaches to top roles was justified in the increased acrobatics of the sport, which required larger bodies to lift gymnasts through the movements and catch them if they fell. However, it was also linked to the increased scientific expertise that acrobatics supposedly required. The gendering of coaching was consistent with the prejudicial notion that men were naturally more intelligent and better suited to this work, while women, being more emotional, were better suited to teaching the "feminine" elements and dance. With the support of the FIG, a Soviet coach shared this advice with the Australian Gymnastics Federation, assuring them that this gendered division of labor was common in Soviet gymnastics. This trend became common in many parts of the world, and even where women became leaders, they may have still felt pressure to eschew qualities seen as feminine (like care, listening, collaborating) in order to justify their position in a typically masculine role. This dynamic added a gendered power imbalance between coach and gymnast to the already existing imbalances of expert/novice and adult/child that subordinated gymnasts. Part of the solution to athlete maltreatment in women's gymnastics then, must lie in rebalancing gender in the sport—creating more space for women coaches and leaders who demonstrate caring, compassionate, athlete-centered decision making.

After the Cold War, the migration of former Soviet coaches led to immense improvements to the gymnastics programs of Western nations around the world. The technical knowledge they brought with them created new possibilities for Western athletes. But these coaches were not known for cooperating with their colleagues in their new countries. They seldom shared their expertise with other coaches, and in turn, former Eastern-bloc coaches were often treated with mistrust.

Blaming foreign coaches for the problems of abuse and maltreatment in women's gymnastics perpetuates the anticommunist, Red Scare rhetoric that underscored the Cold War in the West. It Others the problem of abuse in women's gymnastics, absolving Westerners of their sins instead of demanding that everyone critically reflect on their own impact on the sport. Almost since the sport's inception, some of the world's most celebrated gymnasts have been subjected to questionable coaching practices. Taken together, these incidents suggest that women's artistic gymnastics has developed insidious cultural practices that have been accepted as the norm to achieve success for their gymnasts. While certainly not present at every gymnasium or at every level, a culture of fear is nonetheless endemic to women's artistic gymnastics around the world and has been for decades. These practices go beyond isolated coaches, pointing to a systemic cultural problem created by administrators, officials, and the gymnastics programs they shape. They are united by a determination not to listen to gymnasts, but instead to prioritize the success of the nation and the continued employment of coaches, officials, and support staff over athlete welfare. This system represents a breakdown in cooperation between sports professionals and the gymnasts themselves. And by the end of 2020, gymnasts were making this known to the public under the social media hashtag "gymnast alliance," which spread throughout Europe and Oceania. But this problem is not unique to gymnastics. The will to sustain the coaches' and officials' employment and promote national interests underpins many elite sports, and has resulted in the de-prioritization of athlete welfare across a number of sports. If the FIG is serious about restoring gymnastics' credibility, it must address the imbalance of power that lies at the heart of these issues.

These issues undermine the potential that gymnastics has as a feminist pursuit. Although space for women's gymnastics was carved out of institutions run by men and designed to promote the West's limited conceptions of what women can and should be, it has also provided opportunities for women to govern, coach, and compete in sports. In doing so, it served an important role in quelling fears that women's participation in sports would position them outside socially accepted femininity or ruin their health. Women's gymnastics thus provided an important example for early advocates of women's sports, which opened the door for women's participation in other sports. It also taught women to have full control and agency over their bodies on apparatuses and in the air, allowing them access risky, challenging experiences that have usually been the preserve of masculinity. But while the gymnastics themselves may have been empowering, the way it has been taught and the narrow feminine values it has espoused have certainly curtailed gymnastics' feminist potential.

Yet, in this new millennium, a number of coaches have proven that gymnastics can be an empowering experience. Protecting an athlete's mind and body can make their sporting experience more sustainable, and around the world careers are lengthening as a result of such practices. An increasing number of gymnasts are going to multiple world championships and Olympic Games, not only competing well into their twenties and sometimes longer, but also still winning at this age. Central to this approach has been collaboration between the gymnasts, their coaches, and support staff. Any question as to the value of such coaching has firmly quashed since both Shawn Johnson and Simone Biles achieved Olympic glory after finding coaches who employed protective, empowering, and collaborative training experiences that focused on fun. Meanwhile, other "older" gymnasts coach themselves, which allows them to choose how they practice in order to find joy in the sport and use their self-knowledge to protect their bodies from injury. This increased maturity allows gymnasts to make informed decisions about training, risk, and reward, and it increases their ability to speak out against abuse. This sees gymnasts access the "master" role in the dynamic between gymnast and coach (or other official), addressing one of the three major imbalances of power in the sport. However, although these adult gymnasts are better equipped to practice gymnastics in a safe manner, they can still be subject to intimidation and retribution for speaking up when it comes to national squad selections.[5]

The FIG too is trying to promote a cultural shift, establishing an ethics foundation that attempts to police inappropriate coaching and other harm in the sport. But with allegations of abuse continuing to surface regularly in all parts of the world, the FIG's initiatives do not appear to be strong enough—or it is too soon to tell how effective they will be, given the Gymnastics Ethics Foundation was only recently established. While the FIG cannot demand how each country creates its elite gymnastics system and team selection criteria, it does have the power to ban coaches and administrators. It could even ban entire nations from international competition if it strengthened the rules and enforced the code of ethics. Moreover, the FIG could tackle some of the prejudices about femininity, compliance, and the necessity of early specialization by revisiting the minimum age rule. This would address a second part of the power imbalance between gymnasts and coaches and officials: that of adult/child. Raising the minimum age would require all countries to develop more sustainable coaching practices and national programs that keep gymnasts in the sport longer, or better yet, allow them to enter the sport later, from a place where athletes can make their own informed decisions about balancing the will to win with long-term health consequences.

In a sport designed to appear passive and effortless, the cost of success has always been hidden. Key to many of the problems in the sport has been an imbalance between those coaches and officials who find paid employment in it, and those athletes who support them. Too often, those athletes have been children, and this expectation has been cemented by successive gymnasts who look or act young and are lauded in the media for their prodigious skill. But gymnasts are once again having longer careers, winning at older ages, and reclaiming their agency, speaking up for social change like the gymnasts of decades ago. In doing so they are acting to restore the equilibrium between them and the coaches and officials who govern the sport.

This balance of power among people is one aspect of the larger story of balance that defines gymnastics. The sport was created to carefully display femininity without challenging masculinity. During the Cold War, nations used women's gymnastics to assert their sporting supremacy. The IOC asserted its role as the authority of international sports, while the FIG found its position at the bosom of the IOC. All of these themes played out in relation to one another, showing that the history of gymnastics has been characterized by efforts to achieve a balance of power. But to be successful and self-sustaining, women's gymnastics needs to look to its feminist roots and listen to the gymnasts. In doing so, it will also return to being a safe, empowering experience for the women at its center.

NOTES

Abbreviations

NOC   National Olympic Committee
OSC   Olympic Studies Centre, Lausanne, Switzerland
USOC   US Olympic Committee

Preface

1. Day, "Historical Perspectives on Coaching," 6.
2. Prochasson, "Les jeux du 'je'."
3. Castan-Vicente, Nicolas, and Cervin, "Women in Sport Organisations."
4. Interviews took place between 2013 and 2018 in a semi-structured manner that, in some cases, included follow-up questions by e-mail. Five participants had been members of the FIG Executive Committee or a FIG technical committee. Five were international coaches and judges who were also highly influential in their national programs (and are sometimes referred to as "administrators" or "officials" in the text). Many fulfilled all of these roles at various stages in their careers. Almost all were once gymnasts themselves.

Introduction

1. "Brace of Balanced Beauties."
2. Dichter, "Diplomatic and International History," 1742.
3. Caute, *Dancer Defects*.
4. Keys, *Globalizing Sport*, 17.
5. See, for instance, the edited volume Wagg and Andrews, *East Plays West*.
6. Shaw, "Politics of Cold War Culture," 59.

7. Llewellyn and Gleaves, *Rise and Fall*; Pieper, *Sex Testing*; Beamish and Ritchie, "Totalitarian Regimes"; Hunt, *Drug Games*; Rinehart, "Cold War Expatriot Sport."

8. *Cold War Games.*

9. Congelio, "In Defense of a Neoliberal America"; Sarantakes, *Dropping the Torch.*

10. Vonnard, Sbetti, and Quin, "Divided but Not Disconnected," 5.

11. Ibid.

12. Mellis, "From Defectors to Cooperators."

13. Dichter and Johns, *Diplomatic Games*; Dichter, "Diplomatic and International History"; Postlethwaite and Grix, "Beyond the Acronyms"; Pigman, "International Sport"; Murray, "Sports Diplomacy."

14. According to Schunz, Scott-Smith, and Langenhove, soft diplomacy includes "non-governmental actors, is substantially linked to 'soft issues' (that is, not security-related or economic issues), and involves 'two-way' rather than one-way exchanges. Typical 'soft issues' which are subject to soft diplomacy are culture, science and higher education." Schunz, Scott-Smith, and Van Langenhove, "Broadening Soft Power," 8.

15. Huggins, *Victorians and Sport*, 52.

16. Saull, *Rethinking Theory and History*, 15.

17. Gleaves, "Doped Professionals and Clean Amateurs"; Gleaves and Hunt, *Global History of Doping*; Paul Dimeo, "Good Versus Evil?"; Sands, "Why Gymnastics?"

18. Hall, *Girl and the Game*, 158; Schweinbenz and Cronk, "Femininity Control."

19. Kimmel, "Men's Responses to Feminism," 262; Messner, "Sports and Male Domination," 200; Hargreaves, *Sporting Females*, 43; Elias and Dunning, *Quest for Excitement*; Anaïs Bohuon, "Afterword," 335.

20. Vertinsky, *Eternally Wounded Woman*, 39, 55–56; Chisholm, "Incarnations and Practices."

21. Vertinsky, "Exercise, Physical Capability," 21–22; Chisholm, "Nineteenth—Century Gymnastics."

22. Cahn, *Coming on Strong*, 4–5.

23. Wamsley, "Womanizing Olympic Athletes," 274.

24. In the period 1952–92, 180 medals were available for any one country to win, with each Olympics holding the possibility of winning: one medal in the team competition, three medals in the all-around competition, three medals in each of the four apparatuses until 1972 and from 1976 onward, two medals in each of the four apparatuses. The Soviet Union competed for 144 of these medals, as it boycotted the 1984 Olympics and no longer competed as one country after 1992. Of these 144 potential medals, the Soviet Union won 93, giving it a success rate of 65 percent. By contrast, its closest contender, Romania, won 39 of 156 potential medals, giving it a success rate of 25 percent. "Official Olympic Games Results."

25. Riordan, *Sport in Soviet Society*.

26. Barker-Ruchti, "Ballerinas and Pixies"; C. O'Brien, "Investigation."

27. Riordan, "Rise, Fall and Rebirth."

Chapter 1. The Origins of Women's Artistic Gymnastics

1. Pfister, "Epilogue," 2052.

2. Krüger and Hofmann, "Development of Physical-Education Institutions."

3. GutsMuths quoted in Naul, *Olympic Education,* 41.

4. Pfister, "Epilogue," 2052.

5. GutsMuths, *Gymnastics for youth,* 87.

6. GutsMuths quoted in Naul, *Olympic Education,* 41.

7. Krüger and Hofmann, "Development of Physical-Education Institutions," 738.

8. See Diem, "Per Henrik Ling," 5.

9. Ibid.

10. Fair, "Physical Culture"; Pfister, "Cultural Confrontations."

11. Pfister, "Cultural Confrontations," 69.

12. "International Gymnastics Federation (FIG) Correspondence" folder (D-RM02-GYMNA/003), OSC.

13. Under the First French Empire, the Confederation of the Rhine was formed from sixteen German states, including Prussia and Austria, between 1806 and 1813.

14. Gerber, *Innovators and Institutions,* 128; Pfister, "Cultural Confrontations."

15. Ibid., 136.

16. Ibid., 137.

17. Pfister, "Cultural Confrontations," 66.

18. Gerber, *Innovators and Institutions,* 135.

19. Ibid., 138.

20. Shephard, *Illustrated History,* 638.

21. See Nolte, *Sokol in the Czech Lands.*

22. Sabri Özçakır, "Heroes!"

23. Sanislo, "Protecting Manliness," 265; and Pfister, "Cultural Confrontations," 74.

24. Pfister, "Cultural Confrontations," 70.

25. Barker-Ruchti, "Stride Jump."

26. Ibid., 22; Vertinsky, "Exercise, Physical Capability," 21.

27. Hargreaves, *Sporting Females,* 77.

28. Chisholm, "Gymnastics."

29. Margaret Coxe quoted in Park, "Embodied Selves," 1521; Chisholm, "Gymnastics," 1292.

30. Chisholm, "Incarnations and Practices," 737.

31. Chisholm, "Disciplinary Dimensions," 443.

32. Ibid., 449.

33. "History."

34. Cervin et al., "Gymnastics' Centre of Gravity," 2.

35. Article 37 of Greek Law BXKA of 1899, in Koulouri, "Introduction," 52.

36. "History."

37. Ibid.; "Gymnastics and Archery," 9.

38. Carpentier and Lefèvre, "Modern Olympic Movement," 1113.

39. Minutes of the IOC Executive Board meetings, Lausanne, October 31, 1927, and Vienna, June 5, 1933, in ibid., 1122, 1114, 1126.

40. Ibid., 1115. See Cervin, Elias, and Quin, "From the Carpet," 245–72.

41. Van Rossem, *Ninth Olympiad*, 655.

42. The Olympics were not held during World War II.

43. "Gymnastics at the 1936 Summer Games."

44. "Gymnastics at the 1948 London Summer Games."

45. Lawrence, "Postponement and Progression."

46. From the late 1960s onward, FIG promoted rhythmic gymnastics as "modern gymnastics."

47. Minutes of IOC Executive Board meeting, Lausanne, June 11, 1932, in Carpentier and Lefèvre, "Modern Olympic Movement," 1115.

48. "Minutes of the Copenhagen Session, 15, 16, 17 May 1950," folder "IOC Archives—Sessions and Executive Committee" (CIO SESS-045ES-PV), OSC.

49. Chisholm, "Incarnations and Practices," 740.

50. Latynina's dominance across all apparatuses at successive Olympics was such that she held the record for most Olympic medals at the age of eighteen for nearly fifty years, in 2012 finally surpassed by US swimmer Michael Phelps.

51. Nauright and Parrish, *Sports around the World*, 2:333.

52. Riordan, *Sport in Soviet Society*, 19–33.

53. Karl Marx quoted in ibid., 59.

54. Riordan, *Sport in Soviet Society*, 137.

55. Riordan, *Sport in Soviet Society*, 162.

56. Ibid., 163.

57. Parks, "Verbal Gymnastics," 31.

58. Ibid.

59. Riordan, *Sport in Soviet Society*, 331–33.

60. Pope, *New American Sport History*.

61. Bottenburg, "Why Are the European and American Sports Worlds So Different?"

62. Montez de Oca, "Muscle Gap," 124.

63. Rider, "Projecting America," 19; Montez de Oca, "Muscle Gap," 132–33.

64. "Timeline."

65. Laptad, "Origin, Development, and Function," 169–71.

66. Montez de Oca, "Muscle Gap," 123.

67. Schultz, *Qualifying Times*, 85.

68. Ibid., 90.

69. Grossfeld, "History."

Chapter 2. From Amateurism to Professionalism

1. Wagg, "Tilting at Windmills?" 328.

2. Rider, *Cold War Games*, 47.

3. Cervin et al., "Gymnastics' Centre of Gravity."

4. Llewellyn and Gleaves, *Rise and Fall*, 9–12.

5. Ibid., 13.

6. Huggins, *Victorians and Sport*, 52.

7. Llewellyn and Gleaves, *Rise and Fall*, 59.

8. Llewellyn and Gleaves quote from Coubertin's memoirs: "Today I can admit it; the [amateur] question never really bothered me. It had served as a screen to convene the Congress designed to revive the Olympic Games. Realizing the importance attached to it in sporting circles, I always showed the necessary enthusiasm, but it was enthusiasm without any real conviction" (*Rise and Fall*, 23).

9. Rider, "Olympic Games."

10. Allison Danzig, "Russia Far Ahead of 68 Other Nations as Olympic Games End in Melbourne," *New York Times*, December 8, 1956.

11. Parks, "Verbal Gymnastics," 30.

12. "Athletics in Russia Impress Brundage," *New York Times*, August 1, 1954; "Brundage Praises Russian Athletes," *New York Times*, August 3, 1954.

13. Hazanov, "Porous Empire," 97–104.

14. "Brundage Praises Russian Athletes."

15. "Brundage Hints at 'Open' Olympics," *Canberra Times*, February 14, 1968.

16. Danzig, "Russia Far Ahead."

17. "Russian Victories Call for Scrutiny of Soviet Amateur Code, Official Says," *New York Times*, March 10, 1954.

18. "Brundage Decries 'State Amateurs'," *New York Times*, October 14, 1953.

19. Ken Moses, "Amateurs? Who Are You Trying to Kid U.S.?" *Melbourne Argus*, June 19, 1956.

20. Rider, "Olympic Games," 7.

21. Llewellyn and Gleaves, *Rise and Fall*, 114.

22. "'Lifers' Grin at Avery's Rule," *Melbourne Argus*, August 3, 1956; "Olympians Put Avery Brundage on the Spot," *Sports Illustrated*, August 27, 1956.

23. Avery Brundage quoted in "State Amateurs Ruled Ineligible," *New York Times*, September 28, 1962.

24. Llewellyn and Gleaves, *Rise and Fall*, 61.

25. Simonton, *History of European Women's Work*, 166.

26. Danzig, "Russia Far Ahead."

27. Yoculan and Donaldson, *Perfect 10*, 12.

28. Wolf and LaBella, "Epidemiology of Gymnastics Injuries," 16.

29. Interview with Hardy Fink, 2014. Fink has held a Brevet judging qualification in MAG since 1969.

30. "Team All Around, Women," Sports Reference. Ages found by accessing biographic information for gymnasts on each of these teams at each summer Olympics. These data can be verified with that supplied by Olympic.org. The Sports Reference Website is now offline, but similar data can be accessed at olympedia.org/event_types/333.

31. Barker-Ruchti, "Ballerinas and Pixies," 50.

32. R. Kerr, "Impact of Nadia Comaneci," 89.

33. Llewellyn and Gleaves, *Rise and Fall*, 152.

34. Arthur Daley, "Sport of the Times: The Impossible Dream," *New York Times,* May 15, 1967.

35. Ibid.; Don Schollander and Duke Savage, "Amateurism Is Dead," *New York Times*, July 14, 1971; Gleaves, "Doped Professionals and Clean Amateurs."

36. Schollander and Savage, "Amateurism Is Dead."

37. Ibid.; Dave Anderson, "The Olympic Flame of Hypocrisy," *New York Times*, February 3, 1976; Llewellyn and Gleaves, *Rise and Fall*, 142.

38. Wenn and Martyn, "Juan Antonio Samaranch's Score Sheet," 310–11.

39. Wenn, "Peter Ueberroth's Legacy," 160.

40. Juan Antonio Samaranch quoted in "Olympics: Amateurism Obsolete," *Canberra Times,* January 30, 1981; Wenn and Martyn, "Juan Antonio Samaranch's Score Sheet," 318–19.

41. Neil Amdur, "An Olympic Issue," *New York Times,* December 26, 1982; "Minutes of the 84th I.O.C. Session: Baden-Baden, 29th September to 2nd October 1981," 1981, folder "IOC Archives—Sessions and Executive Committee" (CIO SESS-049ES-PV), OSC.

42. Although tennis players under the age of twenty had been allowed to participate at Los Angeles, tennis was an exhibition sport at those games.

43. Robert McGill Thomas Jr., "Olympics to Allow Pros in 3 Sports," *New York Times,* March 1, 1985.

44. "Move to Open Up Olympic Games to Professionals," *Canberra Times,* February 14, 1986; "'No Haste' in Allowing Olympic Pros," *Canberra Times,* April 26, 1986.

45. Yuri Titov, "Executive Committee of the F.I.G.: Summary of the Minutes of the Meetings Held in Helsinki on 8th and 9th May 1985," *FIG Bulletin* 128 (March 1986): 96.

46. Yuri Titov, "F.I.G. Executive Committee: Summary of the Minutes of the Meetings Held in Washington from 27th February to 3rd March 1986," *FIG Bulletin* 130 (September 1986).

47. Ibid.

48. "Rules of Eligibility for the Federation Internationale de Gymanstique," *FIG Bulletin* 137 (1988): 125.

49. "Longines Watches—the Partner of Gymnastics," *FIG Bulletin* 125 (September 1985).

50. Yuri Titov, "Report Submitted to the Congress," *FIG Bulletin* 154 (September 1992): 38; and Yuri Titov, "F.I.G. President Report: 1996," *FIG Bulletin* 168 (December 1996): 125–29.

51. Krieger, "Born on the Wings," 429.

52. Lawrie Mifflin, "A Lesson in Gold-Medal Economics," *New York Times,* September 24, 1984. For instance, Kurt Thomas starred in the film *Gymkata*, Mary Lou Retton had her own television show, and Kristie Phillips also transitioned into acting.

53. Kirshenbaum, "Scorecard," 16.

54. Fink interview.

55. Barker-Ruchti, "Ballerinas and Pixies," 49; Riordan, *Sport in Soviet Society*, 235–36, 269–71; Brokhin, *Big Red Machine*, 51.

56. Titov, "Report Submitted to the Congress."

57. Morinari Watanabe, "The President's Report," *FIG Bulletin* 246 (April 2019): 110.

58. Yuri Titov, "F.I.G. President Report: 1996," 128. All dollar amounts are US dollars.

59. Titov, "F.I.G. President Report: 1996," 128.

60. Zina Terrier, "Minutes of the General Assembly, 18–20 October 2016," *FIG Bulletin* 238 (December 2016): 91.

61. Bruno Grandi, "Presidential Report," *FIG Bulletin* 180 (June 2000): 104.

62. "Olympics—-IOC Sports Revenue Rankings," *Reuters*, May 30, 2013, https://www.reuters.com/article/olympics-athletics-revenues-idUSL3N0EA2F620130529; Keith, "Swimming Jumps to Top."

63. "Olympic Marketing Factfile."

64. "82nd General Assembly, Baku, 2nd and 3rd December 2018, Financial Matters," *FIG Bulletin* 246 (April 2019): 131.

65. Watanabe, "President's Report."

Chapter 3. Diplomacy in Gymnastics and the Olympic Movement

1. Keys, *Globalizing Sport*, 2, 7.

2. Llewellyn and Gleaves, *Rise and Fall*, 132.

3. Dichter and Johns, *Diplomatic Games*, 3.

4. Nye, *Soft Power*, x, 5.

5. Schunz, Scott-Smith, and Langenhove, "Broadening Soft Power."

6. Rider, *Cold War Games*.

7. Hoffman, "Reconstructing Diplomacy," 526.

8. Dichter and Johns, *Diplomatic Games*; Dichter, "Diplomatic and International History"; Postlethwaite and Grix, "Beyond the Acronyms."

9. Vonnard, Sbetti, and Quin, *Beyond Boycotts*.

10. Cour, "Evolution of the 'Public'"; Cull, "Public Diplomacy."

11. Rider and Witherspoon, "Making Contact."

12. Saul, "Program That Shattered the Iron Curtain"; Kozovoi, "Foot in the Door"; Prevots, *Dance for Export*, 69.

13. Kondrashina, "Soviet Music Recordings."

14. Fulda, "Emergence of Citizen Diplomacy."

15. Thomas, *Globetrotting*, 3.

16. Carter and Sugden, "USA and Sporting Diplomacy."

17. Barker-Ruchti, "Ballerinas and Pixies," 56; R. Kerr, "Impact of Nadia Comaneci," 94; Varney, "Labour of Patriotism."

18. In her autobiography, Korbut recalled her coach Renald Knysh's words to her: "Smile! Otherwise, the spectator will see how hard you're working, and the

illusion will be lost." Korbut and Emerson-White, *My Story*, 37; Varney, "Labour of Patriotism," 1.

19. Karolyi and Richardson, *Feel No Fear*, 8–9, 12–16, 22, 39.

20. Ibid., 45—51. Comăneci first caught the attention of the gymnastics world when she won the all-around competition against the previously unbeatable Soviets at her first international competition, the 1972 Friendship Cup in Bulgaria. Three years later, in Skien, Norway, Comăneci became the European champion, which was then the third most prestigious all-around title.

21. Deford, "Nadia Awed Ya."

22. Zhang, "Bending the Body for China."

23. Barker-Ruchti, *Women's Artistic Gymnastics*, 147.

24. Dufraisse, *Les héros du sport*, 222–23, 253.

25. Mellis, "From Defectors to Cooperators."

26. Dufraisse, *Les héros du sport*, 224.

27. *Sovetsky Sport* quoted in Riordan, *Sport in Soviet Society*, 379.

28. Gerald Eskenazi, "Even Her Quotes Are Guarded," *New York Times*, March 23, 1973. The 1973 tour was reported to have raised approximately $56,000 at the time.

29. Neil Amdur, "A Soviet Pixie Invades the United States," *New York Times*, March 8, 1973.

30. Ibid.; Gerald Eskenazi, "Olga: Overshadowed; 19,694 Don't Care," *New York Times*, March 24, 1973; Duffy, "Hello to a Russian Pixie."

31. Gerald Eskenazi, "19,000 Go Wild over Olga," *New York Times*, November 16, 1974.

32. Evidence of the 1975 tour can be found in Steve Cady, "Soviet Gymnasts Keep Garden Crowd in a Whirl," *New York Times*, December 8, 1975.

33. Glen Levy, "Olga Korbut's Olympic Journey," *Time*, August 3, 2012.

34. Zaglada, *One Coach's Journey*, 30.

35. Varney, "Labour of Patriotism," 48.

36. Levy, "Olga Korbut's Olympic Journey."

37. Zaglada, *One Coach's Journey*, 31.

38. Cady, "Soviet Gymnasts"; Eskenazi, "Olga: Overshadowed."

39. "Soviet Gym Team Makes U.S. Debut," *New York Times*, March 11, 1973; Amdur, "Soviet Pixie."

40. Duffy, "Hello to a Russian Pixie."

41. Tony Kornheiser, "Olga Korbut, Still the One They Like to Watch," *New York Times*, December 17, 1976.

42. Ibid.

43. Keys, "Soviet Union, Cultural Exchange."

44. Kordas, "Rebels, Robots," 198.

45. Nixon, Scowcroft, and Soviet Women's Gymnastics Team, "Memorandum of Conversation."

46. Eskenazi, "Even Her Quotes Are Guarded."

47. Nixon, Scowcroft, and Soviet Women's Gymnastics Team, "Memorandum of Conversation."

48. "N.B.C. Nightly News"; Nixon, Scowcroft, and Soviet Women's Gymnastics Team, "Memorandum of Conversation."

49. Glen Levy, "Olga Korbut's Olympic Journey," *Time Magazine*, August 3, 2012.

50. Glen Levy, "Olga Korbut's Olympic Journey," *Time Magazine*, August 3, 2012.

51. Riordan, *Sport in Soviet Society*, 378; Horne, *Kissinger*, 157–58, 165; Keys, "Nixon/Kissinger and Brezhnev," 548–49; Office of the Historian, "Chronology."

52. Riordan, *Sport in Soviet Society*, 378.

53. In her autobiography, Comăneci recalls, "I was a national treasure because I made my government's rule and way of life look good." Comaneci, *Letters to a Young Gymnast*, 64.

54. "Rumanian Gymnasts to Tour U.S.," *New York Times*, July 21, 1976.

55. Verschoth, "Great Leap Backward"; Russell J. Davis, "The Olympics Revisited: Perfection and Crybabies," *New York Times*, August 29, 1976.

56. Robin Herman, "A New-Look Miss Comaneci at the Garden," *New York Times*, October 10, 1977.

57. Robert Mcg. Thomas Jr. "Women in the Locker Room: 1990; Struggles Are Similar to Those of the 70's," *New York Times*, October 3, 1990.

58. "People in Sports: Miss Comaneci Reported Ill; 5-City U.S. Tour Canceled," *New York Times*, March 2, 1977.

59. "Quake Halts Gymnasts," *New York Times*, 8 March 1977; and "Check Awaits Nadia," *New York Times*, May 1, 1977.

60. Herman, "A New-Look Miss Comaneci at the Garden."

61. "People in Sports," *New York Times*, November 22, 1978.

62. Comaneci, *Letters to a Young Gymnast*, 111–13; "Karoly, Coach of Miss Comaneci, Defects to the US," *New York Times*, April 8, 1981.

63. "People in Sports," *New York Times*, November 22, 1978.

64. Prados, "Notes"; Rubinstein, "Soviet Imperialism."

65. Mason, "Bridge to Change," 283.

66. Guttmann, "Cold War and the Olympics," 559.

67. Sarantakes, *Dropping the Torch*, 12.

68. Gygax, "Raisons et prétextes," 491–92. President Carter and the Western media explained the boycott of the 1980 games as a necessary response to the Soviet invasion of Afghanistan. The context of the oil crisis and the loss of US power in neighboring Iran is missing from this version of events. Gygax shows how boycotting the games was discussed by US politicians as early as 1976 and by US and British press as early as 1977. When Carter became president in 1977, he moved away from a policy of détente; the policy of his new administration would be the defense of human rights instead. Gygax finds that "the Soviets were indirectly encouraged to intervene [in Afghanistan] by the Americans, who are now free to make the Soviets pay for this aggression, this 'threat to the free world'." (507).

69. Mertin, "Soviet Union," 238.

70. Eighty-one nations participated in the games and sixty-two boycotted (although not all over the Afghanistan issue). Some athletes from boycotting nations competed under the Olympic Flag, while those from non-boycotting sports in New Zealand competed under the flag of their national Olympic committee, symbolizing their independence from a government opposed to their participation. Although two New Zealand gymnasts, Rowena Davis and Christine Douglas, reached the qualifying benchmark for the 1980 games, New Zealand Gymnastics decided to join the boycott. The British Olympic Association accepted their Olympic invitation, much to the dismay of their government. Conversely, Canada, initially opposed to a boycott, came around to the idea, joined by Israel and Japan.

71. Sarantakes, *Dropping the Torch*, 234.

72. Ellen Berger, "Report of the Chairman of the W.T.C.," *FIG Bulletin* 110 (September 1981): 70.

73. Jenifer Parks, "Nothing but Trouble."

74. "Report on the Meeting at the Oval Office," May 19, 1980, folder "Correspondence of the NOC of the USA January to June 1980" (D-RM01-ETATU/013), OSC.

75. Mellis, "From Defectors to Cooperators," 61.

76. "Timeline."

77. Cervin, Quin, and Elias, "From the Carpet," 259.

78. See folder "Correspondence of the NOC of the USA July to December 1980" (D-RM01-ETATU/014), OSC.

79. "Report on the Meeting at the Oval Office," May 19, 1980, folder "Correspondence of the NOC of the USA July to December 1980."

80. Béla Károlyi quoted in Neil Amdur, "Influence of United States on Olympics Is Slipping," *New York Times,* February 7, 1982.

81. Aggestam and Towns, "Gender Turn in Diplomacy"; Tonnerre, Vonnard, and Sbetti, "Ghost Administrators."

82. Amdur, "Influence of United States."

83. "F.I.G. Assembly General Held at the State University in Moscow on 16th and 17th July 1980," *FIG Bulletin* 106 (September 1980): 76–77.

84. John F. Burns, "Protests Are Issued: Russians Charge 'Gross Flouting' of the Ideals of the Competition," *New York Times,* May 9, 1984.

85. Mertin, "Soviet Union," 243–47.

86. Guttmann, "Cold War and the Olympics," 565.

87. Edelman, "Russians Are Not Coming!," 11.

88. Mertin, "Soviet Union"; Llewellyn, Gleaves, and Wilson, "Historical Legacy."

89. Since its inception in 1976, the American Cup competition has showcased future Olympic champions such as Nadia Comăneci. The FIG added it to the World Cup Series when it redesigned the international competition program in 2011.

90. "Gymnasts 3–13 Sports," telex, March 13, 1984, folder "Correspondence of the NOC of the USA: January to May 1984" (D-RM01-ETATU/021), OSC.

91. Ellen Berger, "Report of the Chairman of the W.T.C.," *FIG Bulletin* 126 (September 1985): 74.

92. Yuri Titov, "Report of the President Yuri Titov," *FIG Bulletin* 127 (December 1985): 49.

93. Mertin, "Soviet Union," 243.

94. Titov, "Report of the President Yuri Titov."

95. Quoted in Keys, "Political Protection," 1161.

96. Keys, "Political Protection."

97. Ibid.

98. David Lange quoted in Keys, "Political Protection," 1172.

99. Lord Michael Killanin (IOC president) to President Jimmy Carter and President Leonid Brezhnev, telex April 23, 1980, folder "Correspondence of the NOC of the USA January to June 1980."

100. An exception to the IOC's past silence on geopolitical issues was its demand that East and West Germany compete as one nation from 1956 to 1964. In this case, the IOC was adamant that it could only recognize one national Olympic committee for Germany, effectively forcing the two Germanies to work together. But in this case, the IOC worked with the national Olympic committees rather than appealing to government leaders, as it began to do in the 1980s. See Hughes and Owen, "Continuation of Politics," 453–54.

101. "Joint Statement," November 21, 1985, folder "Correspondence of the NOC of the USSR 1985" (DRM01-RUSSI/014), OSC.

102. Juan Antonio Samaranch to President Ronald Reagan, November 18, 1986, folder "Reagan (USA)/Gorbachev (USSR) Summit: Correspondence, Releases and Press Cutting" (DRM01-ETATU/059), OSC.

103. Robert Helmick (USOC) and Marat Gramov (USSR NOC), "Memorandum of Mutual Understanding between United States Olympic Comittee and National Olympic Committee of the Union of Soviet Socialist Republics," September 15,1985, folder "Agreement Signed by the NOC of USA 1979–1988" (D-RM01-ETATU/031), OSC.

104. Ibid.

105. Robert Helmick (USOC) and Marat Gramov (USSR NOC), "Protocol to Memorandum of Mutual Cooperation Between N.O.C.S. of U.S.A. And U.S.S.R.," September 15, 1985, folder "Agreement Signed by the NOC of USA 1979–1988."

106. Ibid. There is no mention of gymnastics in these plans.

107. C. O'Brien, "Investigation."

108. S. Miller and Peary, *It's Not about Perfect*, 23–28.

109. Turner Broadcasting System made agreements with the Soviet government agencies: the Committee on Physical Culture and Sport of the Council of Ministers of the USSR, and the USSR State Committee for Television and Radio, to develop the Games. Ted Turner (Turner Broadcasting System) and B. Tageny (Committee on Physical Culture and Sport of the Council Ministers of the USSR and the State Committee for Television and Radio), "Protocol of Intent," May

29, 1985, folder "1st Edition of the Goodwill Games at Moscow (USSR) in 1986" (H-FC040GOODW/001), OSC.

110. Turner and Tageny, "Protocol of Intent."

111. Vassily Senatorov (USSR NOC press attaché) to R. Gafner (IOC director), "Meetings, Talks, Contacts," September 24, 1986, folder "1st edition of the Goodwill Games at Moscow (USSR) in 1986."

112. Helmick and Gramov, "Protocol to Memorandum."

113. Robert Helmick, Dick Pound, and Juan Antonio Samaranch, "Transcript of Mr. Robert Helmick's Remarks at the Executive Board Meeting on 6th December 1985 in Lausanne," 1985, folder "1st edition of the Goodwill Games at Moscow (USSR) in 1986."

Chapter 4. Making and Breaking the Rules

1. Clastres, "Playing with Greece," 9 (paragraph 23).

2. Anthony Giddens, *Capitalism and Modern Social Theory*, 126–27.

3. M. Miller, "American Football."

4. Guttmann, *From Ritual to Record*, 85. Other scholars have supported this analysis, concurring that measurement and the pursuit of records is what differentiates modern sport from traditional games. Eichberg, "Stronger, Funnier, Deadlier."

5. Keys, *Globalizing Sport*, 6.

6. Darbon, *Les fondements du systeme sportif*; Richard Holt, "Allen Guttmann's Alter Ego."

7. Cervin et al., "Gymnastics' Centre of Gravity," 324.

8. Ritzer, *McDonaldization of Society*, 141.

9. Since at least the 1970s, the FIG has used difficulty classifications to encourage or discourage certain skills. If gymnasts and coaches regard a skill as easy, but the FIG has given it a high difficulty level, then payoff for gymnasts performing it is large. By contrast, many coaches and gymnasts decide that it is not worth it to perform certain skills that have a lower difficulty ranking—it is a needless risk.

10. "Minutes of the 49th I.O.C. Session: Mexico City, 17th–21st April 1953," Minutes to Members of the IOC, 1953, folder "IOC Archives—Sessions and Executive Committee" (CIO SESS-049ES-PV), OSC. This is the first example of gymnastics being suggested as a way to reduce the games.

11. IOC to Charles Thoeni (FIG Secretary General), May 26, 1953, folder "Federation Internationale de Gymnastique (FIG): Correspondence 1906–1959" (D-RM02-GYMNA/003), OSC.

12. Avery Brundage (IOC president) to Count Goblet D'Alveilla (FIG President), June 4, 1954, folder "Federation Internationale de Gymnastique (FIG): Correspondence 1906–1959."

13. Charles Thoeni (FIG president), Ginanni (FIG vice president), Pierre Hentges (MTC president), and Berthe Villancher (Women's Technical Committee president) to Avery Brundage (IOC president), April 10, 1958, folder "Federation

Internationale de Gymnastique (FIG): Correspondence 1906–1959" (D-RM02-GYMNA/003), OSC.

14. Avery Brundage (IOC president) to Charles Thoeni (FIG president), June 28, 1958, folder "Federation Internationale de Gymnastique (FIG): Correspondence 1906–1959."

15. Charles Thoeni (FIG president) to Avery Brundage (IOC president), June 10,1959, folder "Federation Internationale de Gymnastique (FIG): Correspondence 1906–1959."

16. Charles Thoeni (FIG president) to Otto Mayer (IOC chancellor), January 25, 1961, folder "Federation Internationale de Gymnastique (FIG): Correspondence 1960–1976" (D-RM02-GYMNA/004), OSC. Charles Thoeni (FIG president), Pierre Hentjes (MTC president), and Berthe Villancher (Women's Technical Committee president) to Avery Brundage (IOC president), January 20, 1961, folder "Federation Internationale de Gymnastique (FIG): Correspondence 1960–1976," emphasis added. Avery Brundage (IOC president) to Charles Thoeni (FIG general secretary), February 3, 1961, folder "Federation Internationale de Gymnastique (FIG): Correspondence 1960–1976."

17. Quin, "History of Swiss Feminine Gymnastics," 658.

18. Korbut's new, acrobatic gymnastics was almost certainly not the only factor behind the timing of this application. Yuri Titov had also ascended to the FIG vice presidency in 1973, and rhythmic gymnastics already had a significant following in the Soviet Union. He was thus pursuing his country's interests. Moreover, with the discipline having been presided over by the FIG for a decade, it had established enough consistency over the competitions to deem it ready for an Olympic berth. All of these factors combined likely lead to the FIG's request for it to be included in the Olympic program. See Cervin et al., "Gymnastics' Centre of Gravity," 318–19, 326.

19. Arthur Gander, "Executive Committee: Extract from the Minutes of the Meetings Held at Stuttgart from 31st January to 3rd February, 1973," *FIG Bulletin* 77 (June 1973): 34. The sport was eventually included in the Olympics, debuting at the 1984 games.

20. Gander, "Executive Committee."

21. Arthur Gander (FIG president) to Henry Banks (IOC Technical Director), November 20, 1973, "Future Olympic Program for Gymnastics," folder "Federation Internationale de Gymnastique (FIG): Correspondence 1960–1976."

22. Indeed, the Soviet Union won eleven medals in gymnastics, to America's zero. Allison Danzig, "Russia Far Ahead of 68 Other Nations as Olympic Games End in Melbourne," *New York Times,* December 8, 1956.

23. Charles Thoeni (FIG general secretary) to Otto Mayer (IOC chancellor), June 20, 1956, folder "Federation Internationale de Gymnastique (FIG): Correspondence 1906–1959."

24. Charles Thoeni (FIG president) to Avery Brundage (IOC president) and Executive Committee Members of the IOC, October 13, 1956, folder "Federation Internationale de Gymnastique (FIG): Correspondence 1906–1959."

25. Olympic Committee of the USSR, Alexei Romanov, and Konstantin Andrianov to Otto Mayer (IOC chancellor), December 20, 1957, folder "Federation Internationale de Gymnastique (FIG): Correspondence 1906–1959."

26. Folder "Federation Internationale de Gymnastique (FIG): Correspondence 1960–1976"; Avery Brundage (IOC president) to Arthur Gander (FIG president), October 26, 1971, "Gymnast John Crosby Wins 8 Medals at Pan American Games," folder "Federation Internationale de Gymnastique (FIG): Correspondence 1960–1976."

27. Arthur Gander (FIG president) to Authorities of the FIG and Affiliated Federations, October 23, 1973, "Gymnastics Program at the Next Olympic Games," folder "Federation Internationale de Gymnastique (FIG): Correspondence 1960–1976."; and Arthur Gander (FIG president) to Dr. Arpad Csanádi (IOC Program Commission president), May 4, 1973, "Adaptation of the Program for Artistic Gymnastics at Future Olympic Games," folder "Federation Internationale de Gymnastique (FIG): Correspondence 1960–1976."

28. Interview with Hardy Fink, 2014 (a member of the Men's Technical Committee who was therefore privy to such conversations, Fink emphasized that Soviet support was necessary and forthcoming in the change to limit contestants to two per country in apparatus finals). Gander to Authorities of the FIG and Affiliated Federations. Minot Simons attributed this FIG change to Soviet gymnasts at the 1974 world championships, claiming the top five placings in the all-around and floor finals, while winning the top four positions on beam. Simons, *Women's Gymnastics*, 21. While this particular event exemplified the lack of diversity in women's artistic gymnastics' medal distribution, the archival correspondence outlined in the preceding notes shows that Simons underestimated the IOC's influence on the FIG. See folder "Federation Internationale de Gymnastique (FIG): Correspondence 1960–1976."

29. Gander to Csanádi.

30. Parks, "Nothing but Trouble," 1559.

31. Gander to Banks.

32. Norbert Bueche, "Official News," *FIG Bulletin* 160 (April 1994).

33. Jackie Fie, "Women's Technical Assembly: Minutes of the Plenary Assembly Held on the Occasion of the 69th Congress of the Fig on May 10 and 11, 1994 at the Palexpo, Geneva," *FIG Bulletin* 162 (December 1994): 105.

34. Karl-Heinz Zschocke, "Opinions: Remembrance of the Compulsory Routines," *FIG Bulletin* 161 (September 1994): 129–31.

35. Interview with Liz Chetkovich, 2014.

36. See, for example, Martin Twerksy, "Olympic Judging Is Fine, but Fairness Is Hard to Come By," *New York Times,* August 20 1972; and "Bias Alleged Again," *New York Times,* February 9, 1976.

37. Cervin, Quin, and Elias, "From the Carpet," 258, 266.

38. "Difficulties Inherent in Gymnastics Judging," *FIG Bulletin* 82 (September 1974): 70.

39. Ibid.

40. Plessner, "Expectation Biases."

41. The value of deductions for these faults has fluctuated over time. For most of gymnastics' history a fall has been a half-point deduction. It is now an entire point deduction.

42. Interview with a brevet judge, 2014.

43. Ibid.

44. Ibid.

45. Associated Press, "U.S. Gymnastics Officials Level Charges," *St. Petersburg (FL) Times*, July 24, 1976.

46. Korbut and Emerson-White, *My Story*, 122.

47. Karolyi and Richardson, *Feel No Fear*, 68.

48. Diamond and Passudettie, "Moscow Diary," 132.

49. Karolyi and Richardson, *Feel No Fear*, 95.

50. Interview with an international judge from the West who also served on FIG committees, 2014. Further evidence is discussed later in this chapter in improvements to judging.

51. Frank J. Cumiskey, "A History of Gymnastics: The Olympiads and the Intervening Years, Chapter VIII," personal review in *International Gymnast*, 1983, folder "Federation Internationale de Gymnastique (FIG): General Information 1924–1986" (D-RM02-GYMNA/011), OSC.

52. Ibid.

53. Plessner, "Expectation Biases"; Ansorge et al., "Bias in Judging"; Ansorge and Scheer, "International Bias."

54. Neil Amdur, "Perfect Scores in Gymnastics Put Judges on Trial," *New York Times*, July 24, 1976.

55. Anita Verschoth, "A Great Leap Backward," *Sports Illustrated*, April 12, 1976.

56. Fink interview.

57. Associated Press, "U.S. Gymnastics Officials."

58. Interview with an FIG official and judge, 2014.

59. Interview with a judge, 2014.

60. Arpad Csanádi (honorary IOC sports director) to Yuri Titov (FIG President), telegram January 13, 1982, "Ref: 150," folder "International Gymnastics Federation: Correspondence 1982–1983" (D-RM02-GYMNA/006), OSC.

61. Raymond Gafner to Yuri Titov, July 20, 1987, "Minutes of the Presidium Meeting, N.O.C. Statutes," folder "Executive Board of the NOC of the USSR: Correspondence 1953–1988" (D-RM01-RUSSI/002), OSC.

62. Ellen Berger, "Women's Technical Committee: Summary of the Minutes of the Meetings Held from 10. To 14.5.1977 in Prague (Czechoslovakia)," *FIG Bulletin* 94 (September 1977): 66; and Titov, "Report of the President" (December 1977).

63. Berger, "Women's Technical Committee."

64. Ibid.

65. "Romania Go in Huff," *Guardian*, May 16, 1977.

66. Comaneci, *Letters to a Young Gymnast*, 61–62; Matt Rendell, "The Perfect Ten," *Guardian*, July 4, 2004.

67. Comaneci, *Letters to a Young Gymnast,* 62.

68. Barnes, "Politicized Gymnastics."

69. "Proposals from the Federations," *FIG Bulletin* 94 (September 1977): 92.

70. "Proposals Made by the Federations," *FIG Bulletin* 84 (March 1975): 81.

71. Ellen Berger, "Report of the Chairman of the F.I.G. Women's Technical Committee," *FIG Bulletin* 130 (September 1986): 83; Browne, "Editorial."

72. Yuri Titov, "Report of the President, Yuri Titov," *FIG Bulletin* 131 (December 1986): 60.

73. Ellen Berger, "Women's Technical Committee: Minutes of the Plenary Assembly Held in Rome on 8th and 9th November 1986," *FIG Bulletin* 132 (March 1987): 112.

74. Simon Burnton, "50 Stunning Olympic Moments. No. 5: Nadia Comaneci Scores a Perfect 10," *Guardian,* December 14, 2011.

75. Canada, Italy, and Sweden first proposed this rule at the FIG Congress in 1988 but Berger, as chair of the women's technical committee, opposed it. Despite Berger's cautions, it was voted in twenty-four to fourteen. "Federations' Proposals," *FIG Bulletin* 137 (June 1988): 133, and Ellen Berger, "W.T.C. Minutes of the Women's Plenary Technical Assembly Held in Seoul/Kor on 12th and 13th September 1988," *FIG Bulletin* 140 (March 1989): 83.

76. Maryann Hudson, "Karolyi Angered Gym Official in '84, Peters Says," *Los Angeles Times,* September 21, 1988.

77. Faehn was the team alternate, so she did not compete.

78. Michael Janofsky, "The Seoul Olympics: Gymnastics; Karolyi Cries Foul as U.S. Slips into 4th," *New York Times,* September 20, 1988.

79. Maryann Hudson, "Karolyi Angered Gym Official in '84, Peters Says," *Los Angeles Times,* September 21, 1988.

80. Janofsky, "Seoul Olympics."

81. Ibid.

82. Interview with an international coach, 2013.

83. Ellen Berger, "Women's Technical Committee: Summary of the Minutes of the Meetings Held in Moutier, from January 28 to February 4, 1992," *FIG Bulletin* 153 (June 1992): 49.

84. Titov, "Report Submitted to the Congress," *FIG Bulletin* 154 (September 1992): 37.

85. Ellen Berger, "Women's Technical Committee: Chairman's Report," *FIG Bulletin* 152 (March 1992): 87.

86. Jackie Fie, "Women's Technical Committee: Summary of the Minutes of the Meeting of 08–12 July, 1996 at Atlanta, USA," *FIG Bulletin* 169 (April 1997): 104.

87. "Gymnastics Tie-Break Rules Changed."

88. Arpad Csanádi (honorary IOC sports director to Yuri Titov (FIG president), December 7, 1981. "84th Session of the I.O.C. In Baden-Baden," folder "IOC Archives—Sessions and Executive Committee."

89. Arpad Csanádi (honorary IOC sports director) to Max Bangerter (FIG secretary general), February 22, 1982, "Ex Aequo," folder "International Gymnastics Federation: Correspondence 1982–1983."

90. Arpad Csanádi (honorary IOC sports director), Yuri Titov (FIG president), and Max Bangerter (FIG secretary general), "Memo on the Meeting between the I.O.C. Honorary Sports Director and the President, Mr Yuri Titov, and the Secretary General, Mr Max Bangerter of the Federation Internationale De Gymnastique," February 3, 1982, folder "International Gymnastics Federation: Correspondence 1982–1983."

91. Yuri Titov (FIG president) to Arpad Csanádi (honorary IOC sports director), June 1982, "Case of Ex Aequo at the Gymnastics Competitions at the Olympic Games," folder "International Gymnastics Federation: Correspondence 1982–1983."

92. Arpad Csanádi (honorary IOC sports director) to Yuri Titov (FIG president), June 18, 1982, "Re: Ex Aequo on Ranking Lists," folder "International Gymnastics Federation: Correspondence 1982–1983."

93. Indeed, only two years later at the LA Olympics, four men tied for the silver medal on vault.

94. Interview with a FIG official, 2014.

95. There were 14 events at the 1992 Olympics, including both men's and women's apparatuses, all-around, and team competitions. "Gymnastics at the 1992 Barcelona Summer Games."

96. "Gymnastics Tie-Break Rules Changed."

97. R. Kerr and Obel, "Disappearance of the Perfect 10."

98. Fink interview.

99. Jackie Fie and Karl-Heinz Zschocke, "Combined Meeting: F.I.G. Men's and Women's Technical Committees February 24, 1995 in Moutier, Switzerland," *FIG Bulletin* 164 (August 1995): 78.

100. Bruno Grandi, "Presidential Report," *FIG Bulletin* 180 (June 2000): 104–6.

101. Fie and Zschocke, "Combined Meeting."

102. Grandi, "Message from the President."

103. Kym Dowdell and George Beckstead, "Men's and Women's Technical Committees: Summary of the Minutes from the Joint Meeting Held on 17.10.98," *FIG Bulletin* 175 (December 1998): 85.

104. Author correspondence with Fink, November 2015.

105. Norbert Bueche, "Official News," *FIG Bulletin* 175 (December 1998).

106. Jackie Fie, "Women's Technical Committee: Summary of the Meeting October 16–20, 1998, in New York, USA," *FIG Bulletin* 175 (December 1998): 81.

107. Jackie Fie, "Women's Technical Committee, St Petersburg, USA, March 1–5, 1999: Summary of the Minutes," *FIG Bulletin* 178 (December 1999): 178.

108. Personal correspondence with Fink.

109. Norbert Bueche, "Disciplinary Measures," *FIG Bulletin* 156 (March 1993).

110. Amanda Turner, "FIG Rejects Appeal; No Worlds for North Korea," *International Gymnast*, October 14, 2010.

111. Amanda Turner, "FIG Rules Against Dong Fangxiao In Age Scandal," *International Gymnast*, February 26, 2010.

112. Ibid.

113. "China 'Accept' Decision."

114. John Leicester, "China Leaves Underage Gymnast in the Cold," *USA Today*, March 12, 2010, http://usatoday30.usatoday.com/sports/olympics/2010–2003–2012–1263849827_x.htm.

115. Ibid.

116. Yang, "Guilty without Trial."

117. See chapter 5 for a discussion of the racialized discourse that surrounded allegations of Chinese age-falsification.

118. "Romanian Gymnasts 'Lied about Age'."

119. Károlyi publicly accused Agache of age falsification at the time, which Simionescu, a member of the women's technical committee for the FIG, denied. Neil Amdur, "Rift over Underage Gymnasts: Soviet Official Denies Charges Passport Checks Made Hotbed of Controversy," *New York Times*, 7 December 1981. Agache confirmed her birth year to *International Gymnast* some years later, validating the Károlyis' claims of her age falsification during her active career. "Former Romanian Star."

120. "Romanian Gymnasts Faked Age."

121. Ibid.

122. The first positive doping test had been at the 1994 world championships but had not concerned medalists. "Official News," *FIG Bulletin* 163 (April 1995): 96.

123. Sands, "Why Gymnastics?"

124. "Press Release: Positive Doping Test, 26th September 2000," *FIG Bulletin* 182 (December 2000).

125. Interview with a former FIG Executive Committee member, 2014.

126. Vivek Chaudhary, "Bitter Pill as Tiny Gymnast Loses Gold," *Guardian*, September 29, 2000; Lisa Dillman, "Romanian Gymnast Caught in Middle," *Los Angeles Times*, September 29, 2000.

127. Gymnasts who have tested positive for furosemide include Do Thi Ngan Thuong (Vietnam, 2008 Olympic Games), Daiane Dos Santos (Brazil, 2009 outside competition), Kristina Goryunova (Russia, 2009 Russian championships), and Luiza Galiulina (Uzbekistan, 2012 Olympic Games).

128. Cadwallader et al., "Abuse of Diuretics."

129. Parks, "Nothing but Trouble."

Chapter 5. Feminine and Feminist?

1. I use "acrobatic" to mean "aerial" and, more often than not, "rotational."

2. Adams, "From Mixed-Sex Sport," 31.

3. FIG, Code of Points (1964), 2, quoted in Barker-Ruchti, "Ballerinas and Pixies," 47.

4. IOC to Charles Thoeni (FIG secretary general), May 26, 1953, folder "Federation Internationale de Gymnastique (FIG): Correspondence 1906–1959 (D-RM02-GYMNA/003), OSC; Charles Thoeni (FIG secretary general) to Baron Eric von Frenckell, November 2, 1953, folder "Federation Internationale de Gymnastique (FIG): Correspondence 1906–1959."

5. Lorber, *Paradoxes of Gender*; Martin, "Gender as Social Institution."

6. West and Zimmerman, "Doing Gender"; Butler, *Gender Trouble*; Butler, *Undoing Gender*.

7. *Official Report*, 478.

8. Chaves and Moreno, "Dance," 11–13; Verbrugge, *Active Bodies*, 88; Vertinsky, *Eternally Wounded Woman*, 56.

9. *Official Report*, 478.

10. Markula and Clark, introduction, xvii.

11. David Best's distinction between aesthetic and purposive sport is interesting, because gymnastics can be seen as pluralistic. Yes, the purpose of the vault is to get over it, but present in the naming of the apparatus is that one must get over the vaulting horse in a specific way. Doing so aesthetically is essential to how the sport is contested. While artistic is a category of aesthetic, Best nonetheless argues that sports cannot be artistic because art must allow for the possibility of expression of moral, social, and political issues. We see this in the story telling of ballets, but not in the ninety-second routines of female gymnasts, even if they draw on similar bodily movements. There are of course, a few exceptions, like Henrietta Ónodi's *West Side Story* routine, where the gymnast acts throughout the performance and pretends to die at the conclusion. Best, "Art and Sport."

12. Markula and Clark, introduction, xviii–xxiii.

13. Dempster uses the term "voluptuously active" when analyzing feminine passivity in the choreography of Martha Graham. Dempster, "Women Writing the Body."

14. *Official Report*, 476.

15. Ibid., 478.

16. Simpson, "Parading Myths," 187–88.

17. ""Vera Caslavska, Czech Gymnast and Dissident—Obituary," *Telegraph* (UK), September 1, 2016.

18. A number of media outlets corroborate Čáslavská's training methods, but the first appearance of the story seems to be from a 1990 *Los Angeles Times* article. Čáslavská was ostracized by the Czech regime after her 1968 protest, so there is only very limited media coverage about her until the Velvet Revolution that dismantled the Communist regime in 1989. "Vera Caslavska, Czech gymnast and dissident—Obituary," *Telegraph*, September 1, 2016.

19. Simons, *Women's Gymnastics*.

20. Steve Cady, "A Citizen of Prague Speaks Her Mind," *New York Times*, February 1, 1969.

21. R. Kerr, "Evolution of Women's Artistic Gymnastics," 49.

22. Berthe Villancher, "Extract from the Minutes of the General Assembly Held on 3rd October, 1971, Madrid: 4. Reports, C) President of T.C.W.," *FIG Bulletin* 71 (December 1971): 51.

23. Vertinsky, *Eternally Wounded Woman*, 23; Pieper, *Sex Testing*, 16, 159; Quin and Bohuon, *Les liaisons dangereuses*.

24. Barker-Ruchti, "Ballerinas and Pixies," 50.

25. A bias toward hiring male coaches for women's gymnastics remains as of this writing. Men coach tumbling, vault, and bars, while women usually coach only beam and dance on floor. R. Kerr and Cervin, "Ironic Imbalance."

26. Tomizawa, "The Great Czech Gymnast Vera Caslavska."

27. Mertin, "Presenting Heroes," 477–79.

28. Mellis, "From Defectors to Cooperators," 64.

29. The European championships were one of the most prestigious gymnastics events. They were held the year after and the year before the Olympics, while the world championships were contested in the remaining year. Year 1: Olympic Games; year 2: European championships; year 3: world championships, year 4: European championships.

30. Kerr, "Evolution of Women's Artistic Gymnastics," 51.

31. Ibid., 53.

32. Ibid., 50.

33. With his subsequent pupils, Rastorotsky created two of the most essential skills in modern gymnastics: the Yurchenko vault and the Shaposhnikova on the uneven bars.

34. Barker-Ruchti, *Women's Artistic Gymnastics*, 147.

35. Neirick, *When Pigs Could Fly*.

36. Wamsley and MacDonald, "Child's Play," 339.

37. Chisholm, "Acrobats, Contortionists, and Cute Children," 418.

38. Michael Suponev quoted in R. Kerr, "Evolution of Women's Artistic Gymnastics," 62.

39. See Roslyn Kerr, "Evolution of Women's Artistic Gymnastics," 60–61; Barker-Ruchti, "Ballerinas and Pixies," 56.

40. Varney, "Labour of Patriotism," paragraph 1.

41. Valery Nagy, "Women's Technical Committee: Extract of the Minutes from Meetings Held at London, October 23, 1973," *FIG Bulletin* 82 (March 1974): 40. With regard to the overexaggerated back bends: "The women's technical committee agreed upon doing everything possible to eliminate these movements and submitted the problem to the FIG medical commission" (40).

42. Some gymnasts continued to compete variations of the Korbut loop on the bars but did so anxious to avoid any pause. Eventually the FIG banned skills that required the gymnast to stand on the bars, specifically outlawing the Korbut loop a decade later. Valery Nagy, "Provisions in Prospect for the Artistic Gymnastics World Championships to Be Held in 1974 and to Come into Effect on January 1st, 1974," *FIG Bulletin* 81 (June 1974): 65; and Nagy, "Women's Technical Committee: Extract," 39.

43. Valery Nagy, "Women's Technical Committee: Provisions in Prospect for the Artistic Gymnastics World Championships to Be Held in 1974 and to Come into Effect on January 1st, 1974," *FIG Bulletin* 81 (June 1974): 64.

44. Berthe Villancher, "Women's Artistic Gymnastics Competitions, Olympic Games—Munich 1972: Technical Report," *FIG Bulletin* 75 (December 1972): 20.

45. Valery Nagy, "Minutes of the Meetings of the W.T.C. Held at Stuttgart from 21st–30st January, 1973," *FIG Bulletin* 77, no. 2 (June 1973): 41.

46. Ibid., 45.

47. Associated Press, "Olga Korbut Threatening Retirement over Dispute," *Nashua (NH) Telegraph*, 16 July 1973.

48. Dufraisse, *Les héros du sport*, 223–24.

49. Nagy, "Women's Technical Committee: Extract," 40. With regard to the back salto: "The FIG Medical Commission should occupy themselves with this question" (40).

50. Nagy, "Minutes of the Meetings of the W.T.C.," 45.

51. Berthe Villancher, "Extract from the C.E. Minutes of the Meeting of the Assembly General Held on 29th and 30th October, 1970, in Ljubljana: Report of the President of the Women's Technical Committee," *FIG Bulletin* 67 (December 1970): 43.

52. Berthe Villancher, "Standard for Certain Apparatus," *FIG Bulletin* 70 (August 1971): 51.

53. Maurer, *Uneven Bars*, 8.

54. Villancher, "Standard for Certain Apparatus," 51.

55. Nagy, "Minutes of the Meetings of the W.T.C.," 43.

56. Valery Nagy, "Women's Technical Committee: Minutes of the Meetings Held from 15th–29th October, 1974 at Varna," *FIG Bulletin* 86 (March 1975): 70.

57. The FIG even alluded to this view when in 2013 it noted that changing the rules would not necessarily result in beautiful, artistic routines like in the 1970s and 1980s. See R. Kerr and Obel, "Disappearance of the Perfect 10," 327. Fan views can be seen in a Facebook group with more than sixteen thousand members dedicated to celebrating gymnastics before the 1990s—see "Gymnastics—A Golden Era," *Facebook*.

58. Villancher, "Extract from the Minutes," 51.

59. Barker-Ruchti, *Women's Artistic Gymnastics*, 179.

60. Arthur Gander, "'53rd Assembly General, Extract from the Minutes of the Assembly General Held at Berne-Switzerland on 29th and 30th May 1975: President's Report," *FIG Bulletin* 85 (June 1975): 38.

61. Men's artistic gymnastics has artistic goals similar to women's artistic gymnastics. However, they too were constructed on gendered ideals, particularly strength and control on apparatuses designed to demonstrate such traits (e.g., still rings, pommel horse, and parallel bars). Vault, high bar, and floor came to appear very similar to women's artistic gymnastics vault, uneven bars, and floor in the context of acrobatization, although the remnants of the divergent goals can be seen most explicitly in the women's music, choreography, and dance

requirements on the floor exercise. Both disciplines had goals of demonstrating different, gendered qualities; however, both were considered artistic.

62. For examples of how gendered expectations worked against women in other sports, see Schultz, "Going the Distance," and Lynne Emery, "Examination." After the 1928 Olympics, the women's 800-meter race was banned for the next thirty-two years, owing to depictions of female athletes "fainting" at the finish line, endangering their health. Rather than being an accurate reflection of the events (no one fainted; one woman lay down to rest after she had completed the race), it was more a reflection of the contemporary rhetoric surrounding women and physical activity spilling over from the nineteenth century and pervading most women's sports throughout the twentieth century.

63. Villancher, "Extract from the Minutes," 51–52.

64. Nagy, "Minutes of the Meetings of the W.T.C.," 43.

65. Valery Nagy, "Women's Technical Committee: Extract of the Minutes from the Meetings Held at Vienna from 22nd–25th April, 1976," *FIG Bulletin* 90, no. 3 (September 1976): 53.

66. Deford, "Nadia Awed Ya." Deford wrote: "Comaneci could have won 9.95s across the board, earned just as many gold medals, been every bit as good, and attracted about one-half the publicity for herself and for women's gymnastics."

67. Barry Lorge, "Comaneci Finally Wins Two Golds as Judging Controversies Continue," *Washington Post*, July 26, 1980; "Olympics, the Games"; Verschoth, "A Great Leap Backward."

68. Duncan, "Hermeneutic of Spectator Sport," 72.

69. Chisholm, "Acrobats, Contortionists, and Cute Children," 439.

70. Deford, "Nadia Awed Ya."

71. Krustyo Krustev, "Age Limits for the Olympics?" *FIG Bulletin* 97 (June 1978): 55–59.

72. Arpad Csanádi (honorary IOC sports director) to Yuri Titov (FIG president), 7 December 1981, "'84th Session of the I.O.C. in Baden-Baden," folder "International Gymnastics Federation: Correspondence 1977–1981" (D-RM02-GYMNA/005), OSC.

73. Beamish and Ritchie, "Totalitarian Regimes"; Pieper, *Sex Testing*.

74. "Family" is the FIG's term for a group of vaults that share the same general entry but may vary in the second flight phase.

75. "Yurchenko Vault." According to Yurchenko herself, though, she and her coach Rastorotsky were inspired after seeing a male gymnast perform it in the Soviet Union. But when Victor Levinkov did it in 1979, it was not well received within the men's gymnastics community, and the vault disappeared from competition until the twenty-first century. Recall that until 2001, the men vaulted lengthways over the horse, while women voted widthways.

76. T. Benn and B. Benn, "After Olga," 178.

77. Mike Reilley, "Is New Vault Lifting Gymnasts into Danger?" *Chicago Tribune*, June 27, 1988.

78. Young-Hoo, Virginia, and In-Sik, "3-D Analysis." The authors of this study identified the Yurchenko layout and the Yurchenko layout full twist as the two most frequently performed vaults at the 1988 Olympic Games.

79. Maryann Hudson, "A Gym Tragedy: Mother Says U.S. Athlete Fell into a Coma Because of Treatment at a Tokyo Hospital," *Los Angeles Times*, June 27, 1988; Ryan, *Little Girls in Pretty Boxes*, 25.

80. Mike Reilley, "It's Dangerous from the Start: Gymnastics: Some Officials and Coaches Wonder If the Spectacular Yurchenko Vault Is Worth the Risk," *Los Angeles Times*, November 17, 1989.

81. Michel Leglise, "Report of the Chairman of the Medical Commission," *FIG Bulletin* 137 (June 1988).

82. Jackie Fie, "Women's Technical Committee: Summary of the Minutes of the Meeting of 16–19 February, 1997 at Rome, Ita," *FIG Bulletin* 170 (July 1997): 84.

83. Until 2001, men and women used the same vaulting horse but men traversed it lengthwise at 135 cm high while women did so widthwise at 125 cm high. With the vaulting table, the height difference for men and women is retained, but otherwise the apparatus is universal. Jackie Fie, "Women's Technical Committee: Summary of the Minutes of the Meeting of 23–28 August, 1997 Lausanne, Sui," *FIG Bulletin* 171 (December 1997): 105; Jackie Fie, "Women's Technical Committee: Summary of the Meeting October 16–20, 1998, in New York, USA," *FIG Bulletin* 175 (December 1998): 80.

84. Deford, "Rising to Great Heights"; Ottum, "It's Up to You, Mary Lou."

85. Deford, "Rising to Great Heights."

86. Congelio, "In Defense of a Neoliberal America," 215–16.

87. When the Eastern bloc boycotted the 1984 Olympics, Romania still attended, revealing tensions within the Eastern bloc.

88. Guoqi, *Olympic Dreams*, 3.

89. Jackie Fie, "Women's Technical Committee: Summary of the Minutes of Meetings Held in Falun (Swe) 01–04 October 1993," *FIG Bulletin* 160 (April 1994): 89.

90. Zhang, "Bending the Body for China."

91. Lyman, "'Yellow Peril' Mystique."

92. Zhang, "Bending the Body for China."

93. Lyman, "'Yellow Peril' Mystique."

94. Yang, "Guilty without Trial," 87.

95. Shakur-Bruno explains that, beyond the unshaded body, the gymnast's hair and bodily features also suggest that the putative gymnast is White. Shakur-Bruno, "Sporting Subjection," 91.

96. Riordan, *Sport in Soviet Society*, 143, 310, 320.

97. While acknowledging that race is a social construct, Black women were nonetheless seen as racial representatives when they stood out as different in this predominantly White sport.

98. Shakur-Bruno, "Sporting Subjection," 71.

99. Susan K. Cahn, "From the 'Muscle Moll'," 352.

100. Pieper, *Sex Testing*, 51.

101. Chisholm, "Acrobats, Contortionists, and Cute Children," 415, 427–428, 442; Shakur-Bruno, "Sporting Subjection," 23, 83–84. Bruno-Shakur argues that freaks are "conceptually if not biologically marked by race." The freak is associated with the pseudoscientific "missing link," the evolutionarily transitional being who stands between man and animal . . . bodies that press at the very boundaries of human" (84).

102. Chisholm, "Acrobats, Contortionists, and Cute Children"; R. Cohen, "Femininity."

103. Their "cuteness" does not protect gymnasts from being routinely sexualized by the media in photo reportage, and scholars point out more generally that gymnasts have a perverse sexual appeal to pedophiles. Chisholm, "Acrobats, Contortionists, and Cute Children"; Shakur-Bruno, "Sporting Subjection"; Barker-Ruchti and Weber, "Bending, Flirting."

104. Chisholm, "Acrobats, Contortionists, and Cute Children," 439.

105. Sztainbok, "Exposing Her Body," 596.

106. Shakur-Bruno, "Sporting Subjection," 112–15.

107. Ibid., 141.

108. There have been exceptional gymnasts who did not train over thirty hours a week, like 2008 Olympic gold medalist Shawn Johnson, as well as many of the adult gymnasts who have had long careers (Oksana Chusovitina et al.). But in general, the gymnastics community demands over thirty hours per week as the standard training time required for elites. Kerr et al., *Coming of Age*; Barker-Ruchti et al., "Gymnasts Are Like Wine."

109. Cheers, "Dianne Durham."

110. Meyers, "Decades of Black Gymnasts."

111. Shakur-Bruno, "Sporting Subjection." Shakur-Bruno's evidence is not clear on this point. Also, Károlyi had only been in the country a short time, and the 1984 games would have been his first in the US system. It is entirely possible that he was not familiar with alternative Olympic selection routes.

112. Shakur-Bruno, "Sporting Subjection," 144.

113. The Black athletes discussed here are predominantly American examples, or examples of women who won prestigious international medals. There are countless other Black women who are part of this story, including Kim Hamilton, the Umeh sisters in Canada, and the Downie sisters in England.

114. Dos Santos 1 and Dos Santos 2 can be alternatively be described as a piked double arabian and a laid-out double arabian, respectively.

115. Larry Rohter, "Athens: Summer 2004 Olympics—Daiane Dos Santos/Brazil Gymnastics; A Nation's Hope Rises Out of Nowhere," *New York Times*, August 8, 2004.

116. Dos Santos's coach, Adrianna Alves, quoted in ibid.

117. P. O'Brien, *Pacific Muse*, 5.

118. "Lines" are highly valued in gymnastics, where many skills demand that each body part is in the same line. For some gymnasts, their joints can be aligned, but their musculature can disturb the visual impact of the alignment. Slimmer gymnasts with longer limbs are often said to have good lines because they do not have bulging muscles that interfere with the perception of the body (or body part) being fully extended in a straight line. "Lines," or lack thereof can therefore be coded language to describe body types and racialized features.

119. Vanessa Williams, "Gabby Douglas's Hair Sets Off Twitter Debate, But Some Ask: 'What's the Fuss?'" *Washington Post*, August 3, 2012; Lauren McEwan, "Gabby Douglas and Her Ponytail: What's All the Fuss About?" *Washington Post*, August 6, 2012; Kelly Whiteside, "Don't Like Gabby Douglas' Hair? Too Bad," *USA Today*, August 6, 2012; Tammerlin Drummond, "Newsflash: Olympic Gymnast Gabby Douglas Is Not Having a Bad Hair Day," *Oakland Tribune*, August 6, 2012.

120. Liz Clarke, "Gabby Douglas, Her Olympics Over, Tearfully Responds to Social Media Critics," *Washington Post*, August 14, 2016; Les Carpenter, "The Hounding of Gabby Douglas: An Unworthy End for a Great American Champion," *Guardian*, August 15, 2016.

121. Black women can be judged harshly for speaking out, but Biles has been able to do so not only because of her bubbly persona on the competition floor and the normalization of Black gymnasts over the preceding two decades, but also because of the precedent set by her more experienced (White) teammate, Aly Raisman. Raisman was initially one of the most prominent contemporary gymnasts to speak about both Nassar and the USA Gymnastics' role in the case, and she did so often.

122. Markula and Clark, introduction, xxiv.

123. Gymnasts were dying not only through traumatic injury like Elena Mukhina, Julissa Gomez, and Sang Lan, but also through anorexia nervosa, like American Christy Heinrich. Ryan, *Little Girls in Pretty Boxes*.

124. McClendon, "Fashionable Addiction."

125. See, for example, Fass and Grossberg, "Preface," xii–xiii.

126. Wamsley and MacDonald, "Child's Play," 339.

127. Wamsley, "Womanizing Olympic Athletes."

128. Kerr et al., *Coming of Age*, 11–12, 17–18.

129. Markula and Clark, introduction, xxiv. Since the Enlightenment, the body has been seen as traditionally feminine, the mind traditionally masculine.

130. Comaneci, *Letters to a Young Gymnast*, 151.

131. Castan-Vicente, Nicolas, and Cervin, "Women in Sport Organisations," 22. Castan-Vicente, Nicolas, and Cervin also discuss the idea of engagement in sport as a form of social resistance, allowing women to explore places not usually available to women. See also Hargreaves, *Sporting Females*.

132. Summers-Bremner, "Reading Irigaray."

133. Barker-Ruchti, *Women's Artistic Gymnastics*, 198.

134. A vast body of sociological, psychological, and medical work reveals mal-

treatment and other harmful behaviors done to the gymnast by a variety of actors (coaches, administrators, officials). The works of Gretchen Kerr and Natalie Barker-Ruchti warrant particular attention. In 2020, gymnasts themselves began publicly sharing the abuses they suffered in the sport under the hashtag gymnast alliance.

Chapter 6. Coaching and Culture

1. Maguire, "Real Politic"; Borges et al., "Coaches' Migration."

2. Verbrugge, *Active Bodies.*

3. Theberge, "Construction of Gender."

4. Initially, judges and committee members had to be women. Although this is no longer the rule, male judges are still uncommon and there have been few, if any, male members serving on the women's technical committee. Cervin, Quin, and Elias, "From the Carpet."

5. Latynina won the all-around in the 1956 and 1960 Olympics, and gold for the team and floor exercise at the 1964 games.

6. Nauright and Parrish, *Sports around the World,* 2.

7. Cheryl Bentsen, "A Dream for Gymnastics," *New York Times,* Nov 12, 1978. There is more information about Muriel Grossfeld's former husband, Abie Grossfeld, also a gymnast and coach. He was even awarded the Frank Bare award for exceptional contributions to US gymnastics by the International Gymnastics Hall of Fame.

8. According to the 1979 Code of Points, "The gymnasts are permitted to be chaperoned by one female coach only and *only she* has the right to take care of the gymnast on the podium. During the three minute warm up she can be assisted by a second trainer (male or female). Both trainers are permitted to be with the team in the arena during the competition" (original emphasis). FIG Women's Technical Committee, *Code of Points—Women,* 12.

9. Day and Carpenter, *History of Sports Coaching,* 4.

10. Cahn, *Coming on Strong,* 260.

11. Ibid.

12. Smith et al., "Deconstructing Hegemonic Masculinity"; Connell and Messerschmidt, "Hegemonic Masculinity"; Mankowski and Maton, "Community Psychology."

13. Smith et al., "Deconstructing Hegemonic Masculinity."

14. R. Kerr and Cervin, "Ironic Imbalance," 2145.

15. Norman, "Feeling Second Best," 98–99.

16. Barker-Ruchti, *Women's Artistic Gymnastics*; R. Cohen, "Femininity."

17. Hargreaves, *Sporting Females,* 202; Pike at al., "Women and Sport Leadership"; Sartore and Cunningham, "Lesbian Label," 482–83.

18. Korbut, Tourischeva, Tamara Lazakovich, and Antonina Koshel had men as their main coaches. It is unclear who coached Lyubov Burda and Elvira Saadi. Golubev, "Olga Korbut."

19. Theberge, "Construction of Gender," 306.

20. Khomutov, as reported by Frances Thompson, "Report on Tour," 17.

21. There was significant overlap between FIG and Soviet officials in the late 1970s, as Yuri Titov was president of the FIG and also resident at the Soviet Sports Committee in Moscow.

22. C. O'Brien, "Investigation," 68.

23. R. Kerr and Cervin, "Ironic Imbalance," 2144, 2147, 2149.

24. Mellis cites the minutes of an emergency meeting of the Fédération Internationale de Football Association in 1957. Mellis, "From Defectors to Cooperators," 69. For a broader time period, see also Braun and Wiese, "Tracksuit Traitors."

25. Mellis, "From Defectors to Cooperators."

26. Mellis, "Cold War Politics," 64.

27. See, for example, Reuveny and Prakash, "Afghanistan War."

28. See, for example, Strayer, *Why Did the Soviet Union Collapse?*

29. Barker-Ruchti, "Ballerinas and Pixies"; Zaglada, *One Coach's Journey*; interview with a former Soviet coach, 2014.

30. Interview with Liz Chetkovich, 2014.

31. Ibid.

32. Marchenko was a world champion in sports acrobatics.

33. For instance, the Liukins established World Olympic Gymnastics Academy, the Brestyan's established Brestyan's Gymnastics, All Olympic Gymnastics Academy is run by Galina Marinova and Artur Akopyan, Béla and Márta Károlyi opened the "ranch."

34. Maguire, "Blade Runners."

35. Kerr and Cervin, "Ironic Imbalance," 2145, 2149.

36. Kerr and Cervin, "Ironic Imbalance," 2144.

37. Interview with an Australian coach-administrator, 2014.

38. Australian coach-administrator interview.

39. Chetkovich interview.

40. Interview with a FIG official, 2014.

41. Interview with a former Soviet gymnast and FIG official, 2014.

42. FIG official interview, 2014.

43. Australian coach-administrator interview.

44. Khomutov as interviewed by Thompson, "Report on Tour."

45. Forbes, "Gymnastics Visit."

46. FIG official interview, 2014.

47. Ibid.

48. Béla Károlyi quoted in R. O'Brien, "Gymnastics Lord Gym."

49. R. O'Brien, "Gymnastics Lord Gym."

50. FIG official interview, 2014. A number of other interviewees had similar comments.

51. Mike Jacki quoted in R. O'Brien, "Gymnastics Lord Gym."

52. R. O'Brien, "Gymnastics Lord Gym."

53. Arthur Daley quoted in Mellis, "Cold War Politics," 73. Arthur Daley was a Pulitzer Prize–winning sports journalist for the *New York Times* who wrote a regular column titled "Sport of the Times."

54. Winter, "Karolyis' Tainted Glory."

55. Diane Pucin, "Moceanu Accuses Karolyis of Abuse," *Los Angeles Times*, July 23, 2008, https://www.latimes.com/archives/la-xpm-2008-jul-23-sp-karolyi23-story .html; Moceanu and Williams, *Off Balance*.

56. Okino, review of *Little Girls and Pretty Boxes*.

57. Sally Jenkins, "Aly Raisman: Conditions at Károlyi Ranch Made Athletes Vulnerable to Nassar," *Washington Post*, March 15, 2018.

58. Comaneci, *Letters to a Young Gymnast*, 51.

59. Stirling and G. Kerr, "Abused Athletes' Perceptions," 233.

60. Selena Roberts, "U.S. Gymnasts Try to Catch Karolyi's Eye," *New York Times*, August 19, 2000.

61. "USA Gymnastics."

62. Jenkins, "Aly Raisman."

63. Emma Brockes, "Simone Biles: 'I Go to Therapy, Because at Times I Didn't Want to Set Foot in the Gym,'" *Guardian*, March 16, 2019, https://www.theguardian .com/sport/2019/mar/16/simone-biles-therapy-times-didnt-want-set-foot-gym.

64. Pucin, "Moceanu Accuses Karolyis."

65. Benton, "Everything You Need to Know."

66. Ibid.

67. Yan, "Karolyi Ranch."

68. Vanessa Atler provides an example of this from 1999 after the 1998 Goodwill Games medalist, a shoo-in for the upcoming Olympics, trained to burnout, exhaustion, and injury after coaches, parents, and USA Gymnastics mismanaged her career. Dvora Meyers, "Former National Champion."

69. Wiedeman, "Full Revolution."

70. Roenigk and Ford, *Heavy Medals*.

71. Scott Reid, "Marcia Frederick, First U.S. Gymnastics World Champion, Shares Story of Abuse," *Orange County (CA) Register*, January 13, 2018, https://www .ocregister.com/2018/01/13/marcia-frederick-first-u-s-gymnastics-world-champion -shares-story-of-abuse/.

72. Korbut's teammates have spoken in support of her allegations. Dynko, Baumgartner, and Shauliuha, "#MeToo in Belarus."

73. Scott Reid, "Gymnasts Accuse Renowned Coach of Sex Abuse," *Orange County (CA) Register*, September 23, 2011, https://www.ocregister.com/2015/01/06/gymnasts -accuse-renowned-coach-of-sex-abuse/.

74. Claims of sexual assault were not limited to coaches. In 2017, 1992 Olympic champion Tatiana Gutsu claimed that teammate Vitaly Scherbo had raped her. Bryan Flaherty, "Amid #Metoo, Former Soviet Gymnast Tatiana Gutsu Accuses Fellow Olympic Gold Medalist of Rape," *Washington Post*, October 17, 2017, https://www .washingtonpost.com/news/early-lead/wp/2017/10/17/former-soviet-gymnast -tatiana-gutsu-accuses-fellow-olympic-gold-medalist-of-rape/.

75. Maryann Hudson, "A Gym Tragedy: Mother Says U.S. Athlete Fell into a Coma Because of Treatment at a Tokyo Hospital," *Los Angeles Times*, June 27, 1988.

76. Turner, "Yelena Mukhina Dies."

77. Polonskaya, "Yelena Mukhina."

78. Ibid.

79. Dufraisse, *Les héros du sport*, 288.

80. Key figures Aly Raisman and Simone Biles accused USA Gymnastics of trying to cover up the Nassar abuse. Investigative reporters allege that USA Gymnastics routinely dismissed reports of sexual abuse unless they came from the victim's parent. The documentary *Athlete A* (dir. Cohen and Shenk) also shows that when parents reported abuse to USA Gymnastics, the organization did not respond by conducting an investigation and did not make the complaints known to others. Marisa Kwiatkowski, Mark Alesia, and Tim Evans, "A Blind Eye to Sex Abuse: How USA Gymnastics Protected Coaches over Kids by Failing to Report Allegations of Misconduct," *Dayton Daily News*, August 4, 2016.

81. Hudson, "Gym Tragedy."

82. Fiona van der Plaat, "Report Clears AIS Gymnast Program," *Canberra Times*, November 30, 1995.

83. See, for example, Varney, "Legitimation and Limitations."

84. "The Warning in Kerri Strug's Heroics," editorial, *New York Times*, August 11, 1996; Dave Anderson, "Just Let Those Kids Be Kids," *New York Times*, July 31, 1992.

85. Michel Leglise, "Medical Commission: Report of the President," *FIG Bulletin* 159 (December 1993): 106.

86. Michel Leglise, "Medical Commission: Chairman's Report," *FIG Bulletin* 166 (March 1996): 140.

87. Thorpe and Wheaton, "Generation X Games."

88. Kelner, "British Gymnastics"; Scott, "Beaten and Starved."

89. Sean Ingle, "Gymnastics Crisis Shows Again Why Athletes Need a Union Fighting Their Corner," *Guardian*, November 13, 2017, https://www.theguardian.com/sport/blog/2017/nov/13/uk-sport-olympics-funding-british-athletes-commission.

90. Heitinga and Köhler, *De onvrije oefening*; Stier, *Blod, svett och tårar*; "Detta har hänt i gymnastik—Sverige," *Dagens Nyheter*, September 14, 2013, https://www.dn.se/sport/detta-har-hant-i-gymnastik-sverige/; "Swiss Gymnastics Team Boss Suspended during Bullying Inquiry," *Associated Press*, July 9, 2020, https://apnews.com/eed95277192e1f11af3e9041063d6137.

91. Australia launched an investigation through the Australian Human Rights Commission. Meanwhile, British Gymnastics arranged an independent review, called the Whyte Report, but some gymnasts have publicly announced their lack of trust in the process and have opted to take legal action instead. Australian Human Rights Commission. "Independent Review" Scott, "Exclusive"; Liz Clarke, "Simone Biles Blasts USA Gymnastics' Settlement Proposal; Aly Raisman Assails 'Massive Cover Up'," *Washington Post*, March 2, 2020, https://www.washingtonpost.com/sports/2020/02/29/simone-biles-aly-raisman-blast-usa-gymnastics-settlement-proposal/.

92. Meyers, "Next Step"; Cervin et al., "Growing Up."

93. Morinari Watanabe, "The President's Report," *FIG Bulletin* 246 (April 2019): 114.

94. Interview with a gymnastics administrator, 2014.

95. Donnelly, "Child Labour"; David, *Human Rights*.

96. Kidd, "Elite Athlete," 300.

97. Comaneci, *Letters to a Young Gymnast*, 26.

98. See, for example, Barker-Ruchti, *Women's Artistic Gymnastics*, 90, 165.

99. Stirling and Kerr, "Abused Athletes' Perceptions," 235.

100. Kidd, "Elite Athlete," 298–300.

101. For instance, Oksana Chusovitina, Becky Downie, and Marta Pihan-Kulesza all coach themselves.

102. Barker-Ruchti et al., "Gymnasts Are Like Wine"; R. Kerr et al., *Coming of Age*; R. Kerr et al., "Coming of Age"; Cervin et al., "Growing Up"; R. Kerr et al., "Role of Setting."

103. Rastorotsky's most famous students include Ludmilla Tourischeva, Natalia Shaposhnikova, and Natalia Yurchenko.

104. Marlen Garcia, "Shawn Johnson's Roots Run from Iowa to Beijing," *USA Today*, August 6, 2008, https://usatoday30.usatoday.com/sports/olympics/beijing/gymnastics/2008-08-06-johnson_N.htm; Morgan, *Gymnastics*; A. Park, "Liang Chow's Gymnastics Coaching Journey."

105. McKayla Maroney on the GymCastic podcast, quoted in Wiedeman, "Full Revolution."

106. Wiedeman, "Full Revolution."

107. Slava Corn, "Safeguarding Working Group," *FIG Bulletin* 246 (April 2019): 134.

108. André Gueisbuhler in Corn, "Safeguarding Working Group," 135.

109. Gymnastics Ethics Foundation, "About."

110. IOC, "Safeguarding Toolkit," https://www.olympic.org/athlete365/safeguarding/#_ga=2.247332996.1660150717.1529649057–1938241981.1529649057, accessed May 8, 2019. President Watanabe also acknowledged that the education toolkit was inspired by the IOC. Watanabe, "President's Report," 117.

111. Watanabe, "President's Report," 117.

112. Ibid., 135.

Conclusion

1. Bruno Grandi, "Before the Sports Press, F.I.G. President Bruno Grandi Explains How Gymnastics Reinforced Its Credibility," e-mailed press release, February 10, 2016, FIG.

2. Professional gymnastics does not become apparent until after 2000, with world cup series and world championships awarding prize money to top athletes, as well as commercial entertainment format gymnastics such as the televised shows *Pro Gymnastics Challenge* (USA, 2013) and *Tumble* (UK, 2014).

3. Grandi, "Before the Sports Press."

4. Bowmile, "Swimming."

5. See, for example, B. Downie and E. Downie, "Our Story," and Tarabini, "Aproveche la cuarentena."

BIBLIOGRAPHY

Primary Sources

ARCHIVES

IOC Archives, Olympic Studies Centre, Lausanne, Switzerland. Includes *FIG Bulletins*.

Olympic Multimedia Library. Accessed online at https://library.olympic.org/default/multimedia-library.aspx?

Secondary Sources

Adams, Mary Louise. "From Mixed-Sex Sport to Sport for Girls: The Feminization of Figure Skating." In *Women in Sports History*, edited by Carol A. Osborne and Fiona Skillen, 29–52. New York: Routledge, 2011.

Aggestam, Karin, and Ann Towns. "The Gender Turn in Diplomacy: A New Research Agenda." *International Feminist Journal of Politics* 21, no. 1 (2019): 9–28. https://doi.org/10.1080/14616742.2018.1483206.

Ansorge, Charles J., and John K. Scheer. "International Bias Detected in Judging Gymnastic Competition at the 1984 Olympic Games." *Research Quarterly for Exercise and Sport* 59, no. 2 (1988): 103–7. https://doi.org/10.1080/02701367.1988.10605486.

Ansorge, Charles J., John K. Scheer, Jan Laub, and James Howard. "Bias in Judging Women's Gymnastics Induced by Expectations of within-Team Order." *Research Quarterly. American Alliance for Health, Physical Education and Recreation* 49, no. 4 (1978): 399–405. https://doi.org/10.1080/10671315.1978.10615552.

Australian Human Rights Commission. "Independent Review of Gymnastics in Australia." September 22, 2020. https://humanrights.gov.au/gymnastics.

Barker-Ruchti, Natalie. "Ballerinas and Pixies: A Genealogy of the Changing Female Gymnastics Body." *International Journal of the History of Sport* 26, no. 1 (2009): 45–62. https://doi.org/10.1080/09523360802500089.

———. "'Stride Jump—Begin!' Swedish Gymnastics in Victorian England." *Sporting Traditions* 22, no. 2 (2006): 13–29.

———. *Women's Artistic Gymnastics: An (Auto-)Ethnographic Journey*. Basel: Edition Gesowip, 2011.

Barker-Ruchti, Natalie, and Julia Weber. "Bending, Flirting, Floating, Flying: A Critical Analysis of Female Figures in 1970s Gymnastics Photographs." *Sociology of Sport Journal* 29 (2012): 22–41.

Barker-Ruchti, Natalie, Roslyn Kerr, Astrid Schubring, Georgia Cervin, and Myrian Nunomura. "'Gymnasts Are Like Wine, They Get Better with Age': Becoming and Developing Adult Women's Artistic Gymnasts." *Quest* 69, no. 3 (2017): 348–65. https://doi.org/10.1080/00336297.2016.1230504.

Barnes, Harry. "Politicized Gymnastics or How Sport Does Not Always Promote Friendship." Declassified document, May 17, 1977. American Embassy Bucharest, US National Archives. http://aad.archives.gov/aad/createpdf?rid=111900&dt=2532&dl=1629.

Beamish, Rob, and Ian Ritchie. "Totalitarian Regimes and Cold War Sport: Steroid 'Ubermenschen' and 'Ball-Bearing Females.'" In Wagg and Andrews, *East Plays West*, 11–26.

Benn, Tansin, and Barry Benn. "After Olga: Developments in Women's Artistic Gymnastics Following the 1972 'Olga Korbut Phenomenon.'" In *Sport Histories: Figurational Studies in the Development of Modern Sports*, edited by Eric Dunning, Dominic Malcolm, and Ivan Waddington, 172–90. London: Routledge, 2004.

Benton, Emilia. "Everything You Need to Know about Bela and Martha Karolyi That Wasn't in HBO's USA Gymnastics Doc." *Women's Health*, May 5, 2019. https://www.womenshealthmag.com/life/a27307279/bela-martha-karolyi-ranch-usa-gymnastics-larry-nassar-abuse/.

Best, David. "Art and Sport." *Journal of Aesthetic Education* 14, no. 2 (1980): 69–80. https://doi.org/10.2307/3332478. http://www.jstor.org/stable/3332478.

Bohuon, Anaïs. "Afterword: Doing History of Gender and Sport—A Feminist Perspective as a French Sports Historian and Practitioner." In Cervin and Nicolas, *Histories of Women's Work*, 327–38.

Borges, Mário, António Rosado, Rita de Oliveira, and Francisco Freitas. "Coaches' Migration: A Qualitative Analysis of Recruitment, Motivations and Experiences." *Leisure Studies* 34, no. 5 (2015): 588–602. https://doi.org/10.1080/02614367.2014.939988.

Bottenburg, Maarten, van. "Why Are the European and American Sports Worlds So Different? Path Dependence in European and American Sports History." In *Sport and the Transformation of Modern Europe: States, Media and Markets 1950–2010*, edited by Alan Tomlinson, Christopher Young, and Richard Holt, 205–25. New York: Routledge, 2011.

Bowmile, Mitch. "Swimming Set to Receive Second Highest I.O.C. Funding among All Olympic Sports." *SwimSwam*, April 25, 2015. http://swimswam.com/swimming -set-to-receive-second-highest-ioc-funding-among-all-olympic-sports/.

"Brace of Balanced Beauties." *Life* 44, no. 2 (January 13, 1958): 8–10.

Braun, Jutta, and René Wiese. "'Tracksuit Traitors': Eastern German Top Athletes on the Run." *International Journal of the History of Sport* 31 no. 12 (2014): 1519–34. https://doi.org/10.1080/09523367.2014.922549.

Brokhin, Yuri. *The Big Red Machine*. New York: Random House, 1978.

Browne, Peggy. "Editorial." *Australian Gymnast* 11, no. 4 (December 1985): 4.

Butler, Judith. *Gender Trouble: Feminism and the Subversion of Identity*. New York: Routledge, 1990.

———. *Undoing Gender*. New York: Routledge, 2004.

Cadwallader, Amy B., Xavier de la Torre, Alessandra Tieri, and Francesco Botrè. "The Abuse of Diuretics as Performance-Enhancing Drugs and Masking Agents in Sport Doping: Pharmacology, Toxicology and Analysis." *British Journal Of Pharmacology* 161, no. 1 (2010): 1–16. https://doi.org/10.1111/j.1476–5381.2010.00789.x.

Cahn, Susan K. *Coming on Strong: Gender and Sexuality in Twentieth-Century Women's Sport*. Cambridge, MA: Harvard University Press, 1995.

———. "From the 'Muscle Moll' to the 'Butch' Ballplayer: Mannishness, Lesbianism, and Homophobia in U.S. Women's Sport." *Feminist Studies* 19, no. 2 (1993): 343–68. https://doi.org/10.2307/3178373.

Carpentier, Florence, and Jean-Pierre Lefèvre. "The Modern Olympic Movement, Women's Sport and the Social Order during the Inter-War Period." *International Journal of the History of Sport* 23, no. 7 (2006): 1112–27. https://doi.org/ 10.1080/09523360600832387.

Carter, Thomas F., and John Sugden. "The USA and Sporting Diplomacy: Comparing and Contrasting the Cases of Table Tennis with China and Baseball with Cuba in the 1970s." *International Relations* 26, no. 1 (2012): 101–21. https://doi.org/10.1177/ 0047117811411741.

Castan-Vicente, Florys, Claire Nicolas, and Georgia Cervin. "Women in Sport Organisations: Historiographical and Epistemological Challenges." In Cervin and Nicolas, *Histories of Women's Work*, 17–48.

Caute, David. *The Dancer Defects: The Struggle for Cultural Supremacy during the Cold War*. Oxford: Oxford University Press, 2003.

Cervin, Georgia, and Claire Nicolas, eds. *Histories of Women's Work in Global Sport: A Man's World?* Basingstoke, UK: Palgrave Macmillan, 2019.

Cervin, Georgia, Claire Nicolas, Sylvain Dufraisse, Anaïs Bohuon, and Grégory Quin. "Gymnastics' Centre of Gravity: The *Fédération Internationale de Gymnastique*, Its Governance and the Cold War, 1956–1976." *Sport in History* 37, no. 3 (2017): 309–31. https://doi.org/10.1080/17460263.2017.1363081.

Cervin, Georgia, Grégory Quin, and Axel Elias. "From the Carpet to the Executive Committee: Women Leading Women's Gymnastics." In Cervin and Nicolas, *Histories of Women's Work*, 245–72.

Cervin, Georgia, Roslyn Kerr, Natalie Barker-Ruchti, Astrid Schubring, and Myrian Nunomura. "Growing Up and Speaking Out: Female Gymnasts' Rights in an Ageing Sport." *Annals of Leisure Research* 20, no. 3 (2017): 317–30. https://doi.org/10.1080/11745398.2017.1310625.

Chaves, Elisângela, and Andrea Moreno. "Dance and the Education of Femininity: Belo Horizonte—MG (1930–1960)." *Pro-Posições* 29, no. 2 (2018): 259–84. https://doi.org/10.1590/1980–6248-2016–0132.

Cheers, Michael. "Dianne Durham: Going for the Gold in '84 Olympics." *Ebony*, September 1983: 52–56.

"China 'Accept' Decision to Strip Them of Olympic Bronze." Sport: Gymnastics, BBC, April 29, 2010. http://news.bbc.co.uk/sport2/hi/other_sports/gymnastics/8649850.stm.

Chisholm, Ann. "Acrobats, Contortionists, and Cute Children: The Promise and Perversity of U.S. Women's Gymnastics." *Signs: Journal of Women in Culture and Society* 27, no. 2 (2002): 415–50. https://doi.org/10.1086/495692.

———. "The Disciplinary Dimensions of Nineteenth-Century Gymnastics for US Women." *International Journal of the History of Sport* 24, no. 4 (2007): 432–79. https://doi.org/10.1080/09523360601157172.

———. "Gymnastics and the Reconstitution of Republican Motherhood among True Women of Civic Virtue, 1830–1870." *International Journal of the History of Sport* 23, no. 8 (2006): 1275–313. https://doi.org/10.1080/09523360600922212.

———. "Incarnations and Practices of Feminine Rectitude: Nineteenth-Century Gymnastics for U.S. Women." *Journal of Social History* 38, no. 3 (2005): 737–63. http://www.jstor.org/stable/3790653.

———. "Nineteenth-Century Gymnastics for U.S. Women and Incorporations of Buoyancy: Contouring Femininity, Shaping Sex, and Regulating Middle-Class Consumption." *Journal of Women's History* 20, no. 3 (2008): 84–112. https://doi.org/10.1353/jowh.0.0026.

Clastres, Patrick. "Olympisme et guerre froide. Du paradigme réaliste au paradigme culturel." *Guerres mondiales et conflits contemporains* 277, no. 1 (2020): 7–25. https://doi.org/10.3917/gmcc.277.0007.

———. "Playing with Greece: Pierre de Coubertin and the Motherland of Humanities and Olympics." *Histoire@Politique: Politique, culture, société* 12, no. 3 (2010). https://doi.org/10.3917/hp.012.0009.

Cohen, Bonni, and Jon Shenk, dir. *Athlete A.* Documentary. San Francisco, CA: Actual Films, 2020. 104 min.

Cohen, Rachel Lara. "Femininity, Childhood and the Non-Making of a Sporting Celebrity: The Beth Tweddle Case." *Sociological Research Online* 18, no. 3 (2013): 1–10. https://doi.org/10.5153/sro.3193.

Comaneci, Nadia. *Letters to a Young Gymnast.* New York: Basic Books, 2004.

Congelio, Bradley J. "In Defense of a Neoliberal America: Ronald Reagan, Domestic Policy, and the Soviet Boycott of the 1984 Los Angeles Olympic Games." In *Defending the American Way of Life: Sport, Culture, and the Cold War,* edited by

Toby C. Rider and Kevin B. Witherspoon, 205–18. Fayetteville: University of Arkansas Press, 2018.

Connell, R. W., and James W. Messerschmidt. "Hegemonic Masculinity: Rethinking the Concept." *Gender and Society* 19, no. 6 (2005): 829–59. https://doi.org/10.1177/0891243205278639.

Cull, Nicholas J. "Public Diplomacy: Taxonomies and Histories." *Annals of the American Academy of Political and Social Science* 616, no. 1 (2008): 31–54. https://doi.org/10.1177/0002716207311952.

Darbon, Sebastien. *Les fondements du systeme sportif: Essai d'anthropologie historique*. Paris: L'Harmattan, 2014.

David, Paulo. *Human Rights in Youth Sports: A Critical Review of Children's Rights in Competitive Sports*. London: Routledge, 2005.

Day, Dave. "Historical Perspectives on Coaching." In *Routledge Handbook of Sports Coaching*, edited by Paul Potrac, Wade Gilbert, and Jim Denison, 5–15. New York: Routledge, 2013.

Day, Dave, and Tegan Carpenter. *A History of Sports Coaching in Britain: Overcoming Amateurism*. New York: Routledge, 2016.

Deford, Frank. "Nadia Awed Ya." *Sports Illustrated,* August 2, 1976: 28–31. https://vault.si.com/vault/1976/08/02/nadia-comaneci-1976-olympics-perfect-scores.

———. "Rising to Great Heights." *Sports Illustrated*, December 24, 1984: 32–44. https://www.si.com/vault/1984/12/24/620535/rising-to-great-heights.

Dempster, Elizabeth. "Women Writing the Body: Let's Watch a Little How She Dances." In *The Routledge Dance Studies Reader*, edited by Jens Giersdorf, Yutian Wong, and Janet O'Shea, 229–35. New York: Routledge, 2010.

Diamond, Peter, and Linda Passudettie. "Moscow Diary: Superb Pageantry and Performances." In *United States Olympic Book*, edited by Parry D. Sorensen, 130–34. Colorado Springs: United States Olympic Committee, 1980.

Dichter, Heather L. "Diplomatic and International History: Athletes and Ambassadors." *International Journal of the History of Sport* 32, no. 15 (2015): 1741–44. https://doi.org/10.1080/09523367.2015.1098621.

Dichter, Heather, and Andrew L. Johns, eds. *Diplomatic Games: Sport, Statecraft, and International Relations since 1945*. Lexington: University Press of Kentucky, 2014.

Diem, Carl. "Per Henrik Ling. On the Occasion of the One Hundredth Anniversary of His Death." *Olympic Review* 5 (1939).

Dimeo, Paul. "Good Versus Evil? Drugs, Sport and the Cold War." In Wagg and Andrews, *East Plays West*, 149–62.

Donnelly, Peter. "Child Labour, Sport Labour: Applying Child Labour Laws to Sport." *International Review for the Sociology of Sport* 32, no. 4 (1997): 389–406. https://doi.org/10.1177/101269097032004004.

Downie, Becky, and Ellie Downie. "Our Story." Twitter, July 10, 2020. https://twitter.com/Bdownie/status/1281312756415827968?s=20.

Duffy, Martha. "Hello to a Russian Pixie," *Sports Illustrated,* March 19, 1973: 24–27. https://vault.si.com/vault/1973/03/19/hello-to-a-russian-pixie

Dufraisse, Sylvain. *Les héros du sport: Une histoire des champions soviétiques (années 1930–années 1980)*. Ceyzérieu: Champ Vallon, 2019.

Duncan, Margaret Carlisle. "A Hermeneutic of Spectator Sport: The 1976 and 1984 Olympic Games." *Quest* 38, no. 1 (1986): 50–77. https://doi.org/10.1080/00336297.1986.10483841.

Dynko, Alyaksandra, Pete Baumgartner, and Andrey Shauliuha. "#MeToo in Belarus: Ex-Teammates Bolster Korbut's Sexual-Assault Charges against Coach." *Radio Free Europe*, May 16, 2018. https://www.rferl.org/a/metoo-in-belarus-ex-teammates-bolster-korbut-s-sexual-assault-charges-against-coach/29230312.html.

Edelman, Robert Simon. "The Russians Are Not Coming! The Soviet Withdrawal from the Games of the XXIII Olympiad." *International Journal of the History of Sport* 32, no. 1 (2015): 9–36. https://doi.org/10.1080/09523367.2014.958669.

Eichberg, Henning. "Stronger, Funnier, Deadlier: Track and Field in the Way to the Ritual of the Record." In *Ritual and Record: Sports Records and Quantification in Pre-Modern Societies*, edited by John Marshall Carter and Arnd Kruger, 123–34. New York: Greenwood, 1990.

Elias, Norbert, and Eric Dunning. *Quest for Excitement: Sport and Leisure in the Civilizing Process*. Oxford, UK: Blackwell, 1986.

Emery, Lynne. "An Examination of the 1928 Olympic 800 Meter Race for Women." *North American Society for Sport History Proceedings and Newsletter*, 1982: 30. https://digital.la84.org/digital/collection/p17103coll10/id/10786/rec/1.

Fair, John D. "Physical Culture." In *Encyclopædia Britannica*, 2018. www.britannica.com/topic/physical-culture.

Fass, Paula S., and Grossberg, Michael. Preface. In *Reinventing Childhood after World War II*, edited by Paula S. Fass and Michael Grossberg, ix–xiii. Philadelphia: University of Pennsylvania Press, 2012.

FIG Women's Technical Committee. *Code of Points—Women*. Switzerland: FIG, 1979. https://727cb751-cae7-4614-8937-d8d4424e57ae.filesusr.com/ugd/59d1d7_946895cf92d54936bfd5d97d841dd5b2.pdf.

Forbes, Warwick. "Gymnastics Visit to the Soviet Union,. *Australian Gymnast* 11, no. 8 (December 1986): 8–10.

"Former Romanian Star Pities Raducan." *IG News Archive: December 2000* 2015, no. 30 (December 23, 2000). https://web.archive.org/web/20010306073500/http://www.internationalgymnast.com/news2000/dec.html.

Fulda, Andreas. "The Emergence of Citizen Diplomacy in European Union-China Relations: Principles, Pillars, Pioneers, Paradoxes." *Diplomacy and Statecraft* 30, no. 1 (2019): 188–216. https://doi.org/10.1080/09592296.2019.1557419.

Gerber, Ellen W. *Innovators and Institutions in Physical Education*. Philadelphia: Lea & Febiger, 1971.

Giddens, Anthony. *Capitalism and Modern Social Theory: An Analysis of the Writings of Marx, Durkheim and Max Weber*. Cambridge: Cambridge University Press, 1971.

Gleaves, John. "Doped Professionals and Clean Amateurs: Amateurism's Influence on the Modern Philosophy of Anti-Doping." *Journal of Sport History* 38, no. 2 (2011): 237–54. https://muse.jhu.edu/article/477766.

Gleaves, John, and Thomas Hunt. *A Global History of Doping in Sport: Drugs, Policy, and Politics*. New York: Routledge, 2016.

Golubev, Vladimir. "Olga Korbut." *Soviet Life* (Washington, DC) 196, no. 1 (January 1973): 56–59.

Goodbody, John. *The Illustrated History of Gymnastics*. London: Stanley Paul, 1982.

Grandi, Bruno. "Before the Sports Press, F.I.G. President Bruno Grandi Explains How Gymnastics Reinforced Its Credibility." FIG press release (e-mail), Doha, Qatar, February 10, 2016.

Greenhill, Jeff, Chris Auld, Graham Cuskelly, and Sue Hooper. "The Impact of Organisational Factors on Career Pathways for Female Coaches." *Sport Management Review* 12, no. 4 (2009): 229–40. https://doi.org/https://doi.org/10.1016/j.smr .2009.03.002.

Grossfeld, Abie. "A History of United States Artistic Gymnastics." *Science of Gymnastics* 2, no. 1 (2010): 5–28.

Guoqi, Xu. *Olympic Dreams: China and Sports, 1895–2008*. Cambridge, MA: Harvard University Press, 2008. http://ebookcentral.proquest.com/lib/uwa/detail .action?docID=3300133.

GutsMuths, Johann Christoph Friedrich. *Gymnastics for youth: Or, A practical guide to healthful and amusing exercises for the use of schools. An essay toward the necessary improvement of education, chiefly as it relates to the body*. London: J. Johnson, 1800.

Guttmann, Allen. "The Cold War and the Olympics." *International Journal* 43, no. 4 (1988): 554–68. https://doi.org/10.1177/002070208804300402.

———. *From Ritual to Record: The Nature of Modern Sports*. New York: Columbia University Press, 2004.

Gygax, Jérôme. "Raisons et prétextes au boycott américain des jeux Olympiques de Moscou." *Relations internationales*, no. 112 (2002): 487–510.

"Gymnastics and Archery." In *Olympic Encyclopedia*, edited by Monique Berlioux. Lausanne: International Olympic Committee, 1985.

"Gymnastics at the 1936 Summer Games: Women's Team All-Around." Sports Reference, 2016. https://www.sports-reference.com/olympics/summer/1936/ GYM/womens-team-all-around.html.

"Gymnastics at the 1948 London Summer Games: Women's Team All-Around." Sports Reference, 2016. https://www.sports-reference.com/olympics/summer/ 1948/GYM/womens-team-all-around.html (dead).

"Gymnastics at the 1992 Barcelona Summer Games." Sports Reference, 2016. https://www.sports-reference.com/olympics/summer/1992/GYM/ (dead).

Gymnastics Ethics Foundation. "About." https://www.gymnasticsethicsfoundation .org/about, accessed October 11, 2020.

"Gymnastics Tie-Break Rules Changed." Updated June 12, 2012. https://www .foxsports.com/stories/olympics/gymnastics-tie-break-rules-changed.

Hall, Margaret Ann. *The Girl and the Game: A History of Women's Sport in Canada*. Toronto: University of Toronto Press, 2009.

Hargreaves, Jennifer. *Sporting Females: Critical Issues in the History and Sociology of Women's Sports*. London: Routledge, 1994.

Hazanov, Alex. "Porous Empire: Foreign Visitors and the Post-Stalin Soviet State." PhD diss., University of Pennsylvania, 2016.

Heitinga Simone, and Stasja Köhler. *De onvrije oefening: Ex-topturnsters over jaren-lange fysieke en mentale intimidatie als trainingsmethode.* Breda, the Netherlands: De Geus, 2013.

"History." FIG. https://www.gymnastics.sport/site/about.php, accessed April 27, 2019.

Hoffman, John. "Reconstructing Diplomacy." *British Journal of Politics and International Relations* 5, no. 4 (2003): 525–42. https://doi.org/10.1111/1467-856X .00118.

Holt, Richard. "Allen Guttmann's Alter Ego: Sébastien Darbon and the Definition of 'Sport.'" *Journal of Sport History* 44, no. 1 (2017): 58–63.

Horne, Alistair. *Kissinger: 1973, the Crucial Year.* New York: Simon and Schuster, 2009.

Huggins, Mike. *The Victorians and Sport.* London: Cambridge University Press, 2004.

Hughes, R. Gerald, and Rachel J. Owen. "'The Continuation of Politics by Other Means': Britain, the Two Germanys and the Olympic Games, 1949–1972." *Contemporary European History* 18, no. 4 (2009): 443—74. https://doi.org/10.1017/ S0960777309990099.

Hulme, Derek L. J. *The Political Olympics: Moscow, Afghanistan, and the 1980 U.S. Boycott.* New York: Praeger, 1990.

Hunt, Thomas M. *Drug Games: The International Olympic Committee and the Politics of Doping, 1960–2008.* Austin: University of Texas Press, 2011.

Jahn, Friedrich Ludwig. *Die Deutsche Turnkunst für Einrichtung der Turnplätze.* Berlin, 1816.

———. *Runenblätter.* Frankfurt, 1814.

Karolyi, Bela, and Nancy Ann Richardson. *Feel No Fear: The Power, Passion, and Politics of a Life in Gymnastics.* New York: Hyperion, 1994.

Keith, Braden. "Swimming Jumps to Top of IOC Funding Ladder; Three Sports Named for Possible 2020 Inclusion." *Swimswam,* May 29, 2013. https://swimswam .com/swimming-jumps-to-top-of-ioc-funding-ladder-three-sports-named-for -possible-2020-inclusion-2/.

Kelner, Martha. "British Gymnastics: Claims Athletes 'Beaten into Submission' amid 'Culture of Fear.'" *Sky News,* July 6, 2020. https://news.sky.com/story/ british-gymnastics-claims-athletes-beaten-into-submission-amid-culture-of -fear-12022525.

Kerr, Roslyn. "The Evolution of Women's Artistic Gymnastics since 1952." MPhil, University of Sydney, 2003.

———. "The Impact of Nadia Comaneci on the Sport of Women's Artistic Gymnastics." *Sporting Traditions* 23, no. 1 (2006): 87–102.

Kerr, Roslyn, and Camilla Obel. "The Disappearance of the Perfect 10: Evaluating Rule Changes in Women's Artistic Gymnastics." *International Journal of the History of Sport* 32, no. 2 (2015): 318–31. https://doi.org/10.1080/09523367 .2014.974031.

Kerr, Roslyn, and Georgia Cervin. "An Ironic Imbalance: Coaching Opportunities and Gender in Women's Artistic Gymnastics in Australia and New Zealand." *International Journal of the History of Sport* 33, no. 17 (2016): 2139–52. https://doi.org/10.1080/09523367.2017.1283307.

Kerr, Roslyn, Natalie Barker-Ruchti, Astrid Schubring, Georgia Cervin, and Myrian Nunomura. "Coming of Age: Coaches Transforming the Pixie-Style Model of Coaching in Women's Artistic Gymnastics." *Sports Coaching Review* 8, no. 1 (2019): 7–24. https://doi.org/10.1080/21640629.2017.1391488.

Kerr, Roslyn, Natalie Barker-Ruchti, Astrid Schubring, Georgia Cervin, and Myrian Nunomura. *Coming of Age: Towards Best Practice in Women's Artistic Gymnastics. Land, Environment and People Research Report*. Christchurch, NZ: Lincoln University, 2015. https://researcharchive.lincoln.ac.nz/bitstream/handle/10182/6515/Leap%2037-Coming-of-age.pdf;sequence=3.

Kerr, Roslyn, Natalie Barker-Ruchti, Myrian Nunomura, Georgia Cervin, and Astrid Schubring. "The Role of Setting in the Field: The Positioning of Older Bodies in the Field of Elite Women's Gymnastics." *Sociology* 52, no. 4 (2016): 727–43. https://doi.org/10.1177/0038038516674676.

Keys, Barbara. *Globalizing Sport: National Rivalry and International Community in the 1930s*. Cambridge, MA: Harvard University Press, 2006.

———. "Nixon/Kissinger and Brezhnev." *Diplomatic History* 42, no. 4 (2018): 548–51. https://doi.org/10.1093/dh/dhy047.

———. "Political Protection: The International Olympic Committee's Un Diplomacy in the 1980s." *International Journal of the History of Sport* 34, no. 11 (2017): 1161–78. https://doi.org/10.1080/09523367.2017.1402764.

———. "The Soviet Union, Cultural Exchange and the 1956 Melbourne Olympic Games." In *Sport zwischen Ost und West*, edited by Arié Malz, Stefan Rohdewald, and Stefab Wiederkehr, 131–45. Osnabrück: Fibre, 2007.

Kidd, Bruce. "The Elite Athlete." In *Not Just a Game: Essays in Canadian Sport Sociology*, edited by Jean Harvey and Hart Cantelon, 287–308. Ottawa: University of Ottawa Press, 1988.

Kimmel, Michael S. "Men's Responses to Feminism at the Turn of the Century." *Gender and Society* 1, no. 3 (1987): 261–83. http://www.jstor.org/stable/189564.

Kirshenbaum, Jerry. "Scorecard: Bonus-Plus." *Sports Illustrated*, May 31, 1993, 15–16. https://vault.si.com/vault/711028.

Kondrashina, Evegeniya. "Soviet Music Recordings and Cold War Cultural Relations." In *Entangled East and West: Cultural Diplomacy and Artistic Interaction during the Cold War*, edited by Simon Mikkonen, Giles Scott-Smith, and Jari Parkkinen, 193–216. Berlin: de Gruyter, 2018.

Korbut, Olga, and Ellen Emerson-White. *My Story: The Autobiography of Olga Korbut*. London: Arrow, 1993.

Kordas, Ann. "Rebels, Robots, and All-American Girls: The Ideological Use of Images of Girl Gymnasts during the Cold War." In *Girlhood: A Global History*, edited by Jennifer Helgren and Colleen A. Vasconcellos, 195–214. New Brunswick, NJ: Rutgers University Press, 2012.

Koulouri, Christine. "Introduction: Rewriting the History of the Olympic Games." In *Athens, Olympic City, 1896–1906*, edited by Christine Koulouri, 13–53. Athens: International Olympic Academy, 2004.

Kozovoi, Andrei. "A Foot in the Door: The Lacy-Zarubin Agreement and Soviet-American Film Diplomacy during the Khrushchev Era, 1953–1963." *Historical Journal of Film, Radio and Television* 36, no. 1 (2016): 21–39. https://doi.org/10.1080/01439685.2015.1134107.

Krieger, Jörg. "'Born on the Wings of Commerce': The World Championships of the International Association of Athletics Federations." *International Journal of the History of Sport* 33, no. 4 (2016): 418–33. https://doi.org/10.1080/09523367.2016.1159201.

Krüger, Michael, and Annette R. Hofmann. "The Development of Physical-Education Institutions in Europe: A Short Introduction." *International Journal of the History of Sport* 32, no. 6 (2015): 737–39. https://doi.org/10.1080/09523367.2015.1024111.

la Cour, Christina. "The Evolution of the 'Public' in Diplomacy." *Place Branding and Public Diplomacy* 14, no. 1 (2018): 22–35. https://doi.org/10.1057/s41254-017-0093-3.

Laptad, Richard E. "The Origin, Development, and Function of the United States Gymnastics Federation." PhD diss., University of Oregon, 1971.

Lawrence, Blythe. "Postponement and Progression: The Olympics That Helped Shape the Games," *FIG*, March, 27, 2020. https://www.gymnastics.sport/site/news/displaynews.php?idNews=2850.

Llewellyn, Matthew P., and John Gleaves. *The Rise and Fall of Olympic Amateurism*. Urbana: University of Illinois Press, 2016.

Llewellyn, Matthew, John Gleaves, and Wayne Wilson. "The Historical Legacy of the 1984 Los Angeles Olympic Games." *International Journal of the History of Sport* 32, no. 1 (2015): 1–8. https://doi.org/10.1080/09523367.2014.990892.

Lorber, Judith. *Paradoxes of Gender*. New Haven, CT: Yale University Press, 1994.

Lyman, Stanford M. "The 'Yellow Peril' Mystique: Origins and Vicissitudes of a Racist Discourse." *International Journal of Politics, Culture, and Society* 13, no. 4 (2000): 683–747. http://www.jstor.org/stable/20020056.

Maguire, Joseph. "Blade Runners: Canadian Migrants, Ice Hockey, and the Global Sports Process." *Journal of Sport and Social Issues* 20, no. 3 (1996/08/01 1996): 335–60. https://doi.org/10.1177/019372396020003007.

———. "'Real Politic' or 'Ethically Based': Sport, Globalization, Migration and Nation-State Policies." *Sport in Society* 14, no. 7–8 (2011): 1040–55. https://doi.org/10.1080/17430437.2011.603557.

Mankowski, Eric S., and Kenneth I. Maton. "A Community Psychology of Men and Masculinity: Historical and Conceptual Review." *American Journal of Community Psychology* 45, no. 1–2 (2010): 73–86. https://doi.org/10.1007/s10464-009-9288-y.

Markula, Pirkko, and Marianne I. Clark. Introduction. In *The Evolving Feminine Ballet Body*, edited by Pirkko Markula and Marianne I. Clark, xv–xxxiv. Edmonton: University of Alberta Press, 2018.

Martin, Patricia Yancey. "Gender as Social Institution." *Social Forces* 82, no. 4 (2004): 1249–73. https://doi.org/10.1353/sof.2004.0081.

Mason, Courtney W. "The Bridge to Change: The 1976 Montreal Olympic Games, South African Apartheid Policy, and the Boycott Paradigm." In Schaus and Wenn, *Onward to the Olympics*, 283–96.

Maurer, Tracy Nelson. *Uneven Bars: Tips, Rules and Legendary Stars*. Oxford, UK: Raintree, 2017.

McClendon, Alphonso D. "Fashionable Addiction: The Path to Heroin Chic." In *Fashion in Popular Culture: Literature, Media and Contemporary Studies*, edited by Joseph H. Hancock II, Toni Johnson-Woods, and Vicki Karaminas, 67–86. Chicago: Intellect, University of Chicago Press, 2013.

Mellis, Johanna. "Cold War Politics and the California Running Scene: The Experiences of Mihály Iglói and László Tábori in the Golden State." *Journal of Sport History* 46, no. 1 (2019): 62–81. https://doi.org/10.5406/jsporthistory.46.1.0062.

———. "From Defectors to Cooperators: The Impact of 1956 on Athletes, Sport Leaders and Sport Policy in Socialist Hungary." *Contemporary European History* 29, no. 1 (2020): 60–76. https://doi.10.1017/S0960777319000183.

Mertin, Evelyn. "Presenting Heroes: Athletes as Role Models for the New Soviet Person." *International Journal of the History of Sport* 26, no. 4 (2009): 469–83. https://doi.org/10.1080/09523360802658077.

———. "The Soviet Union and the Olympic Games of 1980 and 1984: Explaining the Boycotts to Their Own People." In Wagg and Andrews, *East Plays West*, 235–52.

Messner, Michael. "Sports and Male Domination: The Female Athlete as Contested Ideological Terrain." *Sociology of Sport Journal* 5, no. 3 (1988): 197–211. https://doi.org/10.1123/ssj.5.3.197.

Meyers, Dvora. "The Decades of Black Gymnasts Who Paved the Way for Simone Biles." *Splinter*, July 15, 2016. https://splinternews.com/the-decades-of-black-gymnasts-who-paved-the-way-for-sim-1793860258.

———. "The Next Step for Elite Gymnasts Is to Form a Union." *Deadspin*, January 7, 2019. https://deadspin.com/the-next-step-for-elite-gymnasts-is-to-form-a-union-1831465643.

———. "Former National Champion Speaks Out about USA Gymnastics' Problems with Eating Disorders and Abuse." *Deadspin*, June 12, 2017. https://deadspin.com/former-national-champion-speaks-out-about-usa-gymnastic-1795966537.

Miller, Michael. "American Football: The Rationalization of the Irrational." *International Journal of Politics, Culture, and Society* 11, no. 1 (1997): 101–27. http://www.jstor.org/stable/20019925.

Miller, Shannon, with Danny Peary. *It's Not about Perfect: Competing for My Country and Fighting for My Life*. New York: St Martin's, 2015.

Moceanu, Dominique, with Paul and Teri Williams. *Off Balance: A Memoir*. New York: Touchstone, 2012.

Montez de Oca, Jeffrey. "The 'Muscle Gap': Physical Education and US Fears of a Depleted Masculinity, 1954–1963." In Wagg and Andrews, *East Plays West*, 123–48.

Morgan, Elizabeth. *Gymnastics: Science on the Mat and in the Air*. New York: Lucent, 2018.

Murray, Stuart. "Sports Diplomacy." *The Hague Journal of Diplomacy* 8, no. 3–4 (2013): 191–95. https://doi.org/10.1163/1871191X-12341264.

Naul, Roland. *Olympic Education*. Maidenhead, UK: Meyer & Meyer, 2007.

Nauright, John, and Charles Parrish. *Sports around the World: History, Culture, and Practice*. Santa Barbara, CA: ABC-Clio, 2012.

"N.B.C. Nightly News: Olga Korbut and the U.S.S.R.'S Women's Gymnastics Team." NBC Universal Archives. 1973. http://www.nbcuniversalarchives.com/nbcuni/clip/5112499403_004.do.

Neirick, Miriam. *When Pigs Could Fly and Bears Could Dance: A History of the Soviet Circus*. Madison: University of Wisconsin Press, 2012.

Nixon, President Richard, Brent Scowcroft, and Soviet Women's Gymnastics Team. "Memorandum of Conversation." White House, March 21, 1973. Gerald R. Ford Presidential Library and Museum, National Archives. http://www.fordlibrarymuseum.gov/library/document/0314/1552571.pdf.

Nolte, Claire Elaine. *The Sokol in the Czech Lands to 1914: Training for the Nation*. Basingstoke, UK: Palgrave Macmillan, 2002.

Norman, Leanne. "Feeling Second Best: Elite Women Coaches' Experiences." *Sociology of Sport Journal* 27, no. 1 (2010): 89–104. https://doi.org/10.1123/ssj.27.1.89.

Nye, Joseph S. *Soft Power: The Means to Success in World Politics*. New York: Public Affairs, 2004.

O'Brien, Catherine. "An Investigation of the Processes Which Produce Elite Women Gymnasts in the USSR." PhD diss., Ohio State University, 1979.

O'Brien, Patty. *The Pacific Muse: Exotic Femininity and the Colonial Pacific*. Seattle: University of Washington Press, 2006.

O'Brien, Richard. "Gymnastics Lord Gym: It Has Been 11 Years since Bela Károlyi Defected to Become the Undisputed King of the U.S. Women." *Sports Illustrated*, July 27, 1992: 46–52. https://vault.si.com/vault/1992/07/27/gymnastics-lord-gym-it-has-been-11-years-since-bela-karolyi-defected-to-become-the-undisputed-king-of-the-us-women.

Office of the Historian. "Chronology: United States Relations with Russia: The Cold War: 1945–1949." US Department of State, n.d. https://2001-2009.state.gov/r/pa/ho/pubs/fs/85895.htm#brezhnev_nixon.

"Official Olympic Games Results." International Olympic Committee. http://www.olympic.org/olympic-results, accessed October 2018.

Official Report of the Organizing Committee for the Games of the XVI Olympiad, Melbourne, 1956. Melbourne: W. M. Houson, Government Printer, 1958. https://digital.la84.org/digital/collection/p17103coll8/id/16475.

Okino, Betty. Review, *Little Girls and Pretty Boxes*, by Joan Ryan. Balanced View, *Sports Hollywood*, May 21, 2001. https://web.archive.org/web/20060323203143/http://www.sportshollywood.com/gymnastics3.html.

"Olympians Put Avery Brundage on the Spot." *Sports Illustrated*, August 27, 1956, 28–29. https://vault.si.com/vault/1956/08/27/olympians-put-avery-brundage-on-the-spot.

"Olympic Marketing Factfile: 2019 Edition." International Olympic Committee, updated December 31, 2018. https://stillmed.olympic.org/media/Document%20 Library/OlympicOrg/Documents/IOC-Marketing-and-Broadcasting-General -Files/Olympic-Marketing-Fact-File-2018.pdf.

"Olympics, the Games: Up in the Air." *Time*, August 2, 1976.

Ottum, Bob. "It's Up to You, Mary Lou." *Sports Illustrated*, July 18, 1984, 462–76. https://vault.si.com/vault/1984/07/18/its-up-to-you-mary-lou.

Özçakır, Sabri. "'Heroes! Bring Happiness to Your Motherland! Long Live the Yunaks': The Bulgarian Yunak Gymnastics Movement in the Late Ottoman Period." *International Journal of the History of Sport* 36, no. 2–3 (2019): 186–206. https://doi.org/10.1080/09523367.2019.1630820.

Park, Alice. "Liang Chow's Gymnastics Coaching Journey: From Beijing to West Des Moines." *Time*, July 26, 2012. http://olympics.time.com/2012/07/26/liang -chows-gymnastics-coaching-journey-from-beijing-to-west-des-moines/.

Park, Roberta J. "'Embodied Selves': The Rise and Development of Concern for Physical Education, Active Games and Recreation for American Women, 1776– 1865." *International Journal of the History of Sport* 24, no. 12 (2007): 1508–42. https://doi.org/10.1080/09523360701618933.

Parks, Jenifer. "'Nothing but Trouble': The Soviet Union's Push to 'Democratise' International Sports during the Cold War, 1959–1962." *International Journal of the History of Sport* 30, no. 13 (2013): 1554–67. https://doi.org/10.1080/09523367 .2013.828709.

———. "Verbal Gymnastics: Sports, Bureaucracy, and the Soviet Union's Entrance into the Olympic Games, 1946–1952." In Wagg and Andrews, *East Plays West*, 27–44.

Pfister, Gertrud. "Cultural Confrontations: German Turnen, Swedish Gymnastics and English Sport—European Diversity in Physical Activities from a Historical Perspective." *Culture, Sport, Society* 6, no. 1 (2003): 61–91. https://doi.org/10.1080/ 14610980312331271489.

———. "Epilogue: Gymnastics from Europe to America." *International Journal of the History of Sport* 26, no. 13 (2009): 2052–58. https://doi.org/10.1080/0952336 0903223003.

———. *Gymnastics, a Transatlantic Movement: From Europe to America*. New York: Routledge, 2013.

Pieper, Lindsay Parks. *Sex Testing: Gender Policing in Women's Sports*. Urbana: University of Illinois Press, 2017.

Pigman, Geoffrey Allen. "International Sport and Diplomacy's Public Dimension: Governments, Sporting Federations and the Global Audience." *Diplomacy and Statecraft* 25, no. 1 (2014): 94–114. https://doi.org/10.1080/09592296.2014.873613.

Pike, E., A. White, J. Matthews, S. Southon, and L. Piggott. "Women and Sport Leadership: A Case Study of a Development Programme." In *The Palgrave Handbook of Feminism and Sport, Leisure and Physical Education*, edited by L. Mansfield, J. Caudwell, B. Wheaton, and B. Watson, 809–23. London: Palgrave Macmillan, 2017. https://doi.org/10.1057/978-1-137-53318-0_51.

Plessner, Henning. "Expectation Biases in Gymnastics Judging." *Journal of Sport and Exercise Psychology* 21, no. 2 (1999): 131. https://doi.org/10.1123/jsep.21.2.131.

Polonskaya, Oksana. "Yelena Mukhina: Grown-Up Games." *Ogonyok Magazine*, 1998. http://www.oocities.org/graf_de_la_fer/mukhina-int.html.

Pope, Steven W. *The New American Sport History: Recent Approaches and Perspectives*. Urbana: University of Illinois Press, 1997.

Postlethwaite, Verity, and Jonathan Grix. "Beyond the Acronyms: Sport Diplomacy and the Classification of the International Olympic Committee." *Diplomacy and Statecraft* 27, no. 2 (2016): 295–313. https://doi.org/10.1080/09592296.2016.1169796.

Prados, John. "Notes on the CIA's Secret War in Afghanistan." *Journal of American History* 89, no. 2 (2002): 466–71. https://doi.org/10.2307/3092167.

Prevots, Naima. *Dance for Export: Cultural Diplomacy and the Cold War*. Middletown, CT: Wesleyan University Press, 1998.

Prochasson, Christophe. "Les jeux du 'je': Aperçus sur la subjectivité de l'historien." *Sociétés et représentations* 1, no. 13 (2002): 207–26. https://doi.org/10.3917/sr.013.0207.

Quin, Grégory. "History of Swiss Feminine Gymnastics between Competition and Feminization (1950–1990)." *Sport in Society* 19, no. 5 (2016): 653–66. https://doi.org/10.1080/17430437.2015.1073945.

Quin, Grégory, and Anaïs Bohuon, eds. *Les liaisons dangereuses de la médecine et du sport*. Paris: Éditions Glyphe, 2015.

Reuveny, Rafael, and Aseem Prakash. "The Afghanistan War and the Breakdown of the Soviet Union." *Review of International Studies* 25, no. 4 (1999): 693–708. https://doi.org/10.1017/S0260210599006932.

Rider, Toby C. *Cold War Games: Propaganda, the Olympics, and U.S. Foreign Policy*. Urbana: University of Illinois Press, 2016.

———. "The Olympic Games and the Secret Cold War: The US Government and the Propaganda Campaign against Communist Sport, 1950–1960." PhD diss., University of Western Ontario, 2011.

———. "Projecting America: Sport and Early US Cold War Propaganda, 1947–1960." In *Defending the American Way of Life: Sport, Culture, and the Cold War*, edited by Toby C. Rider and Kevin B. Witherspoon, 13–28. Fayetteville: University of Arkansas Press, 2018.

Rider, Toby, and Kevin Witherspoon. "Making Contact with the Captive Peoples: The Eisenhower Administration, Cultural Infiltration, and Sports Tours to Eastern Europe." *Journal of Sport History* 45, no. 3 (2018): 297–312. https://www.jstor.org/stable/10.5406/jsporthistory.45.3.0297.

Rinehart, Robert E. "Cold War Expatriot Sport: Symbolic Resistance and the International Response in Hungarian Water Polo at the Melbourne Olympics, 1956." In Wagg and Andrews, *East Plays West*, 45–63.

———. "The Rise, Fall and Rebirth of Sporting Women in Russia and the USSR." *Journal of Sport History* 18, no. 1 (1991): 183–99. http://www.jstor.org/stable/43636124.

———. *Sport in Soviet Society: Development of Sport and Physical Education in Russia and the USSR.* Cambridge: Cambridge University Press, 1980.

Ritzer, George. *The McDonaldization of Society.* 5th ed. Los Angeles: Pine Forge Press, 2008.

Roenigk, Alyssa, and Bonnie Ford. *Heavy Medals.* Podcast. ESPN, 2020. https://30for30podcasts.com/heavy-medals/.

"Romanian Gymnasts Faked Age to Compete." *BBC News,* May 2, 2002. http://news.bbc.co.uk/2/hi/europe/1964264.stm.

"Romanian Gymnasts 'Lied about Age.'" *Sports Illustrated,* April 18, 2002. https://web.archive.org/web/20021011031543/http://sportsillustrated.cnn.com/more/news/2002/04/18/romania_ap/.

Rubinstein, Alvin Z. "Soviet Imperialism in Afghanistan." *Current History* 79 (1980): 80.

Ryan, Joan. *Little Girls in Pretty Boxes: The Making and Breaking of Elite Gymnasts and Figure Skaters.* New York: Doubleday, 1995.

Sands, William A. "Why Gymnastics?" *Technique* 19, no. 3 (March 1999): 5–14. https://usagym.org/pages/home/publications/technique/1999/3/whygymnastics.pdf.

Sanislo, Teresa. "Protecting Manliness in the Age of Enlightenment: The New Physical Education and Gymnastics in Germany, 1770–1800." In *Gender in Transition: Discourse and Practice in German-Speaking Europe, 1750–1830,* edited by Ulrike Gleixner and Marion W. Gray, 265–81. Ann Arbor: University of Michigan Press, 2006.

Sarantakes, Nicolas Evan. *Dropping the Torch: Jimmy Carter, the Olympic Boycott, and the Cold War.* Cambridge: Cambridge University Press, 2010.

Sartore, Melanie, and George Cunningham. "The Lesbian Label as a Component of Women's Stigmatization in Sport Organizations: An Exploration of Two Health and Kinesiology Departments." *Journal of Sport Management* 24, no. 5 (2010): 481—501. https://doi.org/10.1123/jsm.24.5.481.

Saul, Norman E. "The Program That Shattered the Iron Curtain: The Lacy-Zarubin (Eisenhower-Khrushchev) Agreement of January 1958." In *New Perspectives on Russian-American Relations,* edited by William Benton Whisenhunt and Norman E. Saul, 229–39. London: Routledge, 2015.

Saull, Richard. *Rethinking Theory and History in the Cold War: The State, Military Power and Social Revolution.* London: Frank Cass, 2001.

Schaus, Gerald P., and Stephen R. Wenn, ed. *Onward to the Olympics: Historical Perspectives on the Olympic Games.* Waterloo, ON: Wilfred Laurier Press, 2007.

Schultz, Jaime. "Going the Distance: The Road to the 1984 Olympic Women's Marathon." *International Journal of the History of Sport* 32, no. 1 (2015): 72–88. https://doi.org/10.1080/09523367.2014.958668.

———. *Qualifying Times: Points of Change in U.S. Women's Sport.* Urbana: University of Illinois Press, 2017. https://doi.org/10.5406/illinois/9780252038167.001.0001.

Schunz, Simon, Giles Scott-Smith, and Luk Van Langenhove. "Broadening Soft Power in EU-US Relations." *European Foreign Affairs Review* 24, no. 2/1 (2019): 3–19. http://www.kluwerlawonline.com/document.php?id=EERR2019016.

Schweinbenz, Amanda Nicole, and Alexandria Cronk. "Femininity Control at the Olympic Games." *Gender, Sport and the Olympics* 9, no. 2 (2010): https://journals .sfu.ca/thirdspace/index.php/journal/article/view/schweinbenzcronk/329.

Scott, Steve. "'Beaten and Starved': Stars Allege Abuse at Heart of British Gymnastics." *ITV News*, July 7, 2020. https://www.itv.com/news/2020-07-06/beaten -and-starved-stars-allege-abuse-at-heart-of-british-gymnastics.

———. "Exclusive: Four Olympians among Former Gymnasts in Talks to Launch Legal Action against British Gymnastics." *ITV News*, September 7, 2020. https:// www.itv.com/news/2020-09-07/exclusive-four-olympians-among-former -gymnasts-in-talks-to-launch-legal-action-against-british-gymnastics.

Shakur-Bruno, Shani. "Sporting Subjection, Sporting Subjectivity: Race, Representation, and Women's Artistic Gymnastics." PhD diss., New York University, 2006.

Shaw, Tony. "The Politics of Cold War Culture." *Journal of Cold War Studies* 3, no. 3 (2001): 59–76. https://doi.org/10.1162/152039701750419510.

Shephard, Roy J. *An Illustrated History of Health and Fitness, from Pre-History to Our Post-Modern World*. Basingstoke, UK: Palgrave Macmillan, 2017.

Simons, Minot, II. *Women's Gymnastics: A History*. Carmel, CA: Welwyn, 1995.

Simonton, Deborah. *A History of European Women's Work: 1700 to the Present*. New York: Routledge, 2002.

Simpson, Pat. "Parading Myths: Imaging New Soviet Woman on Fizkul'turnik's Day, July 1944." *Russian Review* 63, no. 2 (2004): 187–211. http://www.jstor.org/ stable/3664081.

Smith, Rachel M., Dominic J. Parrott, Kevin M. Swartout, and Andra Teten Tharp. "Deconstructing Hegemonic Masculinity: The Roles of Antifemininity, Subordination to Women, and Sexual Dominance in Men's Perpetration of Sexual Aggression." *Psychology of Men and Masculinity* 16, no. 2 (2015): 160–69. https:// doi.org/10.1037/a0035956.

Stier, Jonas. *Blod, svett och tårar: Ledarkulturen inom svensk landslagsgymnastik— belyst och rroblematiserad*. Västerås: Svenska Gymnastikförbundet Och Mälardalens Högskola, 2012. https://www.diva-portal.org/smash/get/diva2:893205/ FULLTEXT01.pdf.

Stirling, Ashley E., and Gretchen A. Kerr. "Abused Athletes' Perceptions of the Coach-Athlete Relationship." *Sport in Society* 12, no. 2 (2009): 227–39. https:// doi.org/10.1080/17430430802591019.

Strayer, Robert. *Why Did the Soviet Union Collapse? Understanding Historical Change*. New York: M. E. Sharpe, 1998.

Summers-Bremner, Eluned. "Reading Irigaray, Dancing." *Hypatia* 15, no. 1 (2000): 90–124. http://www.jstor.org/stable/3810513.

Sztainbok, Vannina. "Exposing Her Body, Revealing the Nation: The Carnival Vedette, Black Femininity and the Symbolic Order." *Social Identities* 19, no. 5 (2013): 592–606. https://doi.org/10.1080/13504630.2013.835508.

Tarabini, Ayelen. "Aproveche la cuarentena para encontrar las palabras adecuadas para despedirme." *Instagram*, April 17, 2020. https://www.instagram.com/ p/B_Dkem7JG5S.

"Team All Around, Women." Sports Reference. http://www.sports-reference.com/
olympics (dead).

Theberge, Nancy. "The Construction of Gender in Sport: Women, Coaching,
and the Naturalization of Difference." *Social Problems* 40, no. 3 (1993): 301–13.
https://doi.org/10.2307/3096881.

Thomas, Damion L. *Globetrotting: African American Athletes and Cold War Politics.*
Urbana: University of Illinois Press, 2012.

Thompson, Frances. "Report on Tour." *Australian Gymnast* 8, no. 3 (October 1978):
16–17. https://www.gymnastics.org.au/images/national/News/Flickin_Back
_Archive/oct_78.pdf.

Thorpe, Holly, and Belinda Wheaton. "'Generation X Games,' Action Sports and
the Olympic Movement: Understanding the Cultural Politics of Incorporation."
Sociology 45, no. 5 (2011): 830–47. https://doi.org/10.1177/0038038511413427.

"Timeline." *USA Gymnastics*, October 3, 2016. https://www.usagymlegacy.org/
timeline/.

Tomizawa, Roy. "The Great Czech Gymnast Vera Caslavska Passes Away, Part 1:
The Gymnast." *The Olympians*, September 16, 2016. https://theolympians.co/
2016/09/16/the-great-czech-gymnast-vera-caslavska-passes-away-part-1-the
-gymnast/.

Tonnerre, Quentin, Philippe Vonnard, and Nicola Sbetti. "Ghost Administra-
tors: Re-Centring Marisa Bonacossa, Lydia Zanchi and Suzanne Otth within
International Sport Organizations." In Cervin and Nicolas, *Histories of Women's
Work*, 101–28.

Turner, Amanda. "Yelena Mukhina Dies." *International Gymnast*, December 24,
2006. http://66.210.158.14/index.php?option=com_content&view=article&id
=38:yelena-mukhina-dies&catid=2:news&Itemid=53.

"USA Gymnastics Agrees to Purchase Karolyi Ranch Gymnastics Facilities." USA
Gymnastics, updated July 25, 2016. https://usagym.org/pages/post.html
?PostID=18960.

Van Rossem, G., ed. *The Ninth Olympiad, Being the Official Report of the Olympic
Games of 1928 Celebrated at Amsterdam.* Translated by Sydney W. Fleming. Netherlands Olympic Committee. Amsterdam: J. H. de Bussy, 1928. https://digital
.la84.org/digital/collection/p17103coll8/id/14512/.

Varney, Wendy. "A Labour of Patriotism: Female Soviet Gymnasts' Physical and
Ideological Work, 1952–1991." *Genders* 39 (June 2004). https://www.colorado
.edu/gendersarchive1998–2013/2004/06/01/labour-patriotism-female-soviet
-gymnasts-physical-and-ideological-work-1952–1991.

———. "Legitimation and Limitations: How the Opie Report on Women's Gymnastics Missed Its Mark." *Sporting Traditions* 15, no. 2 (1999): 73–90. https://
digital.la84.org/digital/collection/p17103coll10/id/5373/rec/1.

Verbrugge, Martha H. *Active Bodies: A History of Women's Physical Education in
Twentieth-Century America.* New York: Oxford University Press, 2017.

Verschoth, Anita. "A Great Leap Backward." *Sports Illustrated,* April 12, 1976,
94–96. https://vault.si.com/.amp/vault/1976/04/12/a-great-leap-backward.

Vertinsky, Patricia. *The Eternally Wounded Woman: Women, Doctors, and Exercise in the Late Nineteenth Century*. Urbana: University of Illinois Press, 1994.

———. "Exercise, Physical Capability, and the Eternally Wounded Woman in Late Nineteenth Century North America." *Journal of Sport History* 14, no. 1 (1987): 7–27. http://www.jstor.org/stable/43609324.

Vonnard, Philippe, Nicola Sbetti, and Grégory Quin. "'Divided but Not Disconnected': Studying a New 'Paradigm' for the History of Sport during the Cold War." In *Beyond Boycotts: Sport during the Cold War in Europe*, edited by Philippe Vonnard, Nicola Sbetti, and Grégory Quin, 1–14. Berlin: De Gruyter Oldenbourg, 2018.

Vonnard, Philippe, Nicola Sbetti, and Grégory Quin, eds. *Beyond Boycotts: Sport during the Cold War in Europe*. Berlin: De Gruyter Oldenbourg, 2018.

Wagg, Stephen. "Tilting at Windmills? Olympic Politics and the Spectre of Amateurism." In *The Palgrave Handbook of Olympic Studies*, edited by Helen Jefferson Lenskyj and Stephen Wagg, 321–36. Basingstoke, UK: Palgrave Macmillan, 2014.

Wagg, Stephen, and David L. Andrews, eds. *East Plays West: Sport and the Cold War*. New York: Routledge, 2007.

Wamsley, Kevin B. "Womanizing Olympic Athletes: Policy and Practice during the Avery Brundage Era." In Schaus and Wenn, *Onward to the Olympics*, 283–96.

Wamsley, Kevin B., and Gordon H. MacDonald. "Child's Play: Decreasing Size and Increasing Risk in Women's Olympic Gymnastics." *Cultural Imperialism in Action: Critiques in the Global Olympic Trust* (2006): 339–46. https://digital.la84 .org/digital/collection/p17103coll10/id/13567/rec/1.

Wenn, Stephen R. "Peter Ueberroth's Legacy: How the 1984 Los Angeles Olympics Changed the Trajectory of the Olympic Movement." *International Journal of the History of Sport* 32, no. 1 (2015): 157–71. https://doi.org/10.1080/09523367 .2014.958665.

Wenn, Stephen R., and Scott G. Martyn. "Juan Antonio Samaranch's Score Sheet: Revenue Generation and the Olympic Movement, 1980–2001." In Schaus and Wenn, *Onward to the Olympics*, 309–24.

West, Candace, and Don H. Zimmerman. "Doing Gender." *Gender and Society* 1, no. 2 (1987): 125–51. http://www.jstor.org/stable/189945.

Wiedeman, Reeves. "A Full Revolution." *New Yorker*, May 23, 2016. https://www .newyorker.com/magazine/2016/05/30/simone-biles-is-the-best-gymnast-in -the-world.

Winter, Jessica. "The Karolyis' Tainted Glory." *Slate*, August 12, 2016. https://slate.com/ culture/2016/08/martha-karolyi-and-her-husband-bela-were-great-coaches -they-also-allegedly-beat-their-gymnasts.html.

Wolf, Sigrid F., and Cynthis R. LaBella. "Epidemiology of Gymnastics Injuries." In *Gymnastics Medicine: Evaluation, Management and Rehabilitation*, edited by Emily Sweeney, 15–26. Cham, Switzerland: Springer Nature, 2019.

Yan, Holly. "Karolyi Ranch Produced Champions and a Culture of Fear, Ex-Gymnasts Say." *CNN*, February 2, 2018. https://edition.cnn.com/2018/02/02/us/karolyi -ranch-gymnastics-abuse-allegations/index.html.

Yang, Michelle Murray. "Guilty without Trial: State-Sponsored Cheating and the

2008 Beijing Olympic Women's Gymnastics Competition." *Chinese Journal of Communication* 7, no. 1 (2014): 80–105. https://doi.org/10.1080/17544750.2013.816752.

Yoculan, Suzanne, and Bill Donaldson. *Perfect 10: The UGA GymDogs and the Rise of Women's College Gymnastics in America*. Athens, GA: Hill Street Press, 2005.

Young-Hoo, Kwon, L. Fortney Virginia, and Shin In-Sik. "3-D Analysis of Yurchenko Vaults Performed by Female Gymnasts during the 1988 Seoul Olympic Games." *International Journal of Sport Biomechanics* 6, no. 2 (1990): 157–76. https://doi.org/10.1123/ijsb.6.2.157.

"Yurchenko Vault." http://www.nataliayurchenko.com/innovations/yurchenko-vault/, accessed October 20, 2019.

Zaglada, Vladimir. *One Coach's Journey from East to West: How the Fall of the Iron Curtain Changed the World of Gymnastics*. Bloomington, IN: Authorhouse, 2010.

Zhang, Tracy Ying. "Bending the Body for China: The Uses of Acrobatics in Sino-US Diplomacy during the Cold War." *International Journal of Cultural Policy* 22, no. 2 (2016): 123–46. https://doi.org/10.1080/10286632.2014.956665.

ILLUSTRATION CREDITS

Figure 1.1 © 1908 IOC—All rights reserved. *London 1908 OG, Artistic Gymnastics, Balance Beam Women—The Danish Team (DEN)*, July 13, 1908, PHO10003813, Olympic Multimedia Library.

Figure 1.2 © 1912 IOC—All rights reserved. *Stockholm 1912 OG, Artistic Gymnastics—A Team Exercise by the Swedish (SWE) Team*, June 29, 1912, PHO10004020, Olympic Multimedia Library.

Figure 1.3 © 1920 IOC—All rights reserved. *Antwerp 1920 OG—Gymnastics Demonstration by the Women Team from Denmark (DEN)*, April 20, 1920, PHO10019677, Olympic Multimedia Library.

Figure 1.4 © 1928 IOC—All rights reserved. *Amsterdam 1928 OG, Gymnastics, Team Competition Women—Members of the French Team (FRA)*, August 7, 1928, PHO10028222, Olympic Multimedia Library.

Figure 1.5 © 1936 IOC—All rights reserved. *Berlin 1936 OG, Artistic Gymnastics—Demonstration of Collective Exercises by the Gymnasts of Tchechoslovakia (TCH)*, August 10, 1936, PHO10001889, Olympic Multimedia Library.

Figure 2.2 © 1976 IOC—All rights reserved. *Montreal 1976 OG, Artistic Gymnastics Women—Balance Beam, Maria Filatova (URS)*, July 18, 1976, PHO10456363, Olympic Multimedia Library.

Figure 2.3 © 1976 IOC—All rights reserved. *Montreal 1976 OG, Artistic Gymnastics, Balance Beam Women—Nadia Comăneci (ROM) 1st*, July 22, 1976, PHO10033368, Olympic Multimedia Library.

Figure 2.4 © 1984 IOC—All rights reserved. *Los Angeles 1984 OG, Closing Ceremony—Jeffrey James FLOAT (USA), Swimmer and Mary-Lou Retton (USA), Gymnast*, August 12, 1984, PHO10514451, Olympic Multimedia Library.

Figure 3.1 © 1976 IOC—All rights reserved. *Montreal 1976 OG, Artistic Gymnastics, Balance Beam Women—Olga Korbut (URS)*, July 18, 1976, PHO10026300, Olympic Multimedia Library.

Figure 3.2 © 1972 IOC/United Archives—All rights reserved. *Munich 1972 OG, Artistic Gymnastics, Uneven Bars Women—Final, Olga Korbut (URS) Weeps after a Low Mark on the Bars*, August 31, 1972, Olympic Multimedia Library.

Figure 3.3 © 1976 IOC/ United Archives—All rights reserved. *Montreal 1976 OG, Artistic Gymnastics Women—Medal Ceremony. Nadia Comăneci (ROM) 1st*, July 21, 1976, PHO10478874, Olympic Multimedia Library.

Figure 3.4 © 1976 IOC—All rights reserved. *Montreal 1976 OG, Artistic Gymnastics, Uneven Bars Women—Nadia Comăneci (ROM) 1e*, PHO11078073, Olympic Multimedia Library.

Figure 3.5 courtesy of the Richard Nixon Presidential Library and Museum (National Archives and Records Administration). Robert Knudsen, *President Nixon standing in the Oval Office with members of the Russian Soviet Women's Gymnastics Team*, March 21, 1973, WHPO-0486–09, Richard Nixon Presidential Library and Museum.

Figure 4.1 © 1920 IOC—All rights reserved. *Antwerp 1920 OG, Artistic Gymnastics, Free System Team, Men—The Team from Denmark (DEN) 1st*, August 22, 1920, PHO10019676, Olympic Multimedia Library.

Figure 4.2 © 1920 IOC—All rights reserved. *Antwerp 1920 OG—Gymnastics Demonstration by the Women Team from Denmark (DEN)*, April 20, 1920, PHO10019674, Olympic Multimedia Library.

Figure 4.3 © 1960 IOC—All rights reserved. *Rome 1960 OG, Rhythmic Gymnastics—Boris Shakhlin (URS) 1st with His Medals*, August 25, 1960, PHO10010747, Olympic Multimedia Library.

Figure 4.4 © 1980 IOC—All rights reserved. *Moscow 1980 OG, Artistic Gymnastics, Women—Elena Davydova (URS) 1st and 2nd*, PHO10517776, Olympic Multimedia Library.

Figure 4.5 © 1976 IOC/United Archives—All rights reserved. *Montreal 1976 OG, Artistic Gymnastics, Floor Exercises Women—Medal Ceremony. Nelli Kim (URS) 1st and Nadia Comăneci (Rom) 3rd*, July 22, 1976, PHO10478855, Olympic Multimedia Library.

Figure 4.6 © 1988 IOC/Richard Harbus—All rights reserved. Richard Harbus, *Seoul 1988 OG, Artistic Gymnastics, Balance Beam Women—Kelly Garrison-Steves (USA)*, September 25, 1988, PHO10416656, Olympic Multimedia Library.

Figure 4.7 © 1992 IOC—All rights reserved. *Barcelona 1992 OG, Artistic Gymnastics, Team Competition Women—Balance Beam, Shannon Miller (USA) 3rd*, July 26, 1992, PHO10373497, Olympic Multimedia Library.

Figure 5.10 © 1976 IOC/United Archives—All rights reserved. *Montreal 1976 OG, Artistic Gymnastics, Women—Olga Korbut (URS) Tenses Up as She Watches the Tally Mount for Nadia Comăneci (ROM)*, July 17, 1976, PHO10483906, Olympic Multimedia Library.

Figure 5.11 © 1980 IOC—All rights reserved. *Moscow 1980 OG, Artistic Gymnastics, Balance Beam Women—Nadia Comăneci (ROM)*, July 19, 1980, PHO10430434, Olympic Multimedia Library.

Figure 5.12 © 2018 IOC/Lukas Schulze—All rights reserved. Lukas Schulze, *Buenos Aires 2018 YOG, Artistic Gymnastics, Vault Women—Qualification, Xijing Tang (CHN)*, October 8, 2018, PHO11095925, Olympic Multimedia Library.

Figure 5.13 © 1984 IOC/United Archives—All rights reserved. *Los Angeles 1984 OG, Artistic Gymnastics, Individual All-Round Women—Balance Beam, Mary-Lou Retton (USA) 1st*, August 3, 1984, PHO10478597, Olympic Multimedia Library.

Figure 5.14 © 1976 IOC/United Archives—All rights reserved. *Montreal 1976 OG, Artistic Gymnastics, Floor Exercises Women—Nelli Kim (URS)*, July 17, 1976, PHO10483938, Olympic Multimedia Library.

Figure 5.15 © 2012 IOC/John Huet—All rights reserved. John Huet, *London 2012 OG, Artistic Gymnastics, Team Competition Women—Final. Balance Beam, Gabrielle Douglas (USA) 1st*, July 31, 2012, PHO10555338, Olympic Multimedia Library.

Figure 5.16 © 2012 IOC/John Huet—All rights reserved. John Huet, *London 2012 OG, Artistic Gymnastics, Individual All-Round Women—Final, Gabrielle Douglas (USA) 1st*, August 2, 2012, PHO10561073, Olympic Multimedia Library.

Figure 5.17 © 2016 IOC/Ian Jones—All rights reserved. Ian Jones, *Rio 2016 OG, Artistic Gymnastics—Floor Exercises Women. Simone Biles (USA) 1st*, August 16, 2016, PHO10933548, Olympic Multimedia Library.

Figure 5.18 © 2016 IOC/Ian Jones—All rights reserved. Ian Jones, *Rio 2016 OG, Artistic Gymnastics—Floor Exercises Women. Simone Biles (USA) 1st*, August 16, 2016, PHO10933529, Olympic Multimedia Library.

Figure 6.1 © 1964 IOC—All rights reserved. *Tokyo 1964 OG, Artistic Gymnastics, Uneven Bars Women—Polina Astakhova (URS) 1st*, October 22, 1964, PHO10010231, Olympic Multimedia Library.

Figure 6.2 © 1988 IOC/Richard Avery Lyon—All rights reserved. Richard Avery Lyon, *Seoul 1988 OG, Artistic Gymnastics, Balance Beam Women—Phoebe Lan Mills (USA) and Her Coach*, September 20, 1988, PHO10418284, Olympic Multimedia Library.

Figure 6.3 © 2016 IOC/Jason Evans—All rights reserved. Jason Evans, *Rio 2016 OG, Artistic Gymnastics, Floor Exercises Women—Final, Alexandra Raisman (USA) 2nd at the End of the Competition,* August 16, 2016, PHO10932458, Olympic Multimedia Library.

Figure 6.4 © 2008 IOC/Hélène Tobler—All rights reserved. Hélène Tobler, *Beijing 2008 OG, Artistic Gymnastics, Beam Women—Shawn Johnson (USA) 1st,* August 19, 2008, PHO10261728, Olympic Multimedia Library.

INDEX

GEORGIA CERVIN is an Honorary Research Fellow at the University of Western Australia and a former international gymnast.

Sport and Society

A Sporting Time: New York City and the Rise of Modern Athletics,
    1820–70   *Melvin L. Adelman*
Sandlot Seasons: Sport in Black Pittsburgh   *Rob Ruck*
West Ham United: The Making of a Football Club   *Charles Korr*
Beyond the Ring: The Role of Boxing in American Society   *Jeffrey T. Sammons*
John L. Sullivan and His America   *Michael T. Isenberg*
Television and National Sport: The United States and Britain   *Joan M. Chandler*
The Creation of American Team Sports: Baseball and Cricket, 1838–72
    George B. Kirsch
City Games: The Evolution of American Urban Society and the Rise of
    Sports   *Steven A. Riess*
The Brawn Drain: Foreign Student-Athletes in American Universities   *John Bale*
The Business of Professional Sports   *Edited by Paul D. Staudohar*
    and James A. Mangan
Fritz Pollard: Pioneer in Racial Advancement   *John M. Carroll*
A View from the Bench: The Story of an Ordinary Player on a Big-Time
    Football Team (*formerly* Go Big Red! The Story of a Nebraska Football Player)
    George Mills
Sport and Exercise Science: Essays in the History of Sports Medicine
    Edited by Jack W. Berryman and Roberta J. Park
Minor League Baseball and Local Economic Development   *Arthur T. Johnson*
Harry Hooper: An American Baseball Life   *Paul J. Zingg*
Cowgirls of the Rodeo: Pioneer Professional Athletes   *Mary Lou LeCompte*
Sandow the Magnificent: Eugen Sandow and the Beginnings of
    Bodybuilding   *David Chapman*
Big-Time Football at Harvard, 1905: The Diary of Coach Bill Reid
    Edited by Ronald A. Smith
Leftist Theories of Sport: A Critique and Reconstruction   *William J. Morgan*
Babe: The Life and Legend of Babe Didrikson Zaharias   *Susan E. Cayleff*
Stagg's University: The Rise, Decline, and Fall of Big-Time Football at
    Chicago   *Robin Lester*
Muhammad Ali, the People's Champ   *Edited by Elliott J. Gorn*
People of Prowess: Sport, Leisure, and Labor in Early Anglo-America
    Nancy L. Struna
The New American Sport History: Recent Approaches and Perspectives
    Edited by S. W. Pope
Making the Team: The Cultural Work of Baseball Fiction   *Timothy Morris*
Making the American Team: Sport, Culture, and the Olympic Experience
    Mark Dyreson
Viva Baseball! Latin Major Leaguers and Their Special Hunger
    Samuel O. Regalado
Touching Base: Professional Baseball and American Culture in the
    Progressive Era (rev. ed.)   *Steven A. Riess*
Red Grange and the Rise of Modern Football   *John M. Carroll*

Hockey: A Global History   *Stephen Hardy and Andrew C. Holman*

Baseball: A History of America's Game   *Benjamin G. Rader*

Kansas City vs. Oakland: The Bitter Sports Rivalry That Defined an Era
   Matthew C. Ehrlich

The Gold in the Rings: The People and Events That Transformed the Olympic
   Games   *Stephen R. Wenn and Robert K. Barney*

Before March Madness: The Wars for the Soul of College Basketball
   Kurt Edward Kemper

The Sport Marriage: Women Who Make It Work Steven M. Ortiz *Steven M. Ortiz*

NFL Football: A History of America's New National Pastime, NFL Centennial
   Edition   *Richard C. Crepeau*

Passing the Baton: Black Women Track Stars and American Identity
   Cat M. Ariail

Degrees of Difficulty: How Women's Gymnastics Rose to Prominence and Fell
   from Grace   *Georgia Cervin*

REPRINT EDITIONS

The Nazi Olympics   *Richard D. Mandell*

Sports in the Western World (2d ed.)   *William J. Baker*

Jesse Owens: An American Life   *William J. Baker*

The University of Illinois Press
is a founding member of the
Association of University Presses.

———————————————————

Composed in 10.25/14 Chaparral Pro
with Univers LT Std display
by Lisa Connery
at the University of Illinois Press
Manufactured by Sheridan Books, Inc.

University of Illinois Press
1325 South Oak Street
Champaign, IL 61820-6903
www.press.uillinois.edu